Lotus® Domino® R5 Clustering

AF763774

STEVE RUSSELL ■ KATHLEEN MCGIVNEY ■ ZELJKA ZORANOVIC

IBM

PH PTR

PRENTICE HALL PTR, UPPER SADDLE RIVER, NEW JERSEY 07458
www.phptr.com

© Copyright International Business Machines Corporation 2001. All rights reserved.

Note to U.S. Government Users—documentation related to restricted rights—use, duplication, or disclosure is subject to restrictions set forth in GSA ADP Schedule Contract with IBM Corp.

Take Note!

Before using this information and the product it supports, be sure to read the general information in Appendix D, "Special notices," on page 235.

PH PTR

© 2001 Prentice Hall PTR
Prentice-Hall, Inc.
Upper Saddle River, NJ 07458

All rights reserved. No part of this book may be reproduced, in any form or by any means, without permission in writing from the author and publisher.

The publisher offers discounts on this book when ordered in bulk quantities. For more information contact: Corporate Sales Department, Prentice Hall PTR, One Lake Street, Upper Saddle River, NJ 07458. Phone: 800-382-3419; Fax: 201-236-7141; E-mail: corpsales@prenhall.com

Printed in the United States of America

Second Edition (November 2000)

This edition applies to Domino Server R5.04a running on Microsoft Windows 2000 Server/Advanced Server and Linux (Red Hat 6.2 and SuSE 6.4) operating systems.

Comments may be addressed to:

IBM Corporation, International Technical Support Organization
Dept. HZ8 Building 678
P.O. Box 12195
Research Triangle Park, NC 27709-2195

When you send information to IBM, you grant IBM a non-exclusive right to use or distribute the information in any way it believes appropriate without incurring any obligation to you.

© Copyright International Business Machines Corporation 1998, 2000. All rights reserved. Note to U.S Government Users—Documentation related to restricted rights—Use, duplication, or disclosure is subject to restrictions set forth in GSA ADP Schedule Contract with IBM Corp.

ISBN 0-13-060836-X

Prentice-Hall International (UK) Limited, *London*
Prentice-Hall of Australia Pty. Limited, *Sydney*
Prentice-Hall Canada Inc., *Toronto*
Prentice-Hall Hispanoamericana, S.A., *Mexico*
Prentice-Hall of India Private Limited, *New Delhi*
Prentice-Hall of Japan, Inc., *Tokyo*
Pearson Education Asia Pte. Ltd.
Editora Prentice-Hall do Brasil, Ltda., *Rio de Janeiro*

Contents

© Copyright IBM Corp. 1998, 2000

Preface

This redbook provides you with the information you need to understand how to plan, design, install, configure, and manage Lotus Domino clusters. Domino is a leading groupware application that provides collaborative workgroup tools such as e-mail, database access and calendar management. These functions have become critical for the day-to-day operations of many companies. For such businesses, downtime, that is, loss of one or more of these tools due to server or software failure, can have a significant impact on business results.

One way to manage the risk of downtime is to implement clustered systems. Clusters are groups of servers treated as a single computing resource that provides services to network users. When a server in the cluster fails, its workload is passed to one or more other members of the cluster until corrective action is taken and the failed server can be brought back into operation again.

In contrast with other clustering technologies, such as Microsoft Cluster Services, Domino provides its own unique clustering technology that is independent of the underlying operating system. This means that a single cluster can comprise servers running a variety of the operating systems supported by Domino, from OS/390, to AIX, to Windows 2000.

The book focuses on IBM's family of Netfinity servers as the hardware platform of choice. Netfinity servers are Intel-based, industry-standard servers that offer a number of innovative features to provide a stable and reliable platform for business-critical computing. In this book, Microsoft Windows 2000 is often used as the operating system chosen to illustrate particular facets of Domino clustering being considered, but Linux is also used as an alternative and to demonstrate the operating system-independent nature of Domino clusters.

We assume the reader is familiar with Domino operation and terminology.

© Copyright IBM Corp. 1998, 2000

The team that wrote this redbook

This redbook was produced by a team of specialists from around the world working at the International Technical Support Organization, Raleigh Center.

Steve Russell is a Certified Consulting IT Specialist at the International Technical Support Organization, Raleigh Center, where he manages residencies and produces redbooks related to IBM Netfinity servers. Before joining the ITSO, Steve had a Technical Marketing role, working in the UK as a member of the IBM Netfinity organization in EMEA. Prior to that, he spent nearly 15 years managing and developing PC-based hardware and software projects at IBM's Hursley laboratory in the UK. He holds a degree in Electrical and Electronic Engineering, and is a member of the Institution of Electrical Engineers and a Chartered Engineer.

Kathleen McGivney is an Advisory IT Specialist for Lotus Professional Services in Southern California. She is a Certified Lotus Professional (CLP) in Release 5 in both System Administration and Application Development, as well as a Principal CLP in both System Administration and Application Development in R4. She has worked on many Notes and Domino projects in the past five years, including major mail migrations, global Notes/Domino deployments, and Domino-based Internet and intranet sites, and has written more lines of LotusScript code than she would care to remember.

Zeljka Zoranovic is a Senior IT Specialist for Notes and Domino in IBM Global Services at IBM Canada, Toronto. For the last six years she has worked on Lotus Notes/Domino network design and deployment, large mail migrations to Notes and Domino, Internet connectivity, and supporting Domino servers on OS/2, Windows NT, AIX, OS/390 and Linux. Before joining the IBM in 1996, she spent four years working on LAN implementation and eight years on automotive design. She is a Domino R4 CLP and R5 CLP in System Administration. She holds a Bachelor's degree in Mechanical Engineering and a Masters degree in Information Systems.

The team: (left-to-right) Zeljka, Steve, and Kathleen

This is the second edition of this redbook. Our thanks to the authors of the first edition:

Enrica Bellia
Fiona Collins
Lori Fucarile
Anssi Nummi

Thanks also to the following people for their invaluable contributions to this project:

Jeffery Conley	Lotus Technical Relationship Manager, IBM RTP
Michael Robinson	Senior Software Engineer, Database Performance Group, Iris
Razeyah Stephen	Domino Performance Engineer, Iris
Brenda Clark	IT Architect, IBM Canada
Steven Vanderbok	Project Manager, Lotus Professional Services
Abe Cohen	Program Manager, North America Marketing, Lotus

Comments welcome

Your comments are important to us!

We want our Redbooks to be as helpful as possible. Please send us your comments about this or other Redbooks in one of the following ways:

- Fax the evaluation form found in "IBM Redbooks review" on page 255 to the fax number shown on the form.
- Use the online evaluation form found at **ibm.com**/redbooks
- Send your comments in an Internet note to redbook@us.ibm.com

Chapter 1. Domino clustering overview

If your Domino server is down or inaccessible, what happens? Users get upset, productivity goes down, and worst of all your customers may go elsewhere. Domino clustering addresses these issues by providing high availability and scalability for your Domino servers.

Many different things can cause unexpected server downtime: operating system or application failures, network problems, or hardware failures are all obvious examples. Even planned downtime can decrease your users' productivity. With Domino clustering, when one Domino server in the cluster is unavailable, users are automatically redirected to a backup server. To the users, this gives the appearance that the "system" is up, even if their primary mail or application server is down. Domino clustering helps in meeting customer service level agreements. And, newly introduced with Release 5, the Domino Internet Cluster Manager allows clustering for Web clients, which helps provide 24 x 7 Web site availability.

Domino clustering has been available and in use by customers for several years. Lotus first released Domino clustering as *Notes for Public Networks*, an offering for telecommunication and Internet service providers as part of Domino R4.0. As a result, several of the large telecommunication and Internet service providers are now using clusters of as many as six Domino servers to provide Domino failover support to their customers.

Lotus released Domino clustering and the Domino Advanced Services license for general customer use with Domino R4.5. Now, with Domino R5.0 Enterprise Server, Domino clustering is included in the Domino server license, and has been enhanced to support failover and load balancing of Web browsers using the Internet Cluster Manager (ICM). Note that Domino clustering is provided with the Domino Enterprise Server license, not with the Domino R5 Application Server and Mail Server licenses.

Lotus' focus with Domino clustering is to address growing requirements from customers for Domino messaging and enterprise applications to be highly available and scalable. Clustering effectively combines a set of systems and their applications, coordinating them to provide higher availability and scalability and to enable more efficient use of resources than is possible with a single system.

Domino clustering provides intelligent failover, and balances the load due to client requests based on the content asked for by the user. Instead of accessing a particular database on a single system, clients are directed to

© Copyright IBM Corp. 1998, 2000

replicas of the database that are distributed among the systems in the cluster. Cluster replication keeps the data in all replicas tightly synchronized. Domino maintains information about the replicas, and on server availability, in order to direct users to the best available server that contains the content they desire. While many clustering solutions available today provide either failover or load balancing, Domino clustering provides both failover and dynamic load balancing for Notes and Web clients accessing the Domino server.

Domino clustering is not hardware or operating system specific. In addition, no unique hardware or software is required; it can be installed on your existing servers. Domino also supports clustering of heterogeneous hardware and operating system platforms. You can fail over users from a Windows 2000 server to a UNIX server, an AS/400 or S/390 system, or to any other platform that supports Domino.

Since Domino clustering is integrated into the core Domino server, you use the Domino Administration Client and other familiar Domino administrative tools to manage and monitor cluster servers, distribute databases among the cluster members and manage users. The Domino Administration Client, in particular, provides a graphical interface that allows administrators to monitor and manage their cluster servers and move users and databases within the cluster very easily.

1.1 Domino clustering or operating system clustering?

Domino clustering uses database replicas to provide failover and load balancing of users accessing Domino applications. Operating system (OS) clustering, such as SUN clustering, Microsoft Cluster Services and IBM AIX HACMP, can provide failover of the operating system and other server tasks and applications, including Domino. Each approach has its own strengths, and they are, in many ways, complementary to each other. Using a combination of OS clustering and Domino clustering can further improve a system's availability to users. You can also deploy network load balancing to further increase the availability and scalability of your Domino infrastructure.

We examine one example of this combination of clustering technologies in Chapter 6, "Domino and Windows 2000 clustering" on page 163.

1.2 Who uses Domino clustering and why?

Today, customers use Domino clustering for the following reasons:

- High availability of critical applications
- Increased scalability to cope with growing workloads
- Migrations of hardware platform, operating system, or Domino version
- Disaster preparedness

If you have critical Domino applications that require 24 x 7 availability, Domino clustering can help you achieve this by creating multiple replicas of your applications within a Domino cluster. Users accessing clustered applications receive improved availability because, if the server they are using goes down, their requests are redirected to another available Domino server that houses the applications being used.

Domino clustering provides scalability. You have the ability to add servers to the Domino cluster and to increase the number of application replicas in order to meet increased workload demands. For example, if an application is on one server and usage of that application increases, the application can be replicated to another server and, through the use of Domino load balancing, users are dynamically redirected to the alternative server.

Domino can also assist in migrations or upgrades of hardware and software. For example, one customer wanted to migrate to Release 5 from Release 4.6. To achieve this, the customer built new servers to provide the Domino R5 environment. These new servers were then clustered with the existing R4 servers. Each of the R4 servers was then set to an unavailable state and Domino's clustering technology failed the users over to the new R5 environment without any interruptions in service.

Other customers have executed server consolidation and platform migration plans by transferring users from a number of existing smaller servers to one large Domino server by using clustering. All servers were added to a Domino cluster and users were then redirected from their smaller servers to the larger Domino server with no disruptions.

Many customers are developing disaster recovery plans for their data centers. Domino clustering can play an integral part in such plans by locating a cluster node in an off-site disaster recovery location and using Domino clustering over a wide area network (WAN) connection. The remote server is kept in tight synchronization with the production servers in the cluster, and is used only in the case of a disaster.

To optimize WAN clustering, it is strongly recommended that your WAN connection to any off-site server has comparable speeds to your LAN. Throughput rates should be thoroughly tested using realistic workloads prior to implementation to make sure that performance requirements are met.

The following table summarizes the functions that are supported by Domino clustering:

Table 1. Functions supported by Domino clustering

Function	Domino clustering
Provides server failover	Yes
Dynamic load balancing	Yes
Content routing of users	Yes
Maximum number of nodes in a cluster	6
Supports mixture of OS platforms	Yes (even within the same cluster)
Supports clusters spanning LAN segments (campus-wide clusters, "geo-clusters" across geographies)	Yes

1.3 New features in Domino Release 5

With the release of the Domino R5 Enterprise Server, customers have been provided with a number of new features that allow them to enhance the availability and scalability of their Domino infrastructure. Some of these new features are enhancements to the existing features in Release 4. However, many of these features are completely new and will be covered in greater detail throughout this book.

This section provides an overview of the new features available with the Release 5 Domino Enterprise Server that specifically relate to high availability and scalability.

1.3.1 Internet Cluster Manager

Internet Cluster Manager (ICM) is a new feature introduced with Domino R5. It is an enhancement to Domino's basic clustering features that allows dynamic load balancing and failover of Web browsers (HTTP and HTTPS). In earlier releases of Domino, failover and load balancing were available only for Notes clients. Now the ICM server task extends Domino's clustering benefits to Web clients.

HTTP clients direct requests for Domino applications to the ICM. The ICM task maintains information about the availability of servers in the Domino cluster, and the distribution of databases among the servers. The ICM determines the best server to receive a particular client request and directs the request to that server.

The Internet Cluster Manager can do the following:

- Monitor back-end Domino servers for availability
- Check the Domino HTTP Web service for availability
- Disallow any new connections to servers that are out of service
- Provide failover (redirect clients) to the best available server
- Provide load balancing by setting availability thresholds for your Domino servers
- Support virtual IP addresses and map ports
- Provide content routing for your clients

Internet Cluster Manager is a powerful tool that lets you extend the benefits obtained from using Domino clustering for your Notes clients to the Web. The ICM can help you to keep your customer service level agreements by ensuring that your Domino Web site is up and running even if the primary Domino Web server is down. The ICM can also help to maximize utilization of your Domino infrastructure with its load-balancing capabilities.

1.3.2 Calendaring and scheduling

Collaborative calendaring and scheduling now supports failover and load balancing in Domino R5. Your users will be more productive since they can continue to schedule meetings with their colleagues even when their mail server is out of service.

There are some limitations to these functions, however. For example, you can schedule a meeting inviting a user whose clustered home mail server is not available. The invited person is then able to accept or decline the invitation and the invitee's mail database is updated accordingly. If you now try to check the schedule of the person you wish to invite (a free time search), the search may not show that the person is busy in the relevant time slot. Only information that was entered prior to his or her home mail server failure is shown correctly. This is also true for group calendars.

Prior to Domino R5, the calendaring and scheduling-related server tasks did not fail over in the cluster. If a user attempted to schedule a meeting with another user whose mail server was down, an error would be returned. In addition, if the users' mail servers were particularly busy, response time during a scheduling operation could be affected. Domino R5 allows dynamic load balancing and failover for calendaring and scheduling operations.

1.3.3 Other enhancements to Domino clustering

Before the release of Domino R5, if a user's mail server went down, any new mail agents that the user had enabled in his mail file would not run on the backup server. In Domino R5, Synchronous New Mail Agents will allow your mail users to have an agent that runs on their mail no matter where it is deposited. When a user's mail server is out of service, the mail will get deposited on the backup mail server and an agent can still process the information.

Type-ahead and addressing features now let users who want to type user names or search for addresses to perform those functions on the backup server when their primary server is out of service. In Domino versions prior to R5, type-ahead addressing would not work properly when the user's primary mail server was unavailable. Users would have to select the recipient's name from the address dialog box.

Unread marks are now synchronized for users who are directed to a backup server when their primary server is out of service. In earlier releases, unread marks were maintained only on the user's primary mail server. Users who failed over to a backup server would see unread marks for documents that they had read on their primary server, and when they resumed work on their primary server, documents that they had read on the backup server would appear as unread. Domino R5 clustering synchronizes unread marks within the cluster.

1.3.4 Transaction logging

Transaction logging is a new feature that debuted with Domino R5 Server. With transaction logging enabled, the Domino system captures database changes and writes them to a transaction log instead of manipulating the database directly. Transactions that have been logged are transferred to the databases as another server task. This offers a vast improvement over Domino Release 4 in server restart times, database integrity, and system availability. It also greatly shortens the time it takes to run the database fixup task if the server is rebooted after a crash. In short, transaction logging alone will increase server performance and availability for your users.

In earlier versions of Domino, each transaction in a database (creating, modifying, and deleting documents, view changes, etc.) had to be committed to the disk in order to be considered a successful transaction. This could be very time-consuming on a busy server. Modifications could occur on different parts of a database or across multiple databases. Making the appropriate updates meant that the server's disk heads had to move over large areas of the disk to get to the proper track and sector for the data that was changed or updated.

Repositioning the head in this "random" manner added to the total time required to complete a transaction. As a result, as the number of database users on an R4 server increased, so did the number of transactions and the average transaction completion time. Waiting for commits to complete (as opposed to returning from the operation and "trusting" that the system would eventually get the data to disk) was necessary so that, in the event of a system failure, the fixup task could ensure the integrity of the databases and restore them to a known state.

With transaction logging enabled, instead of waiting for the data to be committed to the disk, each transaction is recorded in the transaction log, allowing control to return to the application very rapidly. The relevant database is updated some time later, as the transactions logs are worked through. This offers performance improvement in two ways. Each transaction is written to the log, and subsequently the disk, in a *sequential* manner. This decreases the "random" repositioning of the disk head for each transaction, resulting in faster commits to the disk. In addition, in the case of a server crash, the time needed for the fixup task to run is drastically decreased, because the server can simply "pick up where it left off" by reading the transaction log and determining which transactions still need to be committed to the disk.

Note

To obtain maximum benefit from transaction logging, it is important to locate the transaction logs on a separate physical disk to other system data. If, for example, you place the logs on the same disk as your databases, the log files will still be subject to non-sequential accesses.

Transaction logging offers direct benefits with regards to Domino clustering. Since Domino clustering is event-driven, each time a transaction is committed to disk, the transaction is replicated to the other nodes in the cluster. In the case of a server crash on a very active server, the other nodes in the cluster might have to wait until the original server restarts and performs the Fixup task on the database before they receive the database changes. With transaction logging, if one server goes down, the other servers in the cluster can read the transaction log and continue writing the changes to disk while the original server is still down.

Using transaction logging in conjunction with Domino clustering will enhance your servers' performance and availability.

1.4 IBM xSeries and Netfinity servers

Selecting the appropriate IBM xSeries or Netfinity server to run Lotus Domino is not always as easy as selecting a file server for your network. Each Domino server can provide a variety of different functions, such as electronic mail, database, intranet or Internet Web server, or combinations thereof. With Domino Release 5, you can provide services to a wider variety of clients: Notes clients, Web browsers, Internet standard-based e-mail clients and, through Notes, to PDA devices such as the IBM WorkPad or 3Com Palm Pilot.

By understanding the functions your individual Domino servers will perform, you can better identify the hardware configuration that you require. Domino Release 5 benefits from many performance improvements over its predecessor. Changes to database structure, thread processing and buffer usage all contribute to a two to five times increase in the number of users supported over Release 4 on the same hardware.

The following section outlines the features of the xSeries and Netfinity server products. Although this information was accurate when it was written, server hardware is updated frequently to utilize emerging technologies. For the most current compatibility information, please refer to the IBM Netfinity servers Web page at:

`http://www.pc.ibm.com/us/eserver/xseries/index.html`

IBM xSeries and Netfinity servers provide you with the following features:

1. Latest Pentium III technology

   Up to eight-way Pentium III Xeon symmetric multiprocessing (SMP) in a mix of tower and rack-mountable models.

2. Leading performance

   A choice of high-speed intelligent disk subsystems, SCSI controllers, Serial Storage Architecture (SSA), and Fibre Channel adapters and drives deliver excellent Domino R5 performance.

3. Storage flexibility

Advanced features allow you to expand disk arrays while the server is still running using IBM Logical Drive Migration technology with IBM ServeRAID adapters. A similar function is also provided in IBM Fibre Channel products.

4. Advanced Systems Management devices

   Each server may have an Advanced Systems Management (ASM) device in its specification. This is either an optional adapter or, in the more powerful systems, a standard adapter or integrated chip set. ASM devices allow you to communicate with your servers using Netfinity Manager. This management software is included with every server and is used to configure and monitor many of each system's features. Using this feature allows you to diagnose server problems, even if your server cannot be accessed via the normal network.

5. Complete manageability software suite

   In addition to the Netfinity Manager software for proactive server management and control, IBM includes a Capacity Management tool for upgrade planning, and integrated uninterruptible power supply (UPS) management for safe application shutdown. All are provided as standard with IBM servers to reduce your total cost of ownership.

6. Extensive hardware management integration

   Disk drive alerting with self-monitoring and reporting technology (SMART) and predictive failure analysis (PFA) provide pre-failure notification for disk drives and other server subsystems (please see specifications for details for each system). This enables full “lights out” remote management including key component status as well as remote power and restart with the ASM devices mentioned in number 4.

7. High availability

   System downtime is minimized by building error and fault-tolerance features into the servers. Error checking and correcting (ECC) memory, redundant array of independent disks (RAID) subsystems with hot-swappable disk drives, redundant power supply units and cooling fans, hot-swap PCI adapters and failover of faulty network cards and RAID controllers all help to ensure your server is kept running.

8. Compatibility and performance

   IBM engineering teams conduct ongoing compatibility testing, certification testing, and performance measurement and optimization to help ensure that IBM servers, network operating systems, and Lotus Domino run seamlessly together.

9. IBM Start Up Support and IBM Warranty

IBM Start Up Support provides, at no additional charge, telephone assistance for IBM and selected third-party hardware, and software, for the first 90 days of ownership. IBM servers are also covered by IBM's three-year limited on-site warranty.

10. TechConnect

A comprehensive program designed exclusively for networking professionals provides unique solution-based technical information, training and certification opportunities, and more.

11. Lotus Domino included

A Lotus Domino Server license and five Notes client licenses are included at no additional cost.

1.5 Focus of this redbook

The focus of this redbook is to describe how to implement Domino clusters using Domino R5. The examples used in the book are based on Domino R5 Version 5.04a, which was the most recent release at the time of writing. Where relevant, we discuss the differences between Domino clustering in Release 5 and Release 4.

All examples in this redbook are on Netfinity hardware. The operating systems used in our lab environment were Microsoft Windows 2000, Red Hat Linux, and SuSE Linux.

For additional information, you may find the following sources useful:

- `http://www.notes.net`
  See articles in the Iris Today Webzine - search on "clustering". (Iris Associates is where the developers of Lotus Notes and Lotus Domino work. Iris is a wholly owned subsidiary of Lotus, which is a wholly owned subsidiary of IBM.)
- `http://www.lotus.com/enterpriseserver`
  This is the Domino Enterprise Server Web page.
- `http://www.notesbench.org`
  Performance-related information from the NotesBench Consortium, an independent organization dedicated to providing Domino and Notes performance information.

The next chapter focuses on the issues to consider when planning a Domino R5 cluster.

Chapter 2. Planning a Domino cluster

This chapter discusses the things you need to consider when applying Domino clustering to meet your business needs. The chapter helps you to:

- Define server roles within a cluster
- Define database characteristics
- Define user characteristics
- Select hardware for the Domino clustering solution

2.1 Domino clustering

A Domino server cluster is a group of two to six Domino servers in the same Notes domain linked by a network connection. The network connection can be either a standard local area network (LAN) connection or a high-speed WAN connection.

The advantages of Domino clustering are:

- Improved availability

  Clusters provide failover protection for business-critical databases and servers, including passthru server failover to other servers in the cluster. When a server fails, users trying to access databases on the failed server will be automatically redirected to another server in the cluster. This allows users to continue working while their primary server is down.

- Performance optimization

  Workload balancing ensures that user requests on heavily used servers are redirected to other servers in the cluster so that work is evenly distributed throughout the cluster. Server workload balancing helps you achieve optimum system performance.

- Database replicas

  Cluster replication ensures that all replicas of a database within the cluster are kept tightly synchronized. Changes made to a database are immediately passed on to the other members of the cluster that contain replicas of the database. This ensures the consistency of information across the cluster and helps ensure the high availability of data.

- Scalability

  Domino clustering allows you to expand your system as your user base increases. Clustering also allows you to distribute databases and users

© Copyright IBM Corp. 1998, 2000

across clusters to balance the workload on each server. As you accommodate growth, you can move user accounts and databases to other servers in the cluster.

Workload balancing uses similar techniques to failover. User workload for a specific server is managed by the administrator, who adjusts the level at which the server is considered to be too busy. When the load on a server in a cluster reaches this level, additional user requests are redirected to another server in the cluster that has spare capacity. This proves useful in environments where servers experience peak usage times but the increased workload only lasts for a limited time. Workload balancing provides better response times for client requests as well as optimization of existing hardware.

2.2 Planning for Domino clustering

Clustering implementations are broadly divided into two categories. These are *active-active* clusters, in which cluster members are all performing useful work, and *active-passive* clusters, in which one or more machines is idle, doing no useful work until required to stand in for a failed system. In the latter configuration, the idle system is often referred to as a *standby server*.

Domino clusters are generally in an active-active configuration, in which all servers within a cluster actively provide services to clients. The cluster does not contain a standby server. Some types of cluster, in particular those implemented with Microsoft Cluster Services, may be implemented in either active-active or active-passive configurations. These are described in more detail in Chapter 6, "Domino and Windows 2000 clustering" on page 163.

Planning a clustered Domino environment involves decisions in a number of areas:

- Defining the required services from the Domino system.
- Defining database characteristics.
- Defining user characteristics.
- Determining the optimal hardware configuration for your servers.

2.2.1 Defining required services

The first step to take when planning a clustered Domino environment is to identify and define the services that are required in your environment. Some customers wish to implement only mail and standard Domino application services, while others may require other services as well.

The suite of Domino server tasks and services that you may wish to take advantage of include mail routing, Simple Mail Transfer Protocol (SMTP) mail routing, shared mail, Lightweight Directory Access Protocol (LDAP) services, Internet Message Access Protocol (IMAP), Network News Transfer Protocol (NNTP), replication, Hypertext Transfer Protocol (HTTP), passthru, remote access, billing, calendaring and scheduling, ICM, transaction logging, and backup. These server tasks are described in more detail in Chapter 3, “Designing a Domino cluster” on page 39.

After identifying the Domino services that you wish to provide, you should decide which services belong in the cluster. For example, you may want to provide high availability and failover for mail databases and several business-critical applications, but not for IMAP or NNTP services. As mentioned previously, with Domino R5’s introduction of the Internet Cluster Manager (ICM), you also have the option of providing cluster benefits to Web clients.

Since clustering is based on event-driven database replication, you can choose which databases will be clustered on each server. Systems in the cluster may also run several server tasks.

Each server task creates a different amount of workload on the server. For example, mail servers usually do not require many CPU cycles, but consume large amounts of disk space. Conversely, even a relatively small LotusScript application, while taking up a negligible amount of disk space, can cause a high CPU load, depending on the application. The only way to verify the actual CPU workload is to run the application in a test or production environment and use a performance monitor to track CPU performance statistics.

To ensure that your servers perform at optimal levels, you may want to consider dedicating servers for specific tasks. For example, you may want to nominate a server to run the HTTP task. This can be accomplished by editing the NOTES.INI file on all servers in the cluster and removing all unwanted server tasks from the ServerTasks line. In addition, if you have a large number of Domino applications, you can designate servers that house only applications and others that house only mail databases. Some customers have created multiserver clusters with application servers that can fail over to mail servers, and vice versa.

You can create multiple clusters in a Domino domain. There are several requirements for servers in a Domino cluster:

- A server can participate in one cluster at a time
- All the servers in a cluster must be in the same Domino domain
- All the servers in a cluster must share the same set of networking protocols

When you are deciding whether to dedicate a server to a specific task, the decision should be based on the amount of workload generated by the clients accessing that server. To estimate the workload you must know the characteristics of the databases that will reside on your servers. This issue is discussed in the following section.

2.2.2 Defining database characteristics

The next step to take when planning a Domino cluster is to define the characteristics of the databases that your Domino Server clients will be accessing. Understanding your databases' characteristics will help you to make good estimations for the hardware requirements of your Domino cluster. The major characteristics to consider include:

- The number and type of databases in your environment
- The sizes of the databases
- The expected volume of new data, updates, and deletions on a daily, weekly, or yearly basis
- The time sensitivity of data
- The number and distribution of database users
- The location of database replicas among your Domino servers
- The network connections between servers

To make the definition process easier, you may want to create a table that categorizes the characteristics of the databases in your environment. The following sample table illustrates the type of information that should be collected.

Table 2. Significant database characteristics

Database Name	Maximum number of concurrent users	Transaction rate	Number of replicas	Database size	Database growth	Need for high availability
HelpDesk application	10	Medium	1	1, 2 GB	Medium	Medium
Discussion database	500	High	2	2, 5 GB	Fast	High
Business application	350	Medium	2	800 MB	Fast	Very high
Web application	200	Medium	1	1 GB	Medium	Medium
Link library	300	Medium	1	600 MB	Slow	Low

Once you have created a table such as this, it will be easier to determine which of your databases would benefit from improved availability and what kind of impact you can expect the databases to have on your hardware resources. In this example, two databases are growing quickly and have medium or high transaction rates, indicators that they are potentially business-critical, and thus candidates for clustering.

Remember that Web applications will need to be on servers that are running the HTTP server task. If you are planning to dedicate servers for HTTP, you should make note of which databases are used for Web applications.

The number of concurrent users helps determine the amount of memory required for optimum performance. The formula to calculate this is discussed in 2.3, "Planning cluster hardware" on page 21.

In some cases, the statistic for the maximum number of concurrent users may seem misleading; most of the time the concurrent user count may be relatively low, but there will be periods when the user count may be doubled or even quadrupled. If this is the case, utilizing the workload balancing features in Domino clustering would help optimize the use of the hardware in your environment. Workload balancing in this scenario would improve response times for users during the peak hours by distributing client requests across the cluster. You can enable workload balancing by setting the Server_Availability_Threshold parameter in the NOTES.INI file. Workload balancing design and configuration are discussed in detail in Chapter 3, “Designing a Domino cluster” on page 39.

The transaction rate directly affects the CPU load on the server. Cluster replication is event-driven, so every time an addition, deletion, or change is made to a document or database, the change is replicated to all of that database’s replicas within the cluster. Other factors will also affect the overall CPU load and need to be considered. Simple discussion databases with a high transaction rate may not cause as much CPU workload as a complex LotusScript application with a lower transaction rate, so you will need to take the complexity of the application into consideration as well.

Current database sizes and growth rates should provide a good estimation of the disk space needed for the databases. Databases generally tend to grow faster than expected, so it is a good idea to overestimate the amount of disk space your environment will require. Mail databases, in particular, tend to have a very high growth rate, even when database quotas are in place. Keep in mind, too, that you will need space for all the replicas in the cluster. Many customers like to plan for additional capacity that exceeds and sometimes even doubles their disk space estimates, so that they can fine-tune the database distribution within the cluster without having to worry about running out of disk space.

Disk space should be considered very carefully when planning for mail servers. As users start to use more advanced features like attachments, mail message sizes begin to grow. Disk space is also affected by users who tend to keep old messages, even though the messages are no longer needed. When users send messages to multiple recipients, that message is copied to each recipient’s mail file. If those messages have attachments, the potential impact on disk space is significant. You can avoid this problem by implementing shared mail. The shared mail concept and implementation in a clustered environment is discussed in Chapter 3, “Designing a Domino cluster” on page 39 and Chapter 5, “Administering Domino clusters” on page 119.

You can also avoid the problem of users distributing large messages to multiple mail files by implementing a shared database for individual workgroups or for the entire user base. Users should be encouraged to place large attachments or documents in the shared database. They can then distribute them to multiple recipients by creating a document link to the shared database instead of sending a large attachment. This shared database is another good candidate for clustering to provide high availability.

The need for database availability affects the number of replicas that may be distributed among the systems forming the cluster. An important database that is not, however, critical to your operation would typically be distributed to just two servers in the cluster. This would be sufficient to provide an enhanced level of availability at little cost. A database whose availability is essential, on the other hand, should be distributed to more servers within the cluster.

2.2.2.1 Number of replicas for mail databases

In most cases, two replicas of a mail database in a cluster should provide a sufficient level of availability for your mail users, while keeping cluster replication workload low. The transaction rate for mail databases can vary, but for the most part they tend to have a relatively high transaction rate. Since cluster replication is event-driven, every transaction in a mail database results in cluster replication overhead. Mail database replicas should be distributed as evenly as possible among the servers in the cluster to avoid an unreasonable growth of workload on one server in the cluster as a result of the failure of another server in the cluster.

2.2.2.2 Number of replicas for application databases

If an application database has a high transaction rate, the recommendation is that no more than three replicas of the database are created in the cluster. This recommendation allows you to provide high availability while controlling overhead due to cluster replication. Critical databases with relatively low transaction rates may warrant even more replicas than this.

2.2.2.3 Other replication considerations

As already mentioned, cluster replication is event-driven. This means that every time a change, addition, or deletion is made to a document in a database, a cluster replication event is generated. For example, when a document in a mail database is moved to a folder, that change is communicated to all replicas of that database in the cluster. This event-driven cluster replication ensures that all replicas in a cluster are tightly synchronized and up-to-date. It also means that LAN traffic is increased, as well as CPU workload, and memory and disk space requirements for the servers in the cluster.

Creating too many clustered replicas of a heavily used database can decrease the overall performance of the Domino system. There are many factors to be considered when estimating the amount of server workload that any given database will generate. The best way to discover exactly how much impact cluster replication will have on your system is to create a test environment and monitor the statistics. A test environment is also helpful to determine the best way to distribute databases and workload among your clustered servers. Several recommendations to keep in mind are:

- Use a private network for cluster traffic to avoid placing this additional load on the client network.
- Use a fast input/output (I/O) and disk subsystems.
- Dedicate servers for specific tasks, such as HTTP.

2.2.3 Defining user characteristics

The way your users utilize the features of Domino server can also have a significant bearing on your cluster implementation. The amount of workload that a user creates on a server usually depends on his or her familiarity with Domino. Beginners who are not familiar with Domino tend to perform simple operations, such as basic mail tasks, in comparison with more advanced users who may have several databases open simultaneously and perform complex task such as search operations and running agents.

Users can be divided into four broad groups depending on the Domino functions they use, although a typical user's workload is often represented by a combination of these categories. The four categories of user workload we have selected are defined in the following list. They are essentially self-defining, but we have included definitions for completeness:

- *Mail only.* The users in this category only use Notes mail functions, such as sending and receiving mail. They do not use any calendaring and scheduling functions, nor do they access any databases.
- *Mail with calendaring and scheduling.* Users who use Notes mail functions and calendaring and scheduling features are in this category.
- *Database.* Users in this category perform heavy shared database operations, such as making additions and updates to documents, running full text searches, performing view operations and navigating unread documents.
- *Web user.* These are users that access the Domino server using a Web browser. Web clients can use HTTP, POP3, LDAP, or IMAP protocols to perform functions on a Domino server. The corresponding server task must be running on the Domino server to enable the protocol. Web user workload on a Domino server is generally different from the workload generated by a Notes client, because HTTP clients typically open a session to a server to transfer data, and close the session when the operation is completed. Notes client sessions remain open until they are explicitly closed or until the timeout value is exceeded. The actual

workload difference depends greatly on the protocol being used and the type of database that is being accessed on the server.

A typical Notes user can be defined as a mail user with calendaring and scheduling, but mapping users to groups by their characteristics may help you to better understand the requirements for the system. The following table provides an example of a user characteristics distribution:

Table 3. User characteristics distribution

User type	Number of users	Percentage of all users
Mail-only	150	10%
Mail with calendaring and scheduling	600	40%
Database	375	25%
Web	375	25%
Total	1500	100%

In this example, our users can mostly be described as power users performing advanced operations on the servers. Power users tend to create more changes in the databases. This means that more cluster replication events would be created by these users, increasing the server workload. In addition, the number of Web users in this example would indicate that a dedicated HTTP server cluster for Web client requests is worth considering.

2.2.4 Network protocols and topologies

Domino supports several network protocols, including Transmission Control Protocol/Internet Protocol (TCP/IP), Sequenced Packet Exchange (SPX), and Network Basic Input/Output System (NetBIOS) Extended User Interface (NetBEUI). Internal cluster traffic uses only the TCP/IP protocol. This means that you can select any Domino-supported protocol for your clients to connect to the cluster, but you must include TCP/IP for the cluster replication tasks. An additional requirement is for the servers in a cluster to share the same set of protocols. For example, if there are two servers in a cluster, and clients use SPX to connect to the first server and NetBEUI to connect to the second one, each server must run both SPX and NetBEUI for the client traffic, and TCP/IP for the cluster's internal communications.

TCP/IP is a standard protocol supported on every major platform and often a natural choice for new systems. TCP/IP might be a slightly slower protocol in a LAN environment compared to NetBEUI, for example, but a slight performance overhead is acceptable in return for the advantages of using

TCP/IP. These include the ability to route TCP/IP packets and support for subnetting, which offers flexibility in network configuration. In addition, TCP/IP is, of course, the protocol used across the Internet, so you will be preparing for the day when you need to publish Domino-based data and applications on the Web, if you are not doing so already.

Finally, Lotus strongly recommends that TCP/IP should be the only protocol used in a clustered Domino environment. The reason for this is that Domino's failover functions are optimized for TCP/IP, making failovers complete faster than they would when using another protocol. For the remainder of this discussion, therefore, we will focus on the TCP/IP protocol.

Domino clustering does not limit the network topology. It supports every network topology that the platform it is running on supports. Windows 2000 supports all the major topologies including token-ring, Ethernet, FDDI, and ATM. As long as the network adapter is configured and functioning, and the required protocol settings are complete, Domino clustering can operate.

Domino clusters can be implemented on mixed network topologies. For example, if the client network is running over a token-ring infrastructure, the internal cluster traffic could use a private Ethernet network.

Although not essential for clusters, we strongly recommend that you dedicate a private LAN connection for the cluster's internal traffic. If there is no dedicated link between the clustered servers, the cluster replication traffic is transferred over the client network. In the worst case, this may even jam the network, especially if one or more of the clustered servers are attached to a slower network connection.

Finally, there is no architectural reason why a Domino cluster has to be limited to a LAN environment. Domino cluster members can be connected to each other over a WAN link, although the WAN connection should be a high-speed line, providing close to LAN-speed bandwidth, to avoid performance problems.

2.2.5 Supported clients

Release 4 and higher Notes clients can take advantage of the Domino clustering features. With Release 5 Enterprise Server, Web clients can now take advantage of the Domino clustering features as well.

2.3 Planning cluster hardware

When determining the best hardware configuration for the Domino servers in a cluster, several things should be kept in mind. The major differences between planning for a standard Domino server and planning for a clustered implementation are that extra memory and CPU cycles must be reserved to handle the cluster tasks, and the servers in the cluster must be able to cope with the increased workload that will be placed on them if client requests are redirected to them from another server or servers.

Domino clustering will run on any Windows 2000 or Windows NT-compatible hardware, as well as other supported Domino platforms, including S/390, AS/400, RS/6000, Sun, DEC Alpha and others. This book focuses on the Windows 2000 and Linux operating systems running on Netfinity hardware.

Several hardware vendors are members of the NotesBench Consortium. The consortium members are qualified to test their hardware with the NotesBench test program. NotesBench test results can help you to select the appropriate hardware for your particular business needs.

Unlike some clustering technologies, Domino does not require cluster members to be identical servers. If there are two servers in a cluster, the first server could use a RAID disk subsystem and have ECC memory and four Pentium processors installed, while the second server has IDE disks and a single processor. The servers in the Domino cluster can even run on different operating systems; while writing this book, we created a cluster comprising servers running Windows 2000 and Linux.

The most important question to answer when planning the hardware platform for your Domino cluster is whether the hardware is capable of offering the required level of performance for your specific business needs. Hardware bottlenecks are most often due to inadequacies in one or more of the following:

- Memory
- CPU
- Disk I/O
- Disk space
- Network bandwidth

These factors are discussed in more detail in the following sections.

2.3.1 Memory

System memory, sometimes called random access memory (RAM), can become a serious bottleneck in a Domino environment, especially when users perform more advanced functions. Most modern operating systems (including Windows 2000 and Linux) implement a virtual memory system to allow the CPU to manage more data and programs than will actually fit in real memory. When the operating system needs more memory than is physically available in the machine, it starts to use a *page file* on a hard disk to store data that is not currently required, and so make room for new data. When the data that was stored in the page file is required, other data is stored on the disk and the required data is retrieved from the page file.

While this has the benefit of allowing the server to manipulate more data and programs than would be possible without a virtual memory system, there is a performance penalty. The time taken to read and write data from and to the page file is orders of magnitude greater than the time to move data around in RAM, so performance is severely affected as soon as significant paging activity is necessary. Constant paging should be avoided by ensuring there is enough memory installed.

2.3.1.1 User memory

A good approximation to calculate the memory requirement for the active users in your environment is provided by the following formula:

```
Recommended basic memory + (Number of concurrent users / 3) MB
```

The recommended basic memory when running the Domino server on Windows 2000 is 128 MB or more. This algorithm is appropriate for mail and application servers and mail hubs. For example, if you are planning to support 120 concurrent active users on a server, the recommended memory would be 168 MB (128 MB + (120 / 3) MB). However, servers do not conveniently allow configuration with arbitrary amounts of memory, usually providing for increments of 64 or 128 MB. In this case, rounding up to the nearest 64 MB indicates that the actual memory installed should be 192 MB. Note that, for this calculation, we need the number of users that are simultaneously connected, that is to say active users, and not the count of users whose mail files are located on the server. There could be 1,000 users with mail files on a single server, but usually there are significantly fewer users active at any given time.

In addition, if you are planning to provide file and print sharing from the Windows 2000 server, or if you are running other application servers on the machine hosting the Domino server, you will need to add even more memory. Lotus strongly recommends that you do not run Windows file and print sharing services or any application servers, such as SQL Server or IBM DB2, on the same machine that is running the Lotus Domino Server.

2.3.1.2 Replicator memory

You can run multiple instances of the cluster replicator task (CLREPL) to increase performance of the system; however, only one cluster database directory task (CLDBDIR) can be run. It is suggested that you set the number of cluster replicator tasks running on each server in the cluster to the number of servers in the cluster, less one. For example, if you have a four-server cluster, you should set the number of cluster replicator tasks on each server to three.

Lab testing indicated that each cluster replicator task requires about 2 MB of memory. Therefore, the formula to calculate the required memory for cluster replication tasks is:

```
(Number of cluster replicator tasks) x 2 MB
```

Replicator memory need only be considered in environments with large clusters or if the workload is very heavy and several cluster replicator tasks need to be run simultaneously.

2.3.2 Processor

Lotus recommends that you use at least a Pentium-level processor with Domino clustering. The actual requirement for processor power and deciding whether or not you should use multiprocessor systems is dependent on the server and cluster usage. If the cluster is used as a mail server or a database server, increasing CPU cycles or installing a second processor will not provide a significant improvement in the response time, since the bottleneck will usually be either memory or disk I/O rate. If the server is an application server with heavy usage of LotusScript or Java applications, adding CPUs might be the best solution to get rid of the bottleneck.

Clustering in itself does not have an impact on the performance of the individual servers, except for a minimal amount of server-to-server communication that is used to determine availability. After adding servers to a cluster, the CPU utilization rate will remain the same as long as the workload on the servers remains the same. Additional CPU workload comes from maintaining replicas of databases on other servers.

If a new cluster of two servers is created, and all the mail databases on each server are replicated to the other server, the workload on both servers will increase. For example, if two servers with identical hardware configurations have CPU utilization rates of 35% and 40%, the CPU utilization rate on each server when clustered with replication of all databases will most likely be 75%. Keep in mind that the servers are not only handling their original workload, but also duplicating the workload from the other server.

When Domino servers are clustered, event-based replication keeps the information in replicated databases tightly synchronized. The primary reason to implement clustering is to provide high availability of data. In the example discussed above, if one of the servers becomes unavailable, then the remaining server, which has up-to-date replicas of all the databases, can support all the users. While one server in the cluster is down, the other server will handle all the user requests, and cluster replication will not take place. Either server in this scenario clearly has the ability to handle all the user requests when the other server is unavailable.

Often the only way to determine if the CPU is truly the source of the bottleneck is to create a test environment and monitor the CPU load under the real circumstances. With Windows 2000, monitoring is made easy by using the system's Performance tool.

If the processor utilization on a server is constantly near 100%, you should consider either spreading the server workload throughout the cluster, or adding another processor to the overloaded system. Domino servers can take full advantage of symmetrical multiprocessing (SMP) hardware configurations. Servers such as the Netfinity 8500 can support up to eight CPUs in a single system.

Be sure to examine all pertinent performance monitors, not CPU utilization alone. High CPU utilization can also be the result of excessive paging, a malfunctioning adapter card, or simply too many applications running on the server. Windows 2000's Performance tool can help you determine how much CPU each application is consuming as well as the paging rate. If the paging rate is high, adding more memory will probably improve performance and reduce CPU utilization, as discussed in 2.3.1, "Memory" on page 22.

Windows NT

There are some known issues between certain Windows NT Service Packs and Domino, which can cause memory conflicts and high processor utilization. These problems are documented and workarounds have been posted in the Lotus Notes Knowledge Base at:

`http://www.support.lotus.com`

and on the Microsoft Web site at

`http://www.microsoft.com`

If you notice high CPU utilization and have tried all the workarounds listed above, check the support sites of both companies to determine if there is a conflict between the OS and your version of Domino.

2.3.3 Disk input/output

When databases are replicated, all input/output (I/O) activity related to a specific database has to take place for each replica. That is, each server has to manage disk I/O both for its own databases and for those databases for which it hosts clustered replicas. It is apparent, therefore, that paying careful attention to the distribution of a server's databases across its disk subsystem can pay dividends in performance.

When locating database files on a server, place them in an optimal location on the fastest disk hardware available. Use your knowledge of server hardware to place the database where contention for bandwidth is reduced. For example, do not place your database files in the same partition that contains the operating system's swap file. We cover this topic in more detail in 2.3.4, "Disk subsystems" on page 28.

In Domino Release 5, a number of design changes have been made to reduce the opportunity for I/O bottlenecks to occur. The major improvements are:

- Implementing transaction logging
- A new database on-disk structure (ODS)
- New justification for distributing mail files across multiple logical disk units
- The use of multiple MAIL.BOX databases

Each of these I/O optimizations can result in a significant improvement in system performance. We cover each of them in turn below.

2.3.3.1 Transaction logging

In Domino Release 5, transaction logging has been introduced for the first time. This not only helps improve performance by streamlining disk I/O, but also decreases recovery time by logging transactions before they are written to disk. These features help to provide high availability of data and increase database integrity. Using transaction logging in conjunction with Domino clustering can offer a significant increase in system performance. In this section, we will focus on how transaction logging specifically helps to improve disk I/O performance.

Transaction logging is basically provided for reliable data storage and recovery. An added benefit is an increase in system performance. Recent test data has shown that using transaction logging may lower disk and CPU utilization, and improve response times when the server has a heavy workload. System performance improvements due to transaction logging may not be as noticeable when the I/O on the system is low to moderate. The primary reason for this performance improvement is that each transaction on the Domino server is written to sequential data areas on the disk holding the transaction logs.

Without transaction logging, all modifications to databases are committed to disk as they occur. This results in essentially random disk head movement as the head seeks from one database entry to another and between different databases. With transaction logging enabled, all modifications to databases are written sequentially to the transaction logs rather than being written directly to the databases. Control then returns to the process requesting the update. Transactions are transferred to the databases at some later time, when it is convenient for the system to do so. The end result is streamlined disk I/O and faster system performance.

Test data has shown that transaction logging also offers additional system-level performance benefits. At the operating system level, file and disk operations are carried out in a privileged mode that is not directly available to applications. In this privileged mode, all file and disk operations are carried out by the OS kernel. When data is moved to and from the disk, the OS must switch to a kernel thread to handle the task. Disk performance is an important factor. The more time the system spends waiting for I/O to complete, the less time the system spends running the application (in this case, Domino).

Since transaction logging improves the overall I/O rate for Domino, it reduces the time the system spends waiting for disk operations to complete, and therefore increases the time available for the system to spend doing the work of the application. This results in an overall improvement in user-perceived server performance.

2.3.3.2 Database on-disk structure (ODS)

The Domino on-disk structure (ODS) defines how Domino allocates space on the disk to its databases. The Domino R5 database format improves overall database performance. Database operations using the R5 ODS require less I/O than was required to support the ODS for earlier releases of Domino. Therefore, if you are upgrading your existing databases from Release 4, it is strongly recommended that you upgrade your databases to the R5 ODS to take advantage of the I/O improvements. More details on upgrading to the R5 ODS can be found in the Domino R5 Administration Help database.

2.3.3.3 Distributing mail files across logical disk units

To further improve performance, you can use file links to distribute mail files across multiple logical disks. For Windows 2000, you can use directory links; for Linux, you would use symbolic links. With this feature enabled, the Domino router can deliver mail concurrently. This improves I/O performance because the concurrent mail delivery results in concurrent disk I/Os.

A lot can be written about performance improvements that can be gained by careful optimization of your disk subsystem. For more detail on performance and disk subsystems for Netfinity servers, we recommend these two IBM Redbooks:

- *Netfinity Server Disk Subsystems*, SG24-2098
- *Tuning Netfinity Servers for Performance*, ISBN 0-13-040612-0

2.3.3.4 Multiple MAIL.BOX databases

Using multiple MAIL.BOX databases can also enhance your server performance. Recent benchmark data has shown that moving from one to two MAIL.BOX databases offers the most dramatic increase in server performance. Increasing the number of MAIL.BOX databases beyond two produces some further performance gains, but less dramatic than the initial boost from using a second MAIL.BOX.

Having multiple MAIL.BOX databases improves server performance because the mail router can deposit messages into any available MAIL.BOX database. If mail is heavily used on your systems, as it is is most typical installations, the addition of more MAIL.BOX databases makes it easier for the mail router process to deliver mail by reducing contention between users or other server processes that are simultaneously trying to deposit messages in the

MAIL.BOX database. This results in faster message delivery time, which translates to an increase in user-perceived system performance.

2.3.4 Disk subsystems

The following sections briefly discuss the main disk subsystem technologies used by Netfinity servers, including small computer system interface (SCSI), Serial Storage Architecture (SSA), and Fiber Channel. For more detailed information about disk subsystems for IBM Intel-based servers, see *Netfinity Server Disk Subsystems*, SG24-2098.

2.3.4.1 SCSI

The SCSI disk subsystem is the entry-level technology used in Netfinity servers. Desktop personal computers typically use disks with integrated drive electronics (IDE), which are cheaper but have several disadvantages when compared with SCSI subsystems in a server environment, primarily in terms of performance and capacity.

SCSI is a good choice for a server disk subsystem since SCSI offers an excellent compromise among cost, performance and capacity. Up to 15 SCSI drives can be attached to a single SCSI channel, so servers with multiple SCSI channels can support quite a large number of disks.

Using standard SCSI adapters in Windows 2000 results in each disk appearing as a separate drive letter to the operating system. You may find that you have a requirement for data partitions that are larger than the largest single disk. There is also the danger of losing valuable data if a disk fails. Overcoming these limitations is most usefully achieved by using redundant array of independent disks (RAID) technology to drive the SCSI disks (see 2.3.4.2, “RAID” on page 29 below). RAID can also improve availability and disk subsystem performance.

While Windows 2000 offers its own form of RAID (using dynamic volumes) implemented in software, hardware RAID adapters are a better solution, being independent of the operating system and placing no load on the server's CPU. IBM xSeries and Netfinity servers are shipped with SCSI interfaces as standard, and some systems include support for RAID technology as part of their base specification. In addition, optional RAID adapters with up to four independent SCSI channels may be installed in a server. If necessary, several adapters can be installed in the same machine to further increase capacity.

2.3.4.2 RAID

RAID is an acronym for *redundant array of independent disks*. This section provides an introduction to RAID technology. It does not attempt to explain all of the intricacies of RAID configuration. If you are not familiar with RAID concepts and wish to know more, we once again refer you to the redbook *Netfinity Server Disk Subsystems*, SG24-2098.

Five different types of RAID array, referred to as levels, were originally defined. Three of these levels are commonly used in the Intel-based server world, although extensions to RAID beyond the original five levels are becoming more common.

The three most common levels are:

- RAID-0
- RAID-1
- RAID-5

When appropriately configured, a RAID adapter treats a group of disks (an array) as a single entity. An array may contain one or more logical drives, which are seen by the operating system as physical drives. Each logical drive is formatted to a specific RAID level. For simplicity and potential performance benefits, a single logical drive per array is often recommended.

To configure your systems for optimum I/O performance, you should have an understanding of the differences between these different RAID levels:

- A RAID-0 logical drive stripes data across its underlying array in a sequential manner. The addressable space represented by the array is split into blocks. Data is read from or written to the logical drive by accessing a block of data (16 KB, for example) on each disk in turn, cycling through all of the disks in the array. The disk I/O rate for RAID-0 is excellent because disk operations can be executed on several physical disks at the same time. RAID-0 also offers excellent disk capacity. For example, if five 9 GB disks are configured to be a logical disk, a total of 45 GB of disk space is gained. RAID is actually a misnomer in the case of RAID-0 as there is no redundancy of data, since the data on an entire logical disk will be lost if one of the physical disks fails.
- RAID-1 is a mirrored pair of physical disk drives. Mirroring means that the same data is written to both physical disks. This guarantees that the system will be available if one of the physical disks fails, because the data is still available on the second disk. The I/O rate for reads is good, because applications can read from either drive. However, they must write to both drives, resulting in extra I/O for writes, so the write performance is

not as good. RAID-1 is a good choice for environments that require high fault tolerance. However, disk capacity is effectively halved, so RAID-1 is relatively expensive.

- RAID-5 is similar to RAID-0 in the way that data is striped across the underlying array. However, one block in each set of blocks that form a single stripe across the array is reserved for *parity* information. This parity data allows any single block of data from a stripe to be recreated if it becomes unavailable. RAID-5 requires at least three hard disk drives in the underlying array. If a disk in a RAID-5 set fails, the remaining disks contain the information needed to calculate the data on the failed drive. In this way, a disk can fail without any loss of data.

  RAID-5 offers a relatively good I/O rate, because several disk operations can be performed at the same time. However, RAID-5 requires more disk I/Os for each write than the other RAID configurations. For each write operation, multiple disk I/Os are necessary, since the parity data changes when data in its stripe is modified.

Combinations and enhancements of these basic RAID levels, such as RAID-0+1 and RAID-1 Enhanced, can be configured. These are effectively mirrored RAID-0 arrays, extending the capacity of basic RAID-1 to more than a single pair of drives.

Lotus recommends the use of RAID-0+1 or RAID-1 Enhanced for the best performance of Domino databases. This recommendation was developed after the write and read accesses to disk for various workloads was compared. RAID-5 is not recommended for write-intensive applications, since RAID-5 requires three additional I/Os for each write (compared to one additional I/O per write for RAID-0+1 or RAID-1 Enhanced). However, when making a final decision about RAID levels, you should consider the trade-off between cost and performance.

It is important to note that the disk subsystem has redundancy with both RAID-5 and RAID-1 only when all drives are functional; the system will not be fault-tolerant if one of the disks in the array fails. In this state, a RAID array is said to be *critical*. If a second disk were to fail before the original failure is corrected, data loss would be the result. This problem can be minimized by configuring an additional disk to be a *hot spare*.

A hot-spare disk will replace a failed disk in the array, and the system will become fault-tolerant again as soon as the hot-spare disk is synchronized with the array. RAID adapters used in Netfinity servers rebuild data from a failed drive onto a hot-spare disk automatically, minimizing the time the array is in the critical state and helping to maintain high availability.

Most Netfinity servers also offer hot-swap disk subsystems. Hot-swapping allows you to replace and even configure disks on-the-fly without powering down the server.

2.3.5 Storage capacity

When you are determining the amount of hard disk space required to implement Domino clustering, the following things should be considered:

- Operating system requirements
- Paging file
- Lotus Domino program files
- Lotus Domino databases
- Databases replicated from other servers in the cluster
- Transaction logs
- Additional applications, such as backup tools

2.3.5.1 Operating system

According to Microsoft, installing Windows 2000 Advanced Server requires a 2 GB hard drive, of which at least 1 GB must be free. Lotus strongly recommends that you do not run any other application servers or Windows 2000 file and print services on the same machine that is running the Domino server.

Linux is a much more compact operating system and a typical distribution, SuSE Linux 7.0, requires between 150 MB and 6 GB for installation, with a default server installation requiring about 600 MB.

2.3.5.2 Paging file

Random access memory (RAM) is much more expensive than disk space, so many operating systems, including Windows 2000 and Linux, implement virtual memory systems, where disk space is used to extend the capacity of physical RAM. Virtual memory swaps data between RAM and the disk as physical memory becomes fully occupied with data and programs. Access time for the data in the server's RAM is typically 60 ns. SCSI disk access time for data is typically from 8 ms to 12 ms. Therefore, using the virtual memory on the disk is noticeably slower than retrieving the data from RAM. In general, therefore, servers should not page very much except during peak loads.

When Windows 2000 starts, it reserves space on the disk to be used as virtual memory. Microsoft recommends that 1.5 x the amount of physical RAM installed in the system should be reserved for paging, but, in fact, Windows manages the pagefile without your intervention, although you can modify its size and location if you wish by using the System Properties dialog box.

Linux handles its page space in a slightly different way. You have to define one or more swap partitions in your disk subsystem. We discuss Linux partitions in 4.2, "Hardware setup" on page 80.

2.3.5.3 Lotus Domino program files and databases

The Domino R5 Enterprise Server requires a minimum of 750 MB of disk space just for the program code and standard databases, and 1 GB is recommended by Lotus. You can reduce disk consumption somewhat by not installing the Notes help databases on every server.

After defining the database characteristics (as described in 2.2.2, "Defining database characteristics" on page 14), you should be able to define the disk space requirements for the databases. You should also remember to reserve enough disk space for the replicas from other servers in the cluster.

You should reserve about 45 MB of disk space for each Domino mail user. This value might sound high, but mail databases tend to grow very quickly, even when database quotas are applied. Calendar entries and scheduling events also increase the amount of space required by the mail database since they reside there.

2.3.5.4 Transaction logs

If, as recommended, you decide to enable transaction logging on your servers, you should keep the transaction logs on their own separate physical disk, away from the Domino program files, Domino data files, and operating system files. Ideally, the logs should be on a separate, mirrored disk (RAID-1) with its own dedicated controller. This allows sequential access to the logs to take place without being disturbed by accesses to other parts of the disk.

2.3.6 Network bandwidth

Determining the amount of network traffic that a cluster will create is an important consideration when planning a cluster. The best way to do this is to create a test environment and monitor the network bandwidth usage among clustered servers. Many hardware vendors have already performed thorough testing of cluster traffic and its impact on the network. You can find their test results at:

`http://www.notesbench.org`

It is recommended that you create a private LAN to carry cluster traffic. Doing so makes your cluster more efficient by separating the cluster traffic from the other network traffic on your LAN. This will also help avoid the problem of a busy cluster taking up too much bandwidth on your primary LAN. In addition, a private network for your cluster ensures that cluster replication will continue even if problems occur on the primary LAN.

To create a private LAN for your cluster, you must install an additional network interface card (NIC) on each server in the cluster and connect these secondary NICs through a suitable interconnecting hub or switch. All cluster members must be connected to both the primary LAN for client access and the private LAN for cluster communication.

2.3.7 Performance tools

Once your Domino cluster is up and running, you will want to optimize its operation to get the most out of your investment. In Appendix B, "Tuning Domino clusters" on page 217 we provide some Domino-specific information to help you to do so. It is also worthwhile paying attention to the way your operating system is configured.

In this section, we give some brief hints and pointers to sources of information for operating system tuning.

2.3.7.1 Windows 2000 Performance tool

An excellent tool for monitoring resource usage is the Windows 2000 Performance tool (**Start -> Settings -> Control Panel -> Administrative Tools -> Performance**). The Performance tool is well documented in Microsoft materials, so here we will briefly discuss only those monitors that will be most useful when analyzing server bottlenecks.

CPU counters

CPU usage counters that should be checked regularly are Processor:% Processor Time:_Total and Processor:Interrupts/sec:_Total.

The Processor:% Processor Time:_Total counter shows the overall processor utilization. On a single processor machine, it should not exceed 80%. On an SMP machine it should not exceed 50%. Sometimes the processor utilization can go up to 100% for a brief period when applications start or when there is increased keyboard and mouse activity at the server. You should check the average value over a longer period of time; if it exceeds the values suggested above, you may need to make adjustments to your system.

The Processor:Interrupts/sec:_Total counter displays the interrupt rate that the CPU has to service. The keyboard, mouse, and network adapter, for example, all create system interrupts. A high system interrupt rate can indicate a faulty adapter card. When the interrupt rate is very high, the CPU time is wasted serving these requests. Consequently, system performance decreases.

Memory counters

The two main counters to be concerned with for memory usage monitoring are Memory:% Committed Bytes in Use and Memory:Pages/sec.

The Memory:% Committed Bytes in Use counter displays the percentage of the system memory that has been reserved for applications and the operating system. This memory includes both the physical and virtual memory. If the average value is close to 80%, either the operating system paging file size should be increased, or more memory should be added to the system.

The Memory:Pages/sec parameter shows the rate at which memory pages are being moved between RAM and virtual memory. A high paging rate is an indication that memory is being overcommitted by the server. This increases disk workload and can drastically affect overall system performance. The threshold value for this parameter is 5. If the paging rate is too high, you should add more memory to your system or reduce its workload. In general, servers should be paging relatively infrequently in normal operating conditions.

Disk counters

The best counters to check for disk usage are Physical Disk:Avg. Disk Queue Length:Instance and Physical Disk:% Disk Time.

The Physical Disk:Avg. Disk Queue Length:Instance counter is good for monitoring disk I/O rates. It shows the number of disk operation requests queued. If this value is greater than 2, the disk controller or the disk subsystem may be the source of a bottleneck. If only one of the disks shows bad values, you might want to try moving some Notes databases from the busy disk to another disk that is showing no queue. You should also consider improving the disk subsystem. Using faster hard disks or upgrading from, for example, SCSI adapters to RAID controllers will improve system performance.

RAID drives

If you are using RAID technology, remember that the physical disks seen by the operating system are, in fact, the logical drives defined in the underlying RAID arrays.

The Physical Disk:% Disk Time counter displays the percentage of time that the disk subsystem is busy servicing read and write requests. The threshold value for this parameter is 85%. If this value is exceeded, it means that the disk subsystem is busy almost constantly. This may indicate that excessive memory paging is taking place. If paging is the problem, it may be alleviated by adding more memory to the system. Another reason for high disk activity can be a genuine heavy load on the disk system, which can be helped by distributing the data files across the disks, equalizing the workload among physical disks. You can also consider placing Domino databases on a separate disk from the program files.

Activating the statistics-gathering process for the disk subsystem causes a performance overhead of approximately 2% on the system. For this reason, this process should not be running all the time.

To activate the statistics-gathering process for the disk subsystem, enter the following command at the Windows 2000 command prompt:

```
c:\> diskperf -y
```

Once you have finished gathering the statistics, remember to shut off the process. To deactivate the statistics-gathering process for the disk subsystem, enter the following command at the Windows 2000 command prompt:

```
c:\> diskperf -n
```

Interpreting performance data

Remember that the obvious solution isn't always the correct one. As an example, it is possible for a network adapter fault to generate a high number of spurious interrupts. This could be reflected in performance figures as high CPU utilization, since the CPU has to process all of those interrupts. The obvious solution to high CPU utilization might be a CPU upgrade. However, an analysis of the true cause of the inflated figures would reveal the malfunctioning network card.

Similarly, an overly high disk utilization rate may be caused by poor data placement. However, if after a brief analysis, the bulk of the I/O is determined as being to a paging/swap file, this would indicate a memory constraint, and the solution would be to install additional memory.

For more information about tuning your servers to optimize performance under Windows 2000, we recommend *Tuning Netfinity Servers for Performance*, ISBN 0-13-040612-0.

2.3.7.2 Linux performance tools

In a Linux environment, there are a number of ways to improve server performance. Some of these are really only available to experienced Linux users because you may need to recompile the Linux kernel to be able to use them. By doing so, you can switch on all available optimization flags and Intel architecture-specific compiler options to ensure that the code is as fast as possible.

Creating multiple swap partitions and locating them on different physical drives or arrays can also affect performance. However, your server should not be paging excessively during normal operation, so this will have the most effect when the server is experiencing peak loads.

An important monitoring tool for Linux is `top` or one of its graphical variants, such as `KTop` under the KDE GUI. These tools can reveal which tasks are using most of your CPU's resources.

As with many Linux tools, the best way to find out how to use them is to experiment with them yourself. To start, you might refer to the following IBM Redbooks and read the relevant sections about Linux performance tools to find pointers to other tools and references:

- *Red Hat Linux and Netfinity Server Integration Guide,* SG24-5853
- *Netfinity and Caldera OpenLinux Integration Guide*, SG24-5861
- *Netfinity and TurboLinux Integration Guide*, SG24-5862
- *Netfinity and SuSE Linux Integration Guide*, SG24-5863

2.4 Internet Cluster Manager

The Internet Cluster Manager (ICM) allows you to provide Domino clustering services to Web browser clients. This provides your clients with the benefit of improved availability. You can run the ICM on a Domino R5 Enterprise server. The Domino servers should be configured in the same way as a regular Domino cluster prior to configuring the ICM.

ICM supports both the HTTP and HTTPS protocols. It maintains availability statistics about the databases and servers in the cluster. When the ICM receives a client request, it redirects that request to the most available server in the cluster. The ICM code itself can be executed on either a member server of the Domino cluster or outside the cluster altogether. If the ICM is running on a server inside the cluster, it uses the local copy of the Cluster Database Directory (CLDBDIR.NSF) to direct client requests to the appropriate database. If it is running outside the cluster, it accesses a server in the cluster, retrieves the database information from that server's Cluster Database Directory, and redirects the client accordingly.

Test data has shown that the ICM will help to increase server performance. The ICM offers a significant performance boost due to the workload balancing features, while causing only a minimal amount of additional system overhead.

Some hardware tips to consider when planning to use ICM on a server include:

- The more servers you have in the cluster, the more processing power each server will need for communicating with the other clustered servers.
- As you increase the number of tasks executing on a server, the amount of processing power the server will need increases.
- If a server has a large number of users, it will need more memory to keep the performance level high. Use the following formula to get a general idea of the amount of memory you will need:

  ```
  Recommended Domino memory + 1 MB for every three concurrent users
  ```

  For example, if the recommended memory to run Domino alone is 64 MB, and you want to support 180 concurrent users, you will need 124 MB of memory (64 MB + (180 / 3 MB)). In this example, you would install 128 MB, rounding up to the next largest amount of memory that can be configured.
- If you intend to use multiple Cluster Replicators on the servers to improve cluster replication performance, you will need to add more memory to handle the additional workload that each Cluster Replicator adds to the server. Add 2 MB of additional memory for each Cluster Replicator you plan to use.

Additionally, if you plan to run the ICM on a server that is also running the HTTP server task, you should add more memory to handle the additional workload.

2.5 Summary

There is no single correct answer when planning the hardware for Domino clustering. Many variables must be taken into account to tailor the hardware to your specific environment. It is also difficult to predict the future growth of the databases and to predict user behavior. However, there are some approaches to help in this process, such as analyzing disk usage for mail files, preparing for the clustering overhead, and defining user characteristics.

In the chapter, we examined the basics of planning a Domino cluster. Here are the major areas that need to be considered:

- Understand your user profiles and distribution
- Examine the characteristics of your databases (size, growth potential, usage, and so on)
- Determine the roles played by your servers
- Decide how to distribute your data both across the cluster and in terms of disk layout in each server

In the next chapter, we discuss the major design issues to consider when implementing a Domino R5 cluster.

Chapter 3. Designing a Domino cluster

Realizing improved availability of information systems is a goal sought by many IBM customers. Domino's clustering technology offers a powerful and flexible solution to help you to achieve this objective. Understanding how Domino provides improved availability will ensure that you implement a system that meets your objectives.

This chapter includes information that describes how Domino clustering works and discusses important issues to consider when designing a Domino cluster.

3.1 Technical overview of Domino clustering

Before undertaking the design of a Domino clustering solution, you need to understand how a Domino cluster functions. This section provides the technical background to Domino cluster operation.

3.1.1 What is a Domino cluster?

A Domino cluster is a group of interconnected Domino servers configured to provide uninterrupted access to Domino-based networked information resources, including messaging, databases, and other service components. Each Domino cluster comprises up to six Domino servers, within the same Notes domain, that use a common set of networking protocols. Domino servers within a cluster are not restricted to run on a specific operating system or hardware platform. Platforms supported by Domino may be mixed within a single cluster. A domain may contain multiple clusters, but an individual server may only be a member of one cluster.

Domino supports several networking protocols, any of which may be used by clients to connect to the cluster. Replication within the cluster, however, is only supported on a TCP/IP network, so this must be one of the protocols available. Remember that the servers in a cluster must share the same set of protocols. This is because when a Notes client connects to a server using a specific protocol, the client must use the same protocol when it fails over to another server in the cluster. In general, we recommend using TCP/IP for client connections because it will provide better failover performance than other protocols.

© Copyright IBM Corp. 1998, 2000

3.1.2 Domino cluster components

There are several components that make up a Domino server cluster. This section describes how these components work. For details on how to configure and administer a Domino cluster, refer to Chapter 4, “Installing and configuring a Domino cluster” on page 77 and Chapter 5, “Administering Domino clusters” on page 119.

The Administration Process is of great importance in the setup and running of a Domino cluster. When you add a server to a cluster, the Administration Process (AdminP) changes the Server document in the Domino Directory (NAMES.NSF) on the Administration server. Domino submits this request to the Administration Requests database (ADMIN4.NSF) on the server from which the Add Server request was initiated. A separate request is submitted for each server that is added to the cluster.

If you make the above request on the Administration server, the Administration Process immediately acts on the request. If you make the request from another server in the cluster, the ADMIN4.NSF database must first replicate with the Administration server’ ADMIN4.NSF database before the Administration Process can complete the request. Cluster membership changes do not take effect until the added server receives the Domino Directory change.

When you add a server to a cluster, Domino adds the ClusterName and ClRepID fields to the Server document. If the cluster already exists, Domino gets the ClRepID field from the Server document of other member in the same cluster.

The following diagram illustrates how the cluster components interact:

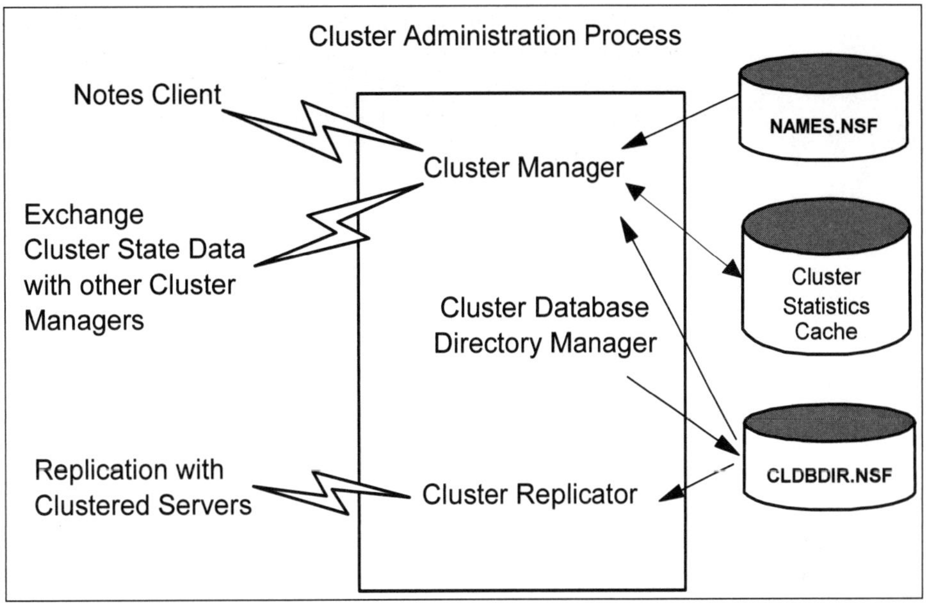

Figure 1. Cluster components

3.1.2.1 Cluster Administration Process

The Cluster Administration Process (CLADMIN) is a Domino add-in task and is responsible for the correct operation of all cluster components, including the configuration (adding/deleting) and launching of other cluster components. On clustered servers, the Cluster Administration Process runs automatically at server startup and whenever the cluster membership changes.

The Cluster Administrator performs many of the housekeeping tasks associated with a cluster. For example, when you add a server to a cluster, the Cluster Administrator starts the cluster tasks: Cluster Database Directory Manager and the Cluster Replicator. It also adds task names (CLDBDIR and CLREPL) to the ServerTasks entry in the NOTES.INI file so that these tasks are launched each time you start the server. The Cluster Administrator also starts the Administration Process, if it is not already running.

3.1.2.2 Cluster Manager task

The Cluster Manager task runs on each server in a cluster, and tracks the status of all members of the cluster. It maintains a list of those servers in the cluster that are currently available, along with information about the workload on each server. When you add a server to a cluster, Domino automatically starts the Cluster Manager on that server. As long as the server remains a member of the cluster, the Cluster Manager is launched each time you start the server or when Domino detects a change in the Domino Directory.

The Cluster Manager polls the other servers in the same cluster and exchanges periodic messages, called probes, with the `NSPingServer` command. The interval for polling is every minute by default but this can be changed by the administrator with the Server_Cluster_Probe_Timeout parameter.

The Cluster Manager tasks include:

- Determining which servers belong to the cluster. It periodically checks the Domino Directory for changes to the ClusterName field in the Server document and the cluster membership list.
- Monitoring server availability and workload in the cluster.
- Informing other Cluster Managers of changes in cluster server availability.
- Redirecting database requests based on the availability of cluster servers (failover).
- Balancing server workloads in the cluster based on the availability of cluster servers.
- Logging failover and workload balance events in the server log file.

3.1.2.3 Cluster Database Directory Manager task

The Cluster Database Directory Manager (CLDBDIR) is a Domino add-in task that runs on all servers in the cluster and creates, populates, and updates the server's Cluster Database Directory (CLDBDIR.NSF). When you add a server to a cluster, the Cluster Database Directory Manager creates a Cluster Database Directory on that server. Adding a database to a clustered server causes the Cluster Database Directory Manager to create a document containing information about the new database in the Cluster Database Directory. Similarly, when you delete a database from a clustered server, the Cluster Database Directory Manager deletes the related document in the directory. The Cluster Database Directory Manager also tracks the status of each database, indicating that databases are "out of service" or "pending delete", for example.

When the Cluster Database Directory on a server is changed, the Cluster Replicator immediately replicates that change to the Cluster Database Directory on all other servers in the cluster.

3.1.2.4 Cluster Replicator task

The Cluster Replicator task (CLREPL) is responsible for the tight synchronization of data among databases and their replicas in a cluster. The

Cluster Replicator is a Domino add-in task that provides continuous event-driven replication among the cluster members. It uses the Cluster Database Directory to determine which databases on which servers have to be updated.

There is a retry mechanism if one of the servers is trying to push changes to a server that is not responding. The changes are then stored in memory until the server comes back up again. The retry time-out for the Cluster Replicator task is initially set to one minute. The time-out value doubles after each failed replication attempt, until the time-out value reaches one hour.

It is recommended that you force a replication for a clustered server to the other servers in the cluster at the server startup to avoid delays in bringing the server's replicas into synchronization. You can do this by using a Program document in the Domino Directory.

See 5.6, "Configuring replication within the cluster" on page 149 for details on replication options within the cluster.

Domino replication

The Cluster Replicator task handles only replications to clustered databases on member servers in the cluster. Domino's standard replicator tasks (REPLICA) is still responsible for the standard replication of changes to and from servers outside the cluster.

3.1.2.5 The Cluster Statistics cache

The cluster statistics are stored in the Cluster Statistics cache on each Domino server in the cluster. There are two kinds of cluster statistics:

- Server.Cluster

  These statistics are related to clustered server activities such as failover, workload balancing events, the server's state within the cluster and information on a specific cluster configuration, such as the server names within the cluster.

- Replica.Cluster

  These statistics are related to cluster replication events, such as the number of documents updated, the number of replica retry events, and the number of bytes received during cluster replications.

See B.2, "Statistics variables descriptions" on page 219 for more details about the statistics parameters.

3.1.2.6 Cluster Database Directory

A Cluster Database Directory (CLDBDIR.NSF) resides on each server in a cluster and contains a directory of all databases within the cluster. The database profile information in this directory provides other cluster tasks and components with the data they need to perform their functions. Every server in a cluster stores a replica of this database. The Cluster Database Directory is created automatically by the Cluster Database Directory Manager task when a clustered server starts up, if it does not already exist. The Cluster Database Directory replica ID number is stored in the Server document of each server in the cluster.

If you lose the Cluster Database Directory on a clustered server, it is recommended that you create a new replica on this server before running the CLDBDIR task. This is because the CLDBDIR task will create a new replica of the Cluster Database Directory itself, adding a document for each database stored on your server, and when a replication occurs with a clustered server, the Cluster Database Directory will then have two documents for each database.

The Cluster Database Directory Manager (CLDBDIR) adds this database to the Cluster Database Directory, and it becomes part of the cluster.

The Cluster Database Directory contains information such as the database name, server, path name, replica ID, and other replication and access attributes for each database on each server in the cluster. This information is used by the Cluster Manager to determine database availability and failover paths.

3.1.2.7 Client cluster components

Domino R5 supports failover and workload balancing of Notes clients, as did previous Domino clustering offerings. R5 also introduces failover support for Web clients (HTTP and HTTPS) accessing Domino clusters.

There are two Notes client cluster components, which are available in Domino R4 and later:

- Cluster-aware Notes client
- Notes API

When the Notes client tries to open a database on a Domino server that is unavailable, the client's cluster cache (CLUSTER.NCF, stored in the client's data directory) provides a list of other servers in the cluster. The Notes client accesses the Cluster Manager on another server in the cluster, which redirects the client to the best available Domino server that holds the database requested by the client. No additional setup is required for Notes clients to take advantage of Domino clustering.

Notes APIs exist to allow applications to be written to take advantage of Domino failover and load balancing.

Web clients

Domino R5 includes a major enhancement to clustering in comparison with previous releases - the Internet Cluster Manager (ICM). Domino clusters can now provide failover and workload balancing for HTTP (and HTTPS, the secure form of HTTP) clients, that is, for anyone who accesses your site through a Web browser. Although Domino 4.6 supported failover and workload balancing for Notes clients, it did not for Web clients.

The ICM can perform the following functions:

- Monitor back-end Domino servers for availability
- Check the Domino HTTP Web service for availability
- Disallow any new connections to servers that are out of service
- Provide failover (direct clients) to the best available server
- Provide load balancing by setting availability thresholds for your Domino servers
- Support "virtual IP addresses" and map ports
- Provide content routing for your clients

HTTP engine support

ICM requires the Domino native HTTP engine. It does not currently support other engines such as Microsoft's IIS.

3.2 Failover and load balancing in a cluster

The two main reasons to implement a Domino cluster are:

- To provide client failover in case of server failure. Using failover, a cluster provides protection for business-critical databases and servers, improving their availability.
- To balance the workload placed on your servers. The load-balancing feature helps Domino administrators to optimize the performance of their Domino systems.

We now examine these two functions in more detail.

3.2.1 Conditions that cause failover

Failover occurs when users make certain requests while they are unable access the server that contains a database they wish to interrogate, or they cannot access the database itself. The following list describes the conditions that can result in users being unable to access servers or the databases they wish to:

- The Domino server is unreachable due to hardware, software or network failures.
- The Domino server is Restricted.
- The Domino server is Busy.
- The Domino server reaches the maximum number of user sessions allowed as specified by the Server_MaxUsers setting.
- The Domino database (replica) is unavailable because it is either marked Out of Service or Pending Delete.

When one of the above situations applies, the following Notes user activities trigger failover when an attempt to access an unavailable system occurs:

- Database-oriented operations:
  - Opening a database from the desktop (double-click the icon or right-click and select **Open**)
  - Opening a database from a bookmark
  - Using a doclink, a viewlink or a database link
  - Using an @command([FileOpenDatabase])
  - Running a LotusScript routine that includes the db.OpenWithFailover call, which opens a database with failover if either the database or server is unavailable
  - A Java function call for opening a database
- Workstation replication
- Home server-oriented operations:
  - Server lookups
  - Composing mail
  - Sending mail
  - Type ahead
  - Name lookups
  - Mail processing agents
  - Meeting invitations
- When all Domino servers are configured to fail over mail transfer and delivery. This can be done by either setting the parameter

MailClusterFailover to 1 in the NOTES.INI files on all Domino R4 servers or enabling cluster failover for all Domino R5 servers for all transfers in the domain or for the last hop only.

- Accessing a Web navigator server in the following situations:
  - Selecting the **Open URL** icon
  - Double-clicking a URL hotspot (HTTP address)

When using the ICM, failover and load balancing work the same for HTTP clients. Domino computes an availability index based on all open sessions, whether they are from Notes clients, HTTP clients, or other Domino servers.

ICM and MaxUsers

The ICM can direct a Web browser client request to a server that has reached its MaxUsers setting, if no other Domino Web server is available, unlike a Domino cluster without ICM providing services to Notes clients only.

When an HTTP client is connected to a server that fails, the client receives a message saying that the server is not responding. To fail over to a different replica, the user must contact the ICM again. The user can do it in one of the following ways:

- Click the **Back** button in the browser one or more times to connect to a page through the ICM
- Use a bookmark
- Type the URL

The user may be required to authenticate with the new server. If the user had previously authenticated to the new server during the browser session, perhaps to access another database, no re-authentication is needed. If both the browser and server support SSL3, and the user selects this option, re-authentication occurs automatically.

3.2.2 Conditions that do not cause failover

Failover does not occur:

- If a server becomes unavailable while a user has a database open
- If a server becomes unavailable while a user is editing a document

  In this situation a user cannot save the document but could copy it to the clipboard, open the database again (which would trigger failover to occur) and then paste it into a replica on a clustered server.

- If you select a database icon and choose any of the following options:
  - **File -> Database -> Properties**
  - **File -> Database -> Access Control**
  - **File -> Database -> Open**
  - **File -> Database -> New Copy**
- If you click a database icon and select **View -> Go To <database view>** from the menu.
- When replicating with a server that is restricted by the administrator or has reached the maximum number of users or the maximum usage level set by the administrator. Also, when replicating with a database marked "Out of Service". Replication occurs regardless of such restrictions, so there is no need for failover to occur.
- When the Mail Router on a Domino R4 mail server attempts to deliver mail while MailClusterFailover is set to 0 or when cluster failover has been disabled for the Domino R5 mail server.
- When running agents, other than the mail pre-delivery agent.
- When you want to use a server as a template server when creating a new database (**File -> Database -> New**).

3.2.3 How failover works for Notes clients

The following figure shows how clustering maintains availability when a Notes client tries to open a database, called SALES.NSF in this example, located on a clustered server (Sun/Universe) that is currently unreachable.

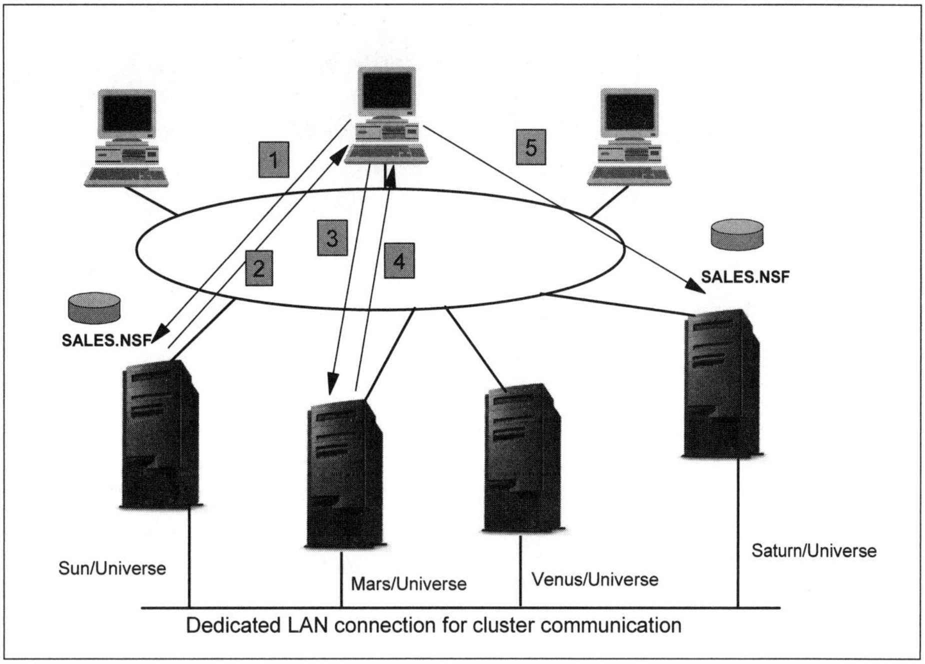

Figure 2. Notes client failover

1. The user clicks on the appropriate bookmark to open the SALES.NSF database on the Sun/Universe Domino server.

2. Without the user being aware of it, the client receives a `Server Not Responding` message because the server is unavailable. The client then searches the CLUSTER.NCF file that is part of the Notes R4+ client.

   If the client code has never before communicated with a server in the cluster, then failover will not work. When the client accesses a server in a cluster for the first time, this file is populated with a list of servers that are members of the cluster, and is kept updated as changes (such as adding or removing servers to or from the cluster) take place.

   A sample CLUSTER.NCF file is shown below:

```
Time=09/05/2000 09:39:47 AM (8525694D:004B11E7)
Galaxy
CN=Mars/O=Universe
CN=Saturn/O=Universe
CN=Sun/O=Universe
CN=Venus/O=Universe
```

3. The client then accesses another server in the list (Mars/Universe in our example).
4. The Cluster Manager of this server determines where replicas of this database file are located. It may or may not be on the server that the client is currently accessing. If the desired database (SALES.NSF) is not on this server, the Cluster Manager gives the client the name of the server in the cluster that contains the replica (Saturn/Universe).
5. The client then accesses that Saturn/Universe to access the required database.

Domino clustered servers usually perform failover by replica ID, but they can also fail over by path:

- By replica ID

  When a user tries to open a database that is not available, the Cluster Manager looks in the Cluster Database Directory for a replica of that database. To find a replica, the Cluster Manager looks for a database that has the same replica ID as the original database.

- By path

  To perform selective replica failover, Domino matches path names, not replica IDs. Failover by path name ensures that where databases use a selective replication formula, users are failed over to the correct database. Failover by path name is triggered when the Cluster Manager finds more than one replica of a database on the same server and assumes that selective replication is used to replicate those databases.

> **Attention**
>
> We recommend that you avoid creating more than one replica of a database on a server under any conditions.

However, if you do have multiple replicas of one database on a server, for example where you have a database containing a subset of documents selected by a formula that some clients will access rather than the full database, you must disable cluster replication for these databases and use scheduled replication to ensure that the selective formula for replication will be used.

3.2.3.1 Failover from a Notes client perspective

When failover occurs, an icon for the new database will appear on the workspace, either stacked on top of the original icon or in a free area on the same workspace page as the original icon. Using the Notes R5 client, even this visible indication is hidden if the user clicks bookmarks instead of the workspace.

The user will remain on the "failover" server even if the first required server comes up, unless the administrator initiates a failback by making the failover server busy (or initiating other failover options).

When the user logs off and on from the Notes client or when he changes the Location document, he will see the mail database's stacked icons reverse themselves and the database icon on the home mail server will be on top again even if the home mail server is still unavailable.

3.2.4 How failover works for Web browser clients

Internet Cluster Manager executes as a task on any server that is running the Domino R5 Enterprise Server license. It acts as a front-end or intermediary to your Web-based applications. HTTP requests are routed to the server running ICM, which in turn routes the requests to other servers in the cluster that are defined to the ICM. These could be requests for Notes databases or requests to a Web server delivering HTML pages to the Web browser client.

Figure 3 on page 52 shows an HTTP (Web browser) client asking a server running ICM (SVR01) to open a database containing Web pages (WEBPAGES.NSF). The database has been replicated on three servers in this cluster, namely SVR02, SVR03, and SVR04. When SVR01 receives the client's request, ICM redirects the client to an available server within the cluster that contains the requested file.

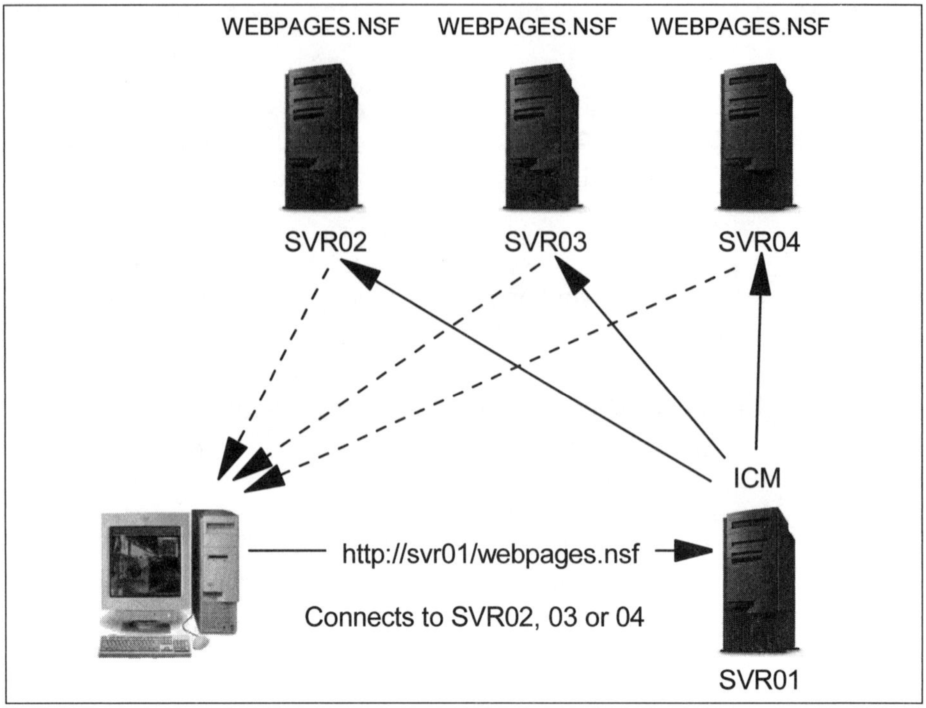

Figure 3. Internet Cluster Manager operation

ICM handles this type of transaction in the following way. ICM periodically sends inquiries to the Web servers in the cluster to determine their status and availability. When a client request is received, ICM looks at the information in the Cluster Database Directory to find a server that has the requested database. The ICM determines the most available server that holds the requested database, and then redirects the client to that server. The client now closes the session with the ICM and opens a new one with the nominated server. The user may see this as a change in the host name in the URL.

In our example, the client sends requests to `http://svr01/webpages.nsf`, but when the new session is established, the browser will display the URL of the nominated server that actually serves the data, such as `http://svr03/webpages.nsf`. It is also possible that the path to the database could also change in the URL, since the database may have a different path on the target server.

The ICM can direct a client request to any Domino server in a cluster, whether it is an R5 server or a server using a prior release of Domino. Only

Domino R5 servers can exploit the ICM, however. To do so, the server has to create URL links that refer back to the ICM. When an R5 server receives a client request, the server generates URLs that include ICM references (the information required to create references to the ICM is contained in each Web server's own Server document). As the user selects URLs that contain these references, the ICM is able to determine the best server to respond to each request, and thus balance the workload and even fail the user over to an alternative server if necessary.

If the ICM redirects the client request to a server running a previous release of Domino, the URLs the server generates will not contain references to the ICM. As the client moves between Web pages, the client with therefore continue to access pages on that same server only. To be able to take advantage of the ICM at that point, the user must select a URL that contains a reference to the ICM.

The discussion above shows how Web clients benefit from using ICM in conjunction with Domino clustering. No information about the Domino cluster is needed by Web clients accessing data held on a cluster; the benefits are gained without making any changes to standard Web browser clients.

3.2.5 How load balancing works in a cluster

Workload balancing redirects user sessions to different servers in the cluster, spreading the overall workload among the available servers in a way that maximizes utilization of cluster resources. The workload balancing feature lets you determine how user workloads are distributed across multiple servers that store cluster replicas of heavily used databases. Additional requests are passed to alternative servers when a server is too busy to take on any more user or server sessions.

When running as part of a cluster, a Domino server constantly monitors its own workload. To measure the workload, the Cluster Manager process on the server monitors the average response time of a representative set of server operations initiated by Notes clients (network time is not considered). The Cluster Manager also probes all the other servers in the cluster to determine their workload.

When the workload on a server exceeds a certain level designated by the administrator (the Server_Availability_Threshold value is zero by default), the server becomes busy and the Domino server rejects subsequent database open requests until the workload falls back below the specified level.

Workload balancing can be triggered in the following situations:

- A Notes client double-clicks on a database icon in the workspace to open a database on a busy server.
- A Web browser client requests a database - ICM checks every time for the least-loaded Domino HTTP server.
- A Notes client or Web browser client tries to launch a doclink, view link or database link that points to a server that is busy.
- A Notes client or Web browser client activates a field, action or button that contains an @Command(FileOpenDatabase) formula and the specified server is busy.
- A LotusScript routine issues a DB.OPENWITHFAILOVER call to open a database on a server that is busy.
- An agent written in Java issues an OpenDatabase method with the failover parameter set to True for a database on a server that is busy.
- An API program issues an NSFDbOpenExtended call to open a database on a server that is busy.

When a cluster-aware Notes client (Notes R4 or later) tries to access a database on a busy server, it receives an error code indicating that the server is busy. The client then contacts the Cluster Manager on one of the servers in the cluster. The Cluster Manager uses the Cluster Database Directory to determine which other servers in the cluster have replicas of the database being requested, and then selects the least busy one to handle the client request. The client then reissues the open request to this server. This target server can be the same one as the original server. On this second request, the open will succeed even if the target server is busy.

3.2.5.1 Workload balancing from a user perspective

Workload balancing is virtually transparent to clients. If they are switched to a different server, the users will see an additional or stacked icon on the desktop. They will not receive an error message or other indication that workload balancing has occurred. Using the Notes R5 client, even this visible indication is hidden if the user clicks bookmarks instead of the workspace.

Workload balancing uses the same process as failover. The main difference is that if all servers in the cluster are busy or there are no other replicas of the required database, the user will be allowed to access the first server that was tried.

3.3 Mail and clustering

The main advantages of using clustering for your Domino-based mail systems are:

- Increased availability of mail databases

  By creating a replica of a mail database you can guarantee mail availability to the user; refer to 3.5.2, "Database distribution across the cluster" on page 66 for more information.

- Mail routing failover

  Even if the user's home mail server is unavailable, a mail message will be delivered to a replica of the user's mail database on a clustered server.

- Integration with the shared mail function

  If you have implemented shared mail on a Domino system, you can fully integrate this feature with clustering by enabling cluster replication of the shared mail database.

The following section will discuss how mail works in a clustered environment and some considerations to take into account when designing a cluster for the mail system infrastructure. For more information about implementing failover for mail, refer to 5.2, "Setting up failover" on page 120.

3.3.1 Mail routing failover

Mail routing is the process of transferring a message from one Domino server to another until the mail routing software locates the server holding the mail file for the recipient. If this server is not available when the router attempts to deliver the mail into a user's mailbox, the router redirects the delivery to the failover Domino server. Thus, users continue to receive mail in real time.

A similar situation applies for outgoing mail. If a user is sending mail and his mail server fails, the Notes router will send the mail message to the failover mail server in the cluster. For information about setting up mail routing in a clustered environment, see 5.2.2, "Setting up mail routing failover" on page 123.

3.3.2 Shared mail

Shared mail, also called Single Copy Object Store (SCOS), is a feature that enables a single copy of a mail message intended for multiple recipients to be stored in a central database on a server. By using a shared mail database to store messages with more than one recipient instead of storing the complete message in each recipient's mail file, you conserve disk space. The amount of space saved can be considerable. If, for example, you send mail to 50 users, all of whom are located on the same server, Domino stores one copy of the mail message instead of 50 copies.

Users can perform all the same tasks with mail messages stored in a shared mail database as they can with messages stored in their own mail files. Using a shared mail database is completely transparent to users. Mail servers configured for SCOS can be clustered. When clustering and shared mail are implemented together, the cluster replicator will automatically keep clustered shared mail databases synchronized. This will not change shared mail features and functions.

To set up shared mail in a cluster, you use the same procedure you use for setting up shared mail with mail databases that are not in the cluster.

To do this, take the following steps:

1. Create an additional shared mail database using the `Load Object Create` command.
2. Link the replica mail file to it using the `Load Object Link` command. This command stores the contents of messages in the shared mail database.
3. Enable shared mail on replica files by entering the command `Load Object Set - Always`. This command ensures that new messages are stored in the shared mail database.

See 5.2.3, “Setting up shared mail in a cluster” on page 129 for more details about setting up shared mail in a cluster. More general information about shared mail can be found in the online help files for the Domino R5 Administrator client.

3.3.3 Clustering in a hub-and-spoke mail infrastructure

A hub-and-spoke mail infrastructure consists of one or more interconnected central servers (hubs), and local Domino mail servers as spokes. The spokes transfer mail via hub servers, and hubs deliver mail to spokes. Hub servers route mail between each other or to higher-level master hub servers in large organizations.

You can provide high availability for mail routing in several ways. For example, you can configure a secondary mail hub server that has a higher defined routing cost than for the primary one. This is done in the Connection document in the Domino Directory.

1. From the Domino Administrator, click the **Configuration** tab and expand the **Server** section.
2. Click Connections.
3. Select the Connection document between the spoke server and Domino server that you want to define as your secondary mail hub, and click **Edit Connection**.
4. If you do not have desired Connection document, you can create one by clicking **Add Connection**.
5. Click the **Replication/Routing** tab (see Figure 4).

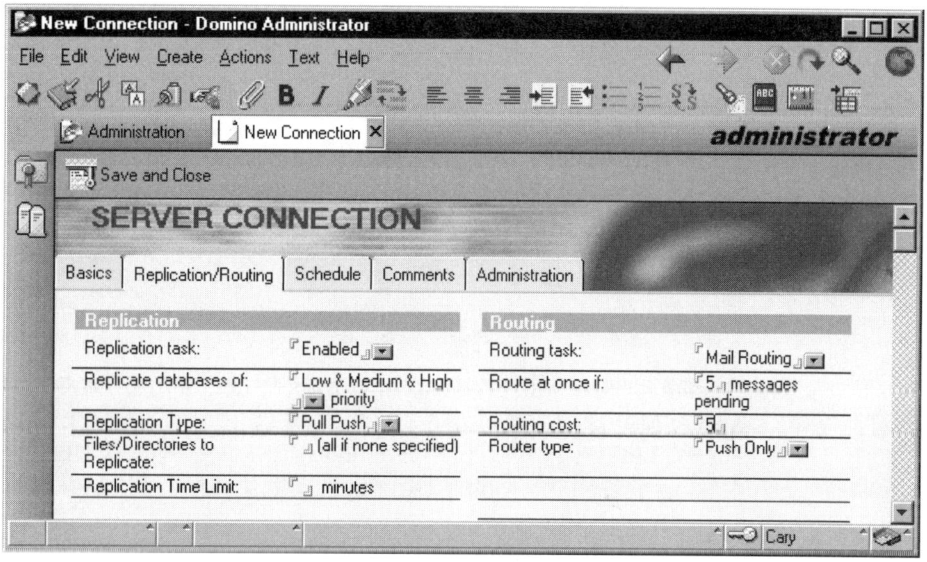

Figure 4. Setting routing cost

6. In the Routing section, change the value in the Routing cost field. By default, the routing cost is 1 for all Connection documents. You should assign a value higher than that if you want to specify that this will be your secondary hub mail server.

Another option to increase availability in a hub-and-spoke infrastructure is to cluster your hub servers. In this case, if one hub mail server is unavailable, the other hub mail server will continue routing messages. This is illustrated in Figure 5:

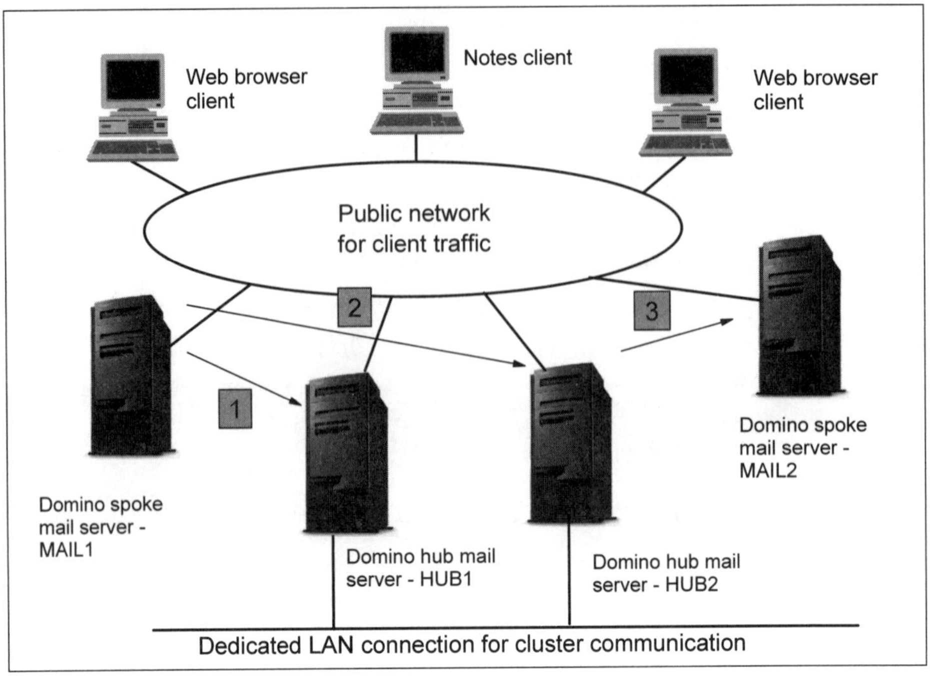

Figure 5. Setting up hub mail servers in a cluster

Domino spoke mail server MAIL1 tries to deliver mail to Domino spoke mail server MAIL2. It attempts to route mail through Domino hub mail server HUB1, but this server is unavailable. However, since HUB1 and HUB2 are clustered, Domino routes messages through HUB2 instead.

3.3.3.1 Multiple mailbox databases

If you have worked with previous releases of Domino, you will know how crucial the server's mailbox (MAIL.BOX) file is to mail operations. MAIL.BOX is a central file for mail transfer and can become a bottleneck in heavily loaded servers. In such cases, you should consider creating multiple mailboxes on each Domino mail server, especially on hub mail servers. This is a new option, available for Domino R5 servers only. Using multiple MAIL.BOX databases allows concurrent processes to handle mail traffic.

You can specify the number of MAIL.BOX databases in the Configuration document, as follows:

1. From the Domino Administrator, click the **Configuration** tab and expand the **Messaging** section.
2. Click **Configurations**.

3. Select the Configuration document for desired server or group of servers, and click **Edit Connection**.
4. If you do not have the desired Configuration document, you can create one by clicking **Add Configuration**.
5. Click the **Router/SMTP -> Basics** tab (Figure 6).
6. Fill in the Number of mailboxes field. The default value is 1, but you can set the number of mailboxes from 1 to 10 for each server that uses this Configuration document.

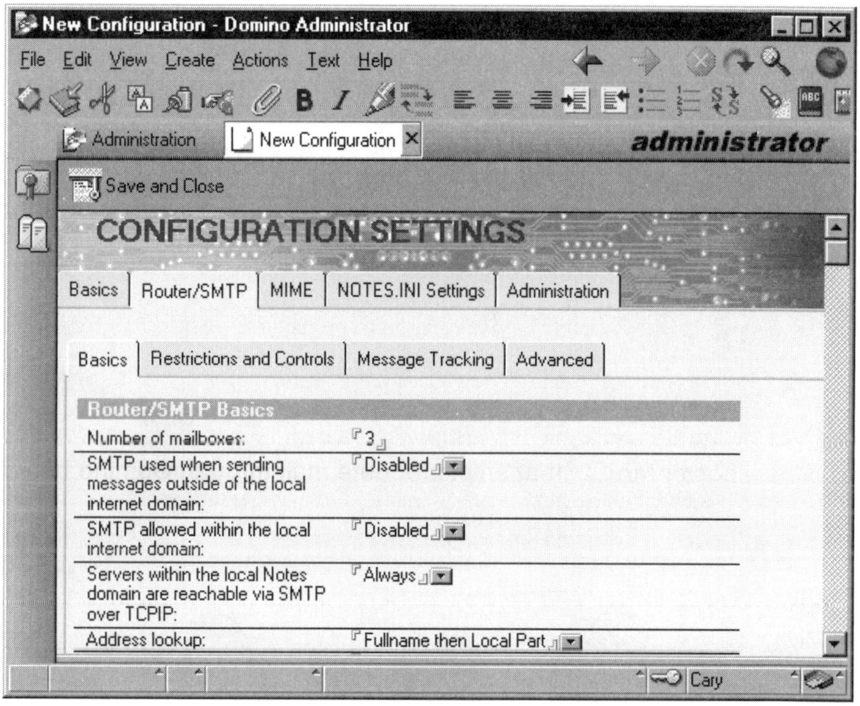

Figure 6. Changing the number of mailboxes

3.4 Passthru servers and clustering

A passthru server is a Domino server that acts as a "stepping stone" to gain access to a destination Domino server. This function is usually used when the destination server does not share a common communications protocol with a workstation or a server (source server) trying to access it. The passthru server necessarily runs protocols used both by the destination server and the source server or workstation.

If the service provided by the passthru server is considered mission critical and you want to gain optimal performance, you should dedicate a server to this role. Dedicated passthru servers typically host neither applications nor mail databases. Access to the passthru server would be limited to those workstations and servers that require access to the destination servers.

A typical use for a passthru server is to provide access for mobile clients that need to access their mail and applications through a dial-up connection. Unfortunately, although a LAN-attached passthru server can operate within a cluster, clustering of passthru servers for dial-up users is not supported. There is an alternative for dial-up users, which we examine next.

3.4.1 Mobile users accessing a cluster

A passthru server is often used to provide access for mobile users. Such users typically call in to a single server over a dial-up modem connection. Once connected to the network, mobile users accessing their mail or application servers through a passthru server can take advantage of a Domino cluster configuration as readily as any other user in the network, as shown in Figure 7:

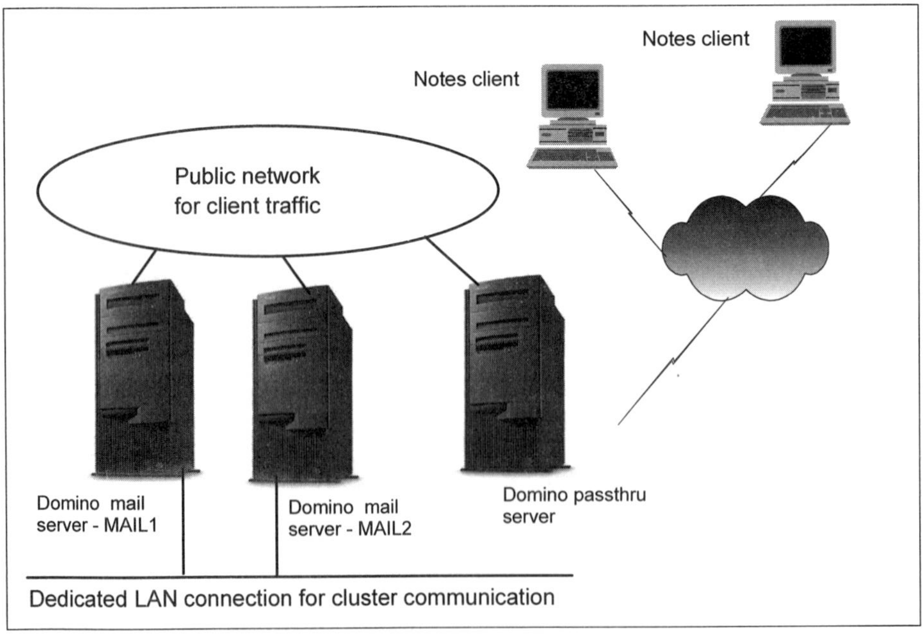

Figure 7. Mobile users accessing a Domino cluster

In this configuration, however, the passthru server may itself be subject to failure and thus loss of service to your mobile users. As previously stated, you cannot use Domino clustering to provide passthru functionality for dial-in access. However, there is a way to provide high availability for your mobile users and that is to implement a *hunt group* of passthru servers. A hunt group uses a telephone network switching mechanism, provided in many private automatic branch exchanges (PABXs), to assign one phone number to multiple dial-up servers.

When a user dials the phone number to access the passthru server, the PABX connects the incoming call to whichever server is available. One phone number represents all passthru servers in the hunt group and the load is spread among the servers. All passthru servers in a single hunt group should be configured to provide access to the same destination servers. Now when one passthru server in the hunt group becomes unavailable, another server in the hunt group is used to make a connection to a destination server.

The users must have a hunt group Connection document that specifies a name and phone number for the hunt group. Also, they should create a Passthru Connection document for each destination server to which they can connect through the hunt group. For more details on creating these documents, refer to Notes R5 Help database, which is shipped with the product.

3.4.2 Clustering LAN-attached passthru servers

You can provide high availability for passthru servers by configuring them in a cluster if you are using local area network connections. Figure 8 on page 62 shows an example of a passthru server cluster. The client workstations use only the NetBEUI protocol, the destination servers use only the TCP/IP protocol, and the two clustered passthru servers run both the NetBEUI and the TCP/IP protocols.

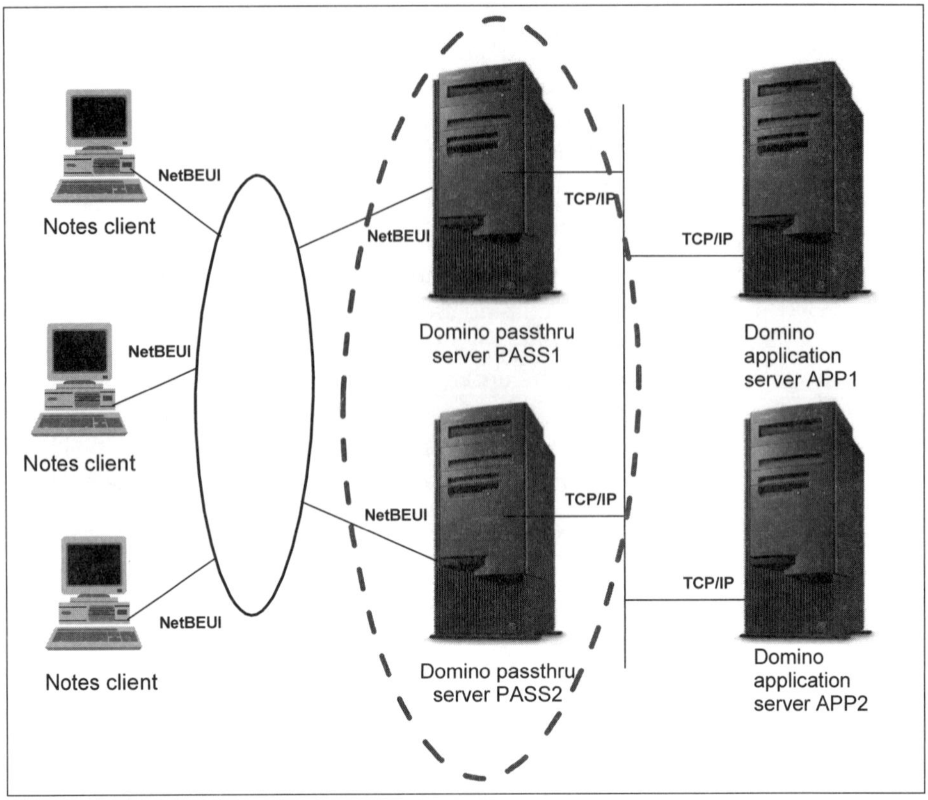

Figure 8. Clustered passthru servers

You have to set up both servers in the cluster using the same passthru configuration settings. Users' Location documents should include the cluster name as the default passthru server name. Remember that, as we discussed earlier in 3.2.3, "How failover works for Notes clients" on page 48, the user must access one of the clustered servers at least once before using the connection to the cluster name. This is because the client cluster cache is not updated with the information about the servers in the cluster until that first access takes place.

3.5 Cluster implementation

When implementing and deploying Domino clusters, several key areas should be considered. These are:

- Server tasks - what will each server be required to do?
- Client workload.

- The distribution of databases throughout the cluster.
- Network implications.
- Load balancing.

Chapter 2, “Planning a Domino cluster” on page 11 outlined some of the issues related to the hardware required for clustering. In this section, we will describe some additional topics related to Domino features to consider when implementing Domino clusters.

3.5.1 Allocating servers to specific tasks

You can designate servers to handle specific Domino tasks. This can improve system efficiency and make administration easier, especially in large organizations. Having allocated server roles, clustering provides a way to ensure access to a desired service on a Domino server by using the failover and workload-balancing features.

Critical server tasks such as mail, replication and passthru tasks particularly benefit from operating in a clustered environment.

Here is a brief explanation of the principal server tasks that you may want to allocate to a specific server:

- Mail

  Mail servers host mail databases, Domino Directory databases, and the calendar and free-time system, and also provide mail routing. Designating these tasks to specific servers reduces network traffic, since mail is routed only between mail servers and some mail is sent to recipients on the same mail server. The reason that you do this is so that you can design a topology that provides efficient mail routing. The design requirements for mail routing are different from those of application replication, for example.

- Hub

  You may want to designate a server purely for hub functions. Hubs replicate databases, route mail from spoke servers, and connect different parts of an organization, such LAN/WAN interconnections.

- Simple Mail Transfer Protocol (SMTP)

  Allocating the SMTP routing function to a specific server is especially useful if your users have Notes mail on your LAN and communicate frequently with Internet mail users. You can even dedicate separate servers for inbound and outbound SMTP routing tasks. In this way, one server could be used for sending messages with destinations outside your local domain and another server for receiving Internet mail intended for your Notes mail users.

Previous releases of Domino server used SMTP Message Transfer Agent (MTA) to route Internet mail. In Release 5, the Domino router routes Internet mail, so every Domino server can perform any necessary conversion and exchange messages with Internet users.

SMTP failover limitation

Failover of SMTP routing is not supported in Domino clusters.

- Application

  By hosting the most important Notes applications used by your organization on a specific server, you can reduce the number of connection documents in the system. This is especially true if these applications do not use mail, since replication requires only one connection document while mail routing requires two. You can group applications by use, load, or functional area on the same server. Where needed, a hub-and-spoke topology provides an efficient replication infrastructure.

- Web

  Nominating specific servers to handle requests from Web browsers reduces the number of systems that have to execute the Domino HTTP engine. In addition, doing so will help to simplify any security measures you need to take to protect servers that are accessed by clients external to your organization, since the servers concerned can be clearly identified.

- Passthru

  Passthru servers allow users to connect to different destination servers through a single server without knowing routing information for the destination servers. Passthru servers usually do not host applications or mail databases. There are some restrictions to implementing passthru servers within clusters, which were discussed in 3.4, “Passthru servers and clustering” on page 59.

- Remote

  Remote servers allow users to access Domino using a modem. Workstation users can connect to a Domino server while traveling, at home, or at another office.

  Also, you can use a remote server to communicate with servers that are not on the same physical network, or with servers belonging to other organizations. A remote server increases security by acting as a single, secure point of entry.

- Gateway

  The gateway function connects Notes and foreign systems. Transferring data between different systems may require the conversion of document formats to and from Notes and the foreign system. In some cases there will be benefits from allocating this task to a specific server.

- Backup

  This function stores critical information as a precaution against malicious or accidental loss and is an especially important task that may benefit from clustering. When you set up a backup server, you must replicate the database you want backed up on that server. If information is lost on your other Domino servers, you can restore it from the backup servers. So, you can take advantage of the cluster replicator updating information on-the-fly for replicas that might be hosted on different operating systems. This is one of the advantages of the flexibility of Domino technology. In addition, you can copy replicas from backup servers to disk, tape, or other removable media.

  The following table summarizes those Domino server tasks that can take advantage of Domino clustering:

Table 4. Server tasks that benefit from clustering

Domino server task	Can take advantage of Domino clustering
Mail	Yes
Hub	Yes
SMTP	No
Application	Yes
Web	Yes, if you implement ICM
Passthru	Yes, for LAN users
Remote	No
Gateway	No
Backup	Yes

3.5.2 Database distribution across the cluster

After you have decided which server tasks will run in your Domino network, and which functions will be clustered, you need to decide how best to distribute the databases within the cluster.

You should take into consideration the potential full load on these servers both in normal operation and when failovers have occurred. Remember to look at each server's CPU utilization, amount of paging, disk queue length, and Notes database and replication statistics.

The two primary questions to be answered are:

- How many replicas of each database are needed?
- How should replicas be distributed among the servers in the cluster?

Here are some factors to consider when determining how many replicas to create in a cluster:

- How critical is each database you plan to cluster?
- The number and distribution of database users.

  You can provide better performance for a large number of users if you spread databases across multiple servers.
- What are the average and peak transaction rates for each database you plan to cluster?
- How much growth are your databases likely to experience?

  If you have many replicas, a large amount of new data can slow down performance.
- How is your organization distributed geographically?
- What type of network connection will you provide for your clustered servers?

  Cluster replication can create a lot of traffic, which can be an issue for a wide area network (WAN) connection.

For mail databases it is suggested that you create one or two replicas on clustered servers. Heavily used application databases may warrant creation of more than this.

How much data redundancy each database requires depends on how frequently users access a database. Obviously the more replicas you create, the more accessible and available the data becomes. Too many replicas, however, can impact Domino server performance, reduce available disk space and overload the cluster replicator tasks. Analysis of performance and traffic patterns once your cluster is operational may provide guidance to help fine-tune your cluster configuration.

3.5.2.1 Mail databases distribution

Database distribution should reflect user distribution. One of the most important objectives of clustering is to provide high availability access. The way you choose to distribute your users' mail databases is an important decision, because failover events will significantly affect the performance of servers. Let us look at the example in Figure 9:

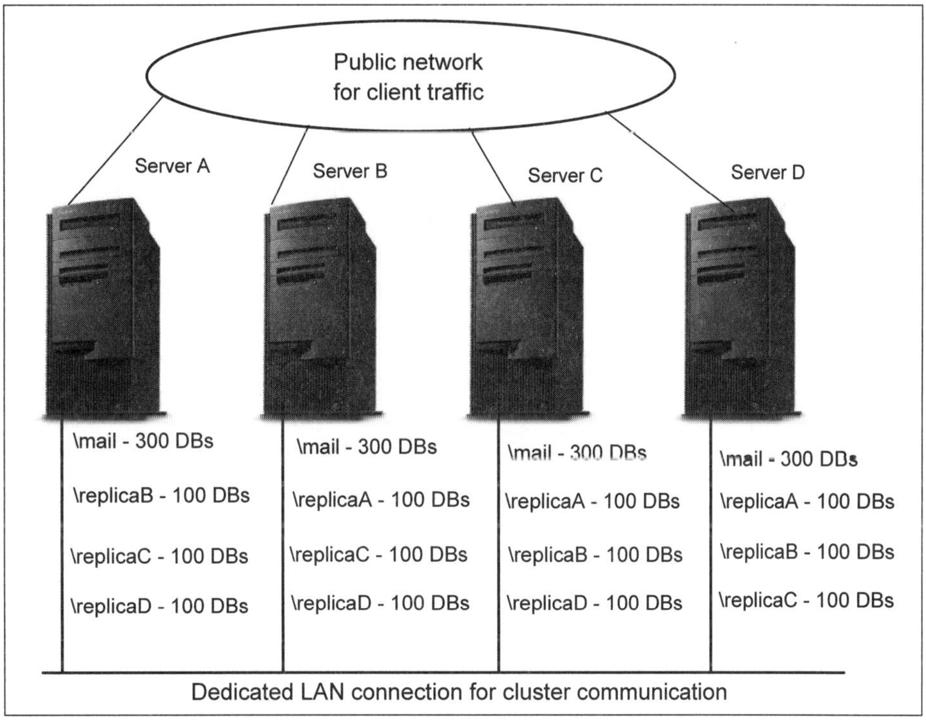

Figure 9. Mail database distribution

Suppose you have 1,200 mail users that you want to put in a cluster with four servers (Servers A, B, C and D). To start, you will probably allocate 300 users to each server in order to place approximately the same load on each server.

To ensure high availability of your users' mail databases, you want to create a replica of each user's mail file on another server in the cluster. You could take all registered users on Server A, for example, and place a replica of their mail files on Server B. This does not make best use of your hardware, however, because if Server A becomes unavailable, all 300 of its users will be redirected to Server B. Servers C and D will not absorb any of the additional load due to the failover, because the necessary databases are only available on Server B.

A better approach is to spread the replicas for each server's registered users across the other three servers. Using Server A as an example again, if its mail databases are spread evenly across the other servers, that is, 100 of Server A's users on Server B, 100 on Server C, and 100 on Server D, a failure of Server A would result in an approximately equal increase in workload for the three remaining servers in the cluster.

Replicas within a cluster have to be created manually by the Domino administrator. Although we have not done so in Figure 9 for simplicity, we recommend that you use a naming convention for directories containing replica databases. For example, distributing replica copies of the mail databases for the 300 registered mail users on Server A equally among three other servers, you might create three mail directories on Server A: mailA_replicaB, mailA_replicaC and mailA_replicaD. This naming convention indicates that for databases in those directories the users' home mail server is Server A and replica copies are on Servers B, C and D respectively.

Looking now at the replica databases on the other servers, the replicas of Server A's databases are stored in the following directories: replicaB_mailA on ServerB, replicaC_mailA on ServerC and replicaD_mailA on ServerD, indicating that the directories contain replicas from Server A. Since the users' home mail server and mail directory are listed in each user's Person document in the Domino Directory, the administrator will quickly be able to locate both copies of a particular user's mail file.

When you create database replicas in a cluster, you must set the same access control list for every replica, so that when users fail over to a different replica they have the same access authority. See Chapter 5, "Administering Domino clusters" on page 119 for more details on creating replicas in a cluster.

Caution

If you have Domino R4.x servers in your cluster, you should keep in mind that mail databases based on the R5 template do not work properly on Domino R4 servers. If mail databases in your cluster are based on the R5 mail template, do not create replicas of them on Domino R4 servers.

3.5.2.2 Application database distribution

Different factors come into play when deciding how to distribute your application databases. This is because some applications are used more frequently than others, and the amount of computing resources required to run them can vary widely. Your Domino administrator should closely monitor the system for usage patterns, especially during peak periods, and adjust cluster resources accordingly. You can change your application distribution easily if your system's performance and distribution requirements change.

Your goal should be to spread the overall workload evenly across all the servers in the cluster. You should also remember to pay attention to the ensuing workload balance under failover conditions. As a starting point, you could distribute the database replicas equally across the other servers in the cluster and then fine-tune the workload following observation of the cluster's performance.

Figure 10 shows an example of application database distribution, using three servers in a Domino cluster:

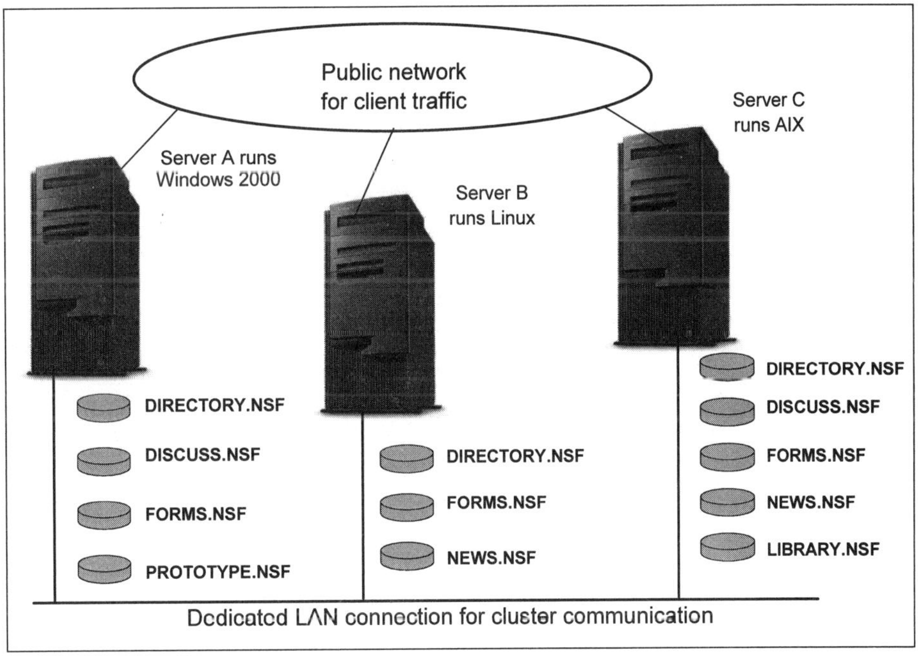

Figure 10. Application database distribution

The three servers in our example cluster are each running different operating system platforms. Replicas are distributed according to each database's usage and the resources of each server, using the following guidelines:

- One replica on each server for databases that are accessed frequently but not subject to high rates of change. DIRECTORY.NSF is a good example.
- Share replicas equally among servers (taking the servers' performance into account) for databases that either must be highly available or that have a high number of open sessions, for example: NEWS.NSF, FORMS.NSF and DISCUSSION.NSF.

3.6 Clustering solutions

In this section we will outline some examples of clustering solutions for Notes and Web browser clients accessing their mail and application servers. All of these solutions will assume LAN connections exist between the clustered servers. Cluster Replicator generates a lot of network traffic, so if you want to implement Domino clustering using WAN connections you need to plan carefully to avoid your WAN becoming a bottleneck.

We describe four clustering solutions: one solution for a Domino cluster providing services to Notes clients, a solution for hub servers, and two solutions for Domino clusters providing services to Web browser clients.

3.6.1 Domino cluster servicing Notes clients

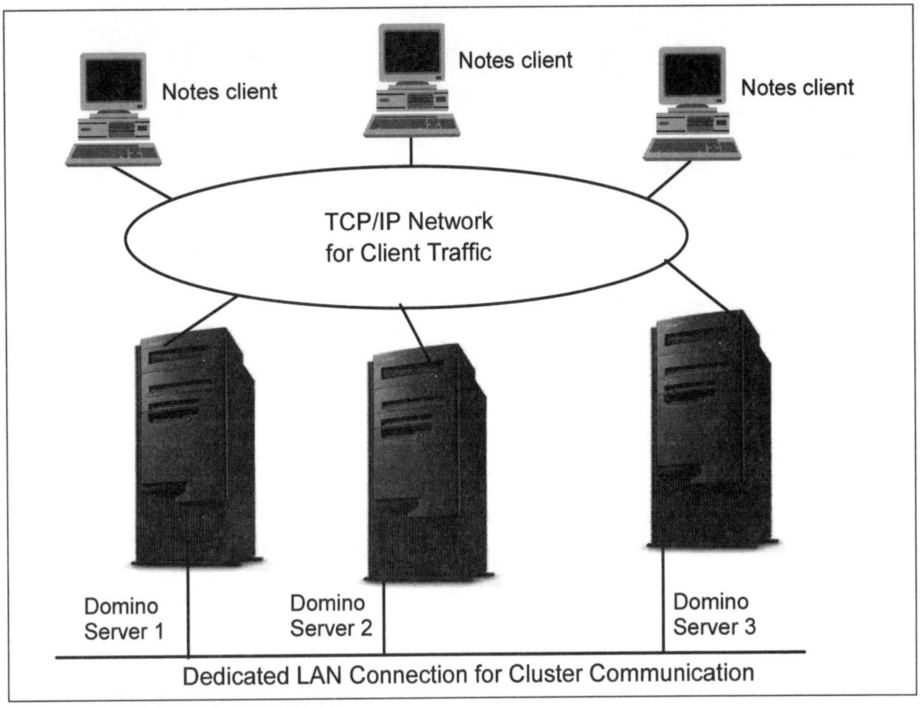

Figure 11. Solution with three Domino servers in a cluster

This basic cluster is very useful for Domino networks, and provides the following features:

- It allows you to spread user mail databases across multiple Domino mail servers and provides failover to two other mail servers if one of the mail servers becomes unavailable.
- It ensures good performance for your mail and application servers.

  You have to take care when distributing replicas among the servers to optimize database availability and server performance. Refer to 3.5.2, "Database distribution across the cluster" on page 66, for information about database distribution.

  If the number of applications or the number of users that will access a given application grows, you can introduce additional Domino servers to the cluster to maintain performance levels. You should remember to pay special attention to the workload of the cluster replicator tasks and intra-cluster network traffic. Remember, also, that cluster replication is event driven, so if you store too many replicas of one database in a cluster, a lot of activity will be generated by the database transaction events. It is recommended that all servers in the cluster use a private LAN to carry cluster replication traffic in order to avoid a network traffic bottleneck on the public LAN.

3.6.2 Clustering for hub servers

If you decide to implement a hub-and-spoke topology for your application servers, it is critical that you ensure high availability of your hub servers. We discussed this in the context of Domino clustering for mail hub servers in 3.3.3, "Clustering in a hub-and-spoke mail infrastructure" on page 56.

To recap, a hub-and-spoke replication topology establishes one or more central servers as hubs, with outlying servers as spokes. Hub servers replicate with each other or with master hub servers. Also, hub servers exchange data updates with their spoke servers. Users usually access the spoke servers.

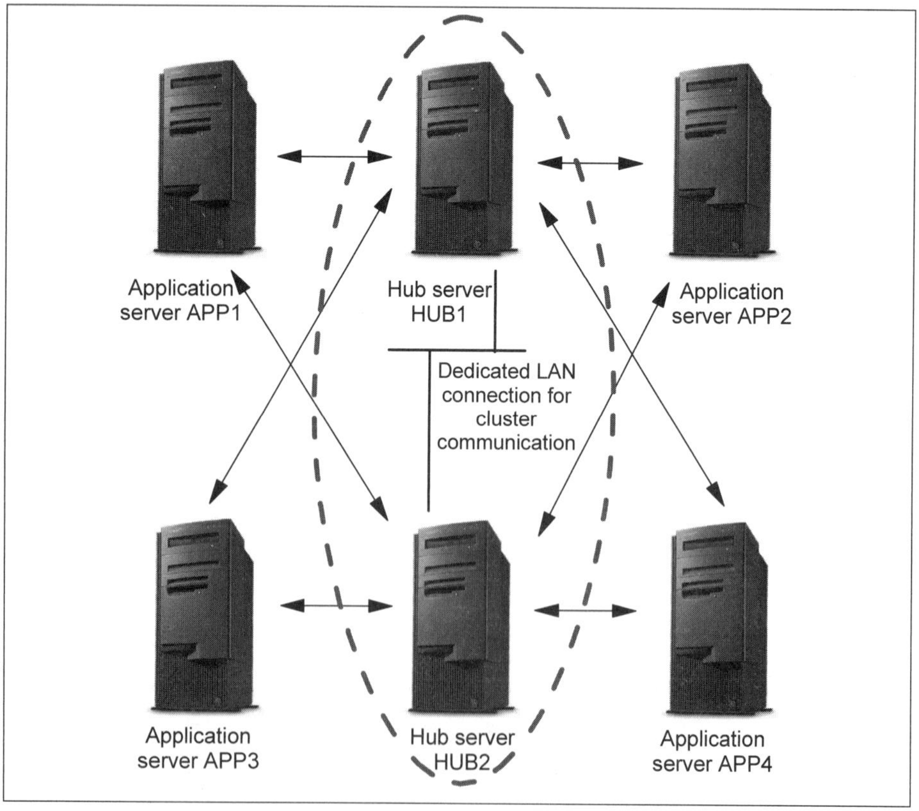

Figure 12. Application hub servers in a cluster

In our example, an application hub (HUB1) is clustered with a server (HUB2) acting as its backup. For the hub servers, we create one Connection document for each spoke server (hub to spoke), so that the hub servers initiate all replications to spokes.

3.6.3 ICM - HTTP clients and Domino clusters

Prior to Domino R5, Domino clusters were able to support only Notes clients. With the introduction of Release 5, Domino now supports failover and load balancing for both Notes and Web browser clients. This function is provided by a new Domino server task called the Internet Cluster Manager (ICM).

The ICM is responsible for managing HTTP and HTTPS (the secure form of HTTP) client requests to a Domino cluster. It does not manage File Transfer Protocol (FTP), SMTP or User Datagram Protocol (UDP) requests. There are other, third-party, load balancing or software products that manage these protocols, should you require this capability.

The ICM does not require any additional hardware. You can install it on any Domino Enterprise Server. It runs on all operating systems and hardware platforms supported by the Domino server. The ICM supports client connections via TCP/IP only. A brief description of how ICM operates follows. For more information, see 3.2.4, “How failover works for Web browser clients” on page 51.

HTTP clients direct requests for a database to the ICM. The ICM maintains availability information about the servers in the Domino cluster and also maintains information about the distribution of databases among the servers. The ICM determines the best server to receive a particular client request and directs the request to that server.

The ICM accepts and processes all URL requests currently supported by the Domino HTTP server, including URLs to do the following:

- Open servers, databases, and views
- Open forms, navigators, and agents
- Open, edit, and delete documents
- Open documents by name from a view
- Open image files, attachments, and OLE objects
- Create search queries

Web client bookmarks

If a Web browser client creates a bookmark for a page being managed by the ICM, the bookmark contains the URL of the back-end Domino server containing the page that is being viewed. The bookmark does not point to the ICM, and thus will not fail over if the server is unavailable in the future.

Only Domino R5 servers can exploit the ICM. In Domino R5, changes were made in Domino HTML generation to direct HTTP clients to the ICM for databases within a cluster. If the ICM redirects the client request to a server running a previous version of Domino, the URLs the server generates do not contain references to the ICM. As the client moves between Web pages, the client continues to access pages on that same server only. To take advantage of the ICM, the user must again select a URL that contains a reference to the ICM.

You can configure ICM to run on a Domino server that is a member of a cluster or on one that is outside the cluster. We now examine both of these cases.

3.6.3.1 ICM running within a cluster

The ICM may run on one or more of the Domino servers in the cluster. ICM availability is improved by running more than one ICM. Typically, you configure all ICMs for the cluster with the same host name in the Domain Name System (DNS) server. In this way, if one of the ICMs is unavailable, Web browser clients can fail over to another ICM while continuing to use the same host name.

If you configure ICM to run on a server in the cluster, there is some performance advantage, since the ICM accesses a local copy of the Cluster Database Directory. In this type of configuration, however, you should make sure that the server running ICM has the capacity to handle the traffic that ICM will generate in addition to the regular cluster and client traffic.

Figure 13 on page 75 shows a Web browser client accessing two ICMs that are running on Domino servers within a cluster. Each ICM can redirect client requests to any Domino HTTP server in the cluster.

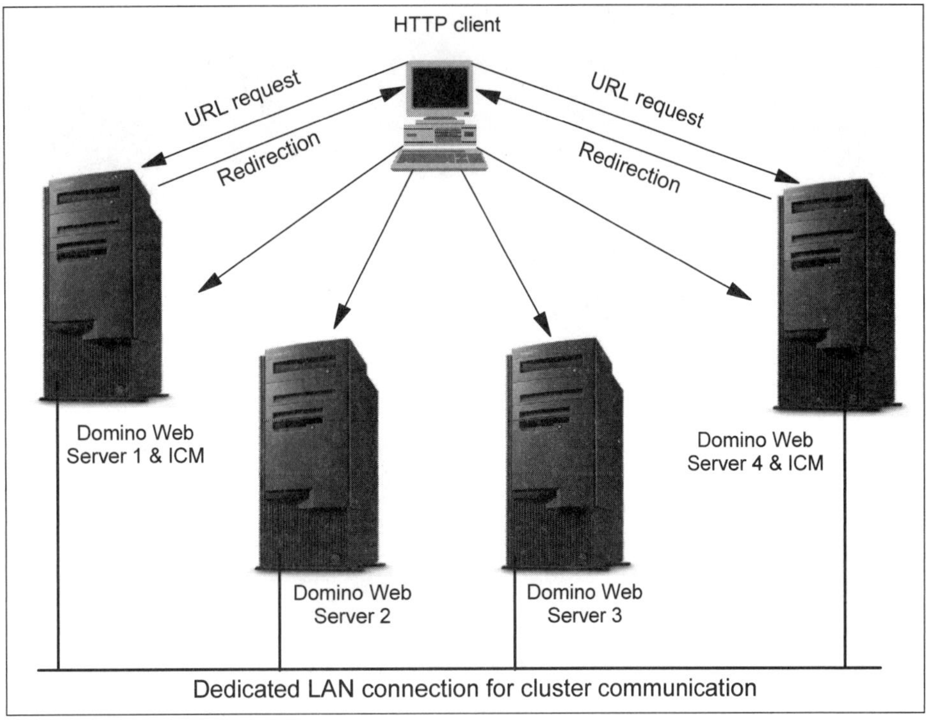

Figure 13. Multiple ICMs within a cluster

3.6.3.2 ICM running outside the cluster

ICM can also be configured to run on a Domino server that is not a member of the cluster. Once again, you can improve the availability of the ICM by configuring more than one ICM so that if one ICM becomes unavailable another one can handle Web browser client requests. If you decide to implement more than one ICM, typically you configure all of them with the same host name in the Domain Name System (DNS) server. You can use an operating system cluster such as Microsoft Cluster Services to provide failover support for the ICMs running outside the cluster.

If desired, it is also possible to implement multiple ICMs on a single physical machine by using Domino Partitioned Servers. You should take care to ensure that a partitioned system is powerful enough to provide the processing power necessary and that it can handle the increased network traffic.

You may decide to dedicate a Domino server to the ICM function. It will run only the basic set of Domino server tasks and will contain only those databases necessary for server operation. Taking this approach will guarantee that the majority of the ICM server's resources are devoted to handling Web client requests. An example is shown in Figure 14:

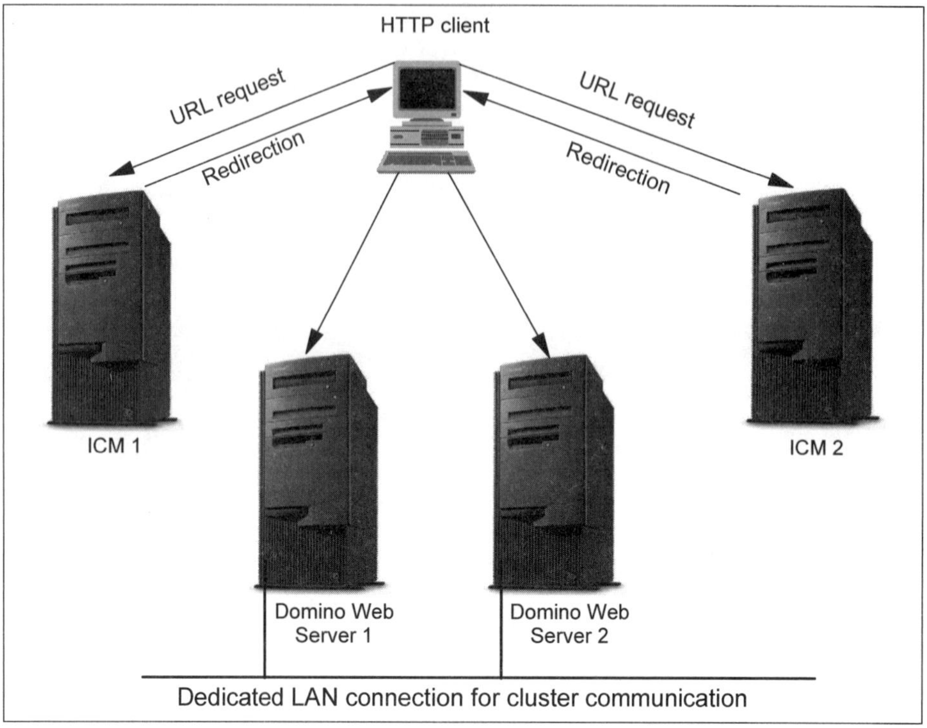

Figure 14. Multiple ICMs outside a cluster

In Figure 14, the real benefit of running multiple ICMs is availability, not increased performance. Adding an ICM will increase performance only in those cases where a single ICM cannot cope with the volume of requests.

3.6.3.3 ICM and security

The ICM supports the current Domino security model used for Web access. However, it does not participate in the authentication process. Requests from Web browser clients are sent to the ICM with no user ID or password. The ICM then redirects requests at the protocol level and it sends target server information back to the client. The Web browser client then requests data from the target Domino Web server. At that time, security checks are made on the target Domino server, which may result in an authentication process taking place between the client and the target server.

The ICM uses SSL for transport level security, using the same certificates that Domino server uses.

Chapter 4. Installing and configuring a Domino cluster

This chapter will cover the installation and configuration steps for clusters using Domino Enterprise Server Release 5.0.4a. Initially, we discuss installing Domino servers running on Windows 2000. Then, in 4.4, "Installing Domino R5 for Linux on IBM Netfinity servers" on page 106, we cover the areas that are significantly different when your servers are running Linux as their base operating system.

We will focus on the following topics:

- Installing a new cluster
- Modifying the cluster configuration (by adding, moving, or deleting a server)
- Upgrading a standard server to a clustered server
- Configuring calendaring and scheduling in a cluster
- Configuring Internet Cluster Manager (ICM)
- Hints and tips for installation problems

We will also discuss specifics of the installation and configuration steps for the Domino Enterprise Server Release 5.0.4a on Linux.

4.1 Prerequisites

In order to install Domino Cluster features, you must have installed and configured a working Windows 2000 server environment. You must also have configured the network protocols that will be used in your Domino environment.

Lotus Domino Enterprise Server requires the TCP/IP protocol for communication between cluster members. You can install and configure other protocols to be used in the Domino environment and the clients can access the databases using those protocols. It is necessary for all servers in a cluster to be configured with a consistent set of network protocols.

© Copyright IBM Corp. 1998, 2000

Protocols

Although other protocols may be used in addition to TCP/IP, we recommend that you use TCP/IP for both client to server and inter-server cluster communications if possible. The Domino cluster solution is optimized for TCP/IP, and provides faster failover times for clients using it than with other protocols.

The minimum system requirements for Domino clustering are listed in the following table.

Table 5. Minimum system requirements for Domino clustering

Feature	Windows 2000	Linux
Operating system	Windows 2000	Red Hat 6.0 (and later) Caldera 2.2 (and later) SuSE 6.3 (and later) TurboLinux 6.0 (and later)
Processor types	133 MHz or higher Pentium-compatible	Intel x86
SMP Support	Yes	Yes
RAM	128 MB or more minimum (256 MB recommended)	64 MB minimum
Disk space	2 GB (with a minimum of 1 GB free space)	750 MB minimum (1 GB or more recommended)
Protocols	TCP/IP SPX SPX II NetBIOS, NetBEUI AppleTalk VINES X.PC	TCP/IP X.PC

System requirements may vary greatly depending on the number of concurrent clients accessing the server, the database sizes, the transaction rate per second, and the number of replicated databases in the cluster.

In general, Domino clustering will require more resources than a standard Domino server. The following list indicates the major factors that influence resource requirements.

- The more replicas you create, the more disk space you need and the more processing power you need for cluster replication.
- The more servers in the cluster, the more processing power each server uses to communicate with the other cluster servers.
- The more server tasks and CPU-intensive applications you run on a server, the more processing power you need.
- The more users a server has to handle concurrently, the more memory the server needs to keep performance acceptable.

All servers in a cluster must run the Domino Release 5 or Release 4.62 Enterprise server license, or the Domino Release 4.5 or Release 4.6 Advanced Services license. All necessary software is included on the Lotus Domino CD-ROM.

To install a Domino cluster, the following conditions must be met:

- All servers in a cluster must be connected using a high-speed local area network (LAN). You can also set up a private LAN to separate cluster traffic from client traffic.
- All servers in a cluster must use TCP/IP and be on the same Notes named network.
- All servers in a cluster must be in the same Domino domain and share a common Domino directory.
- You must specify an administration server for the Domino Directory in the domain that contains the cluster. If you do not specify an administration server, the Administration Process cannot change cluster membership. The administration server does not have to be a member of a cluster or be running the Enterprise Server license.
- Each server in a cluster must have a hierarchical server ID. If any servers have flat IDs, you must convert them to hierarchical IDs to use them in a cluster.
- A server can be a member of only one cluster at a time.
- Each server must have adequate disk space to function as a cluster member.
- Each server must have adequate processing power and memory capacity.

With these prerequisites in place, you can now install Domino.

4.2 Hardware setup

All of the examples discussed in this chapter use the same hardware. The configurations we discuss are genuine ones that we constructed in our server lab. We chose to run Domino on four IBM Netfinity servers: two IBM Netfinity 7000 M10 4-way servers and two IBM Netfinity 5500 servers. The IBM Netfinity 7000 servers were equipped with 2 GB memory, 18 GB disk space on ServeRAID-attached disks, and IBM Token-Ring and IBM Ethernet adapters for network connectivity. All of the hard disks on a particular server were configured as a RAID-5 array, then as a single logical drive within the array. This logical drive then appears to the operating system as a single physical drive. We installed Windows 2000 on the two IBM Netfinity 7000 M10 servers and partitioned the logical drive as shown in the following table:

Table 6. Disk configuration on Windows 2000 server

Drive letter	Space	Component
C:	2 GB	Operating system
D:	4 GB	Paging file
		Domino program files
E:	8 GB	Domino databases
F:	4 GB	Domino transaction log

The two IBM Netfinity 5500 servers were equipped with 256 MB memory, 18 GB disk space on ServeRAID-attached disks, and IBM Token-Ring and IBM Ethernet adapters for network connectivity. All of the hard disks on a particular system were grouped into a RAID-1 array and defined as one logical drive. This logical drive then appears to the operating system as a single physical drive. On these IBM Netfinity 5500 servers we installed two different distributions of Linux. For one server we used Red Hat 6.2, and, for the other, SuSE 6.4.

We partitioned the logical drive as shown in the following table:

Table 7. Disk configuration on Linux server

Mount point	Partition size
/	256 MB
<swap>	See accompanying text
/boot	50 MB
/home	512 MB
/data	4096 MB
/data/log	1024 MB
/opt	1024 MB
/tmp	512 MB
/usr	2048 MB
/var	512 MB

If your server has less than 512 MB of memory, the swap partition should be three to four times the size of your physical RAM. If your RAM size is 512 MB or more, then set the swap partition size equal to the amount of RAM you have in your system. For our configurations, we allocated 1 GB to the Linux swap partition.

Swap partition size limit

Note that the maximum supported swap partition size for the latest kernel 2.2-based Linux distributions is approximately 2 GB. Kernels prior to 2.2 limit swap partitions to 128 MB. For these earlier kernels, larger partitions can be allocated, but waste space, since only the first 128 MB are actually used. To provide more than 128 MB of swap space requires that you configure multiple swap partitions. These can be located inside a disk's extended partition.

The hardware setup used here is not intended as a recommendation. The actual hardware required to provide Notes or Web clients with acceptable response times varies greatly from one installation to another, depending upon many factors including network infrastructure, number of users, and the types of applications and services provided.

To keep our lab systems relatively simple, we used a single array/logical drive configuration as already discussed. You will want to pay more attention to organizing your disk subsystem to optimize performance. Deciding exactly where the various files used by Domino should be located is quite crucial for performance. See 2.3, “Planning cluster hardware” on page 21 to read more about hardware components considerations for your cluster, including a discussion about the disk subsystem.

Disk organization and performance

This scope of this book prevents a detailed discussion of disk organization and the potential impact it can have on server performance. It is, however, worth mentioning one or two items of particular relevance:

- Placing the swap partition on a dedicated drive or on its own RAID array can give performance advantages. Using an array gives the added advantage that multiple disk spindles are active simultaneously, providing greater throughput than for a single disk.
- A similar argument applies for Domino R5’s transaction logs. Whenever possible, a separate dedicated disk drive or array should be used for these logs.

For more information about Domino performance, see the IBM Redbook *Netfinity and Domino R5.0 Integration Guide*, SG24-5313. A useful guide to improving server performance in general is another Redbook, *Tuning Netfinity Servers for Performance*, ISBN 0-13-040612-0.

Figure 15 illustrates the network and the Domino servers we installed in our lab environment:

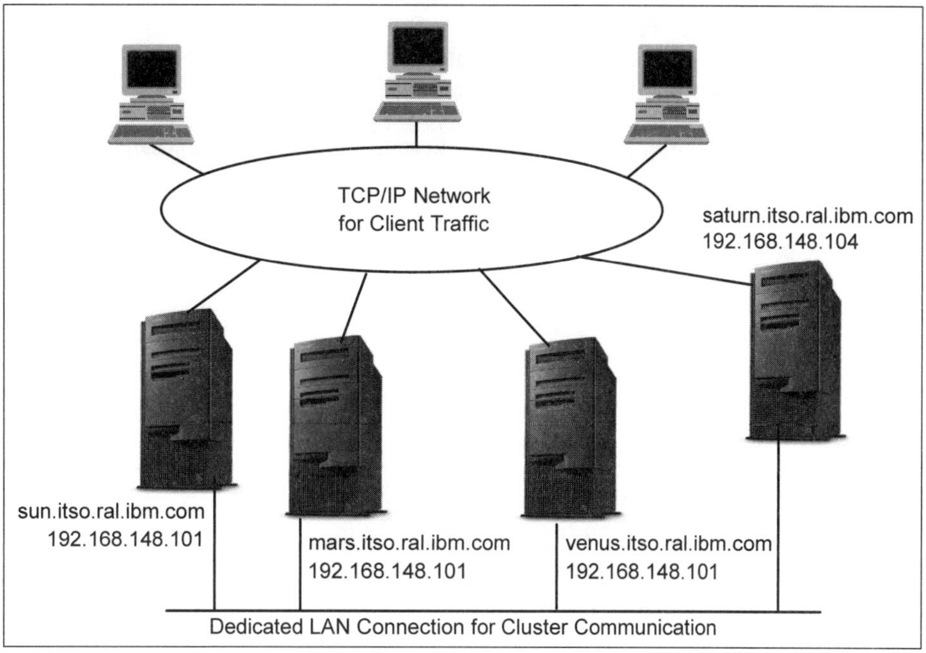

Figure 15. A four-node Domino cluster

All servers were connected using a dedicated Ethernet LAN connection.

We installed a 10/100 Mbps Ethernet adapter in each server, each connected to an Ethernet hub, to create a private network for the cluster traffic. Although this setup requires more hardware than would be necessary if the client network were used for cluster traffic, the resulting solution reduces traffic on the client network, and the additional cost is relatively small.

The network load that the cluster traffic will generate depends on the number of clustered nodes and number of update transactions between nodes. We therefore particularly recommend this approach for Domino clusters that provide service to large numbers of users or that will generate significant cluster traffic.

Lotus Domino Server can use any network topology supported by the underlying operating system.

4.3 Installing a new Domino cluster

In this section we will describe how to install Lotus Domino Enterprise Server and how to configure a cluster.

The installation steps can be summarized as follows:

1. Install the first Domino server.
2. Configure the first Domino server:
   a. Configure the server name, organization and domain.
   b. Configure the ports, protocols and named network.
   c. Start the server.
3. Prepare to install the remaining cluster servers:
   a. Create the certification log.
   b. Register additional servers.
4. Install and configure the remaining cluster servers. For each of them:
   a. Install the program files.
   b. Configure the server name, organization and domain.
   c. Configure the ports and protocols and named network setup.
   d. Start the server.
5. Create the cluster:
   a. Create the cluster using the Domino Directory.
   b. Verify that the cluster database directory file is replicated or replicate the file manually to all the servers in the cluster.
   c. Configure the communication port for the backbone communication between the servers participating in the cluster.
6. Test the cluster.

We now take you through each of these steps in turn.

4.3.1 Installing the first Domino server

Installing the first Domino server consists of the following simple steps. Note that TCP/IP is the only protocol stack used at this point of the cluster installation.

1. Insert the Lotus Domino CD-ROM and start the server installation program from an appropriate directory.
2. Read and accept the license terms.
3. Enter the user registration information.

4. In the Lotus Domino Installation window, select the program and data directories to be used for the Domino server.

   It is a recommended practice to install the Domino data directory on a dedicated partition. In our case we used the drives as defined in Table 6 on page 80.

5. Select the **Domino Enterprise Server** radio button to install a Domino server that includes Domino clustering as shown in Figure 16:

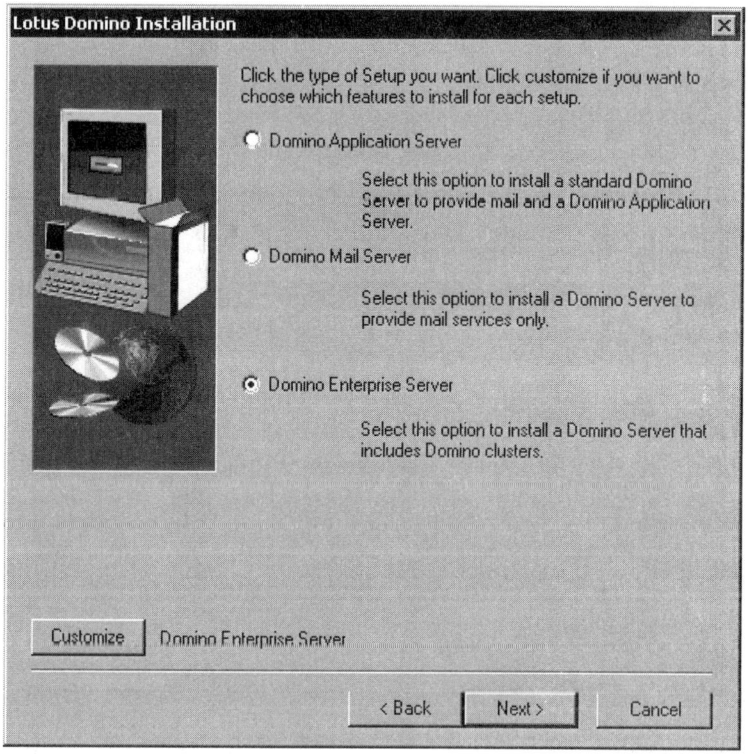

Figure 16. Domino Enterprise Server installation

6. Click **Customize** and select the components you want to install; Domino as an NT service, for example.

7. Installation will add program icons to the Lotus Applications folder. You may type a new folder name.

8. Click **Next** and the installation process will proceed to completion.

4.3.2 Configuring the first Domino server

This section, describing the configuration of the first server, is divided into two parts: the general configuration and the port and named network configuration.

4.3.2.1 General configuration

After the code installation phase has completed, the server must be configured in the same way as a standard Domino server. To configure the first server follow the steps below:

1. Select **Start -> Programs -> Lotus Applications -> Domino Server**. When you start the server for the first time after installation, the Domino setup client will run automatically.
2. Select the **First Domino Server** radio button in the first setup window.
3. Select **Advanced setup** in the second setup window.
4. Select the additional services that you want to run in the New Domino Server third setup window.

> **Web clusters**
>
> If you plan to provide failover benefits to Web clients, you will need to select Domino's HTTP service for installation. Remember to disable the Windows 2000 World Wide Web Publishing service provided by Microsoft's Internet Information Server (IIS) if this is installed.

5. Enter the required information for the Domino server in the last setup window. Figure 17 shows the setup and naming conventions for our lab setup.

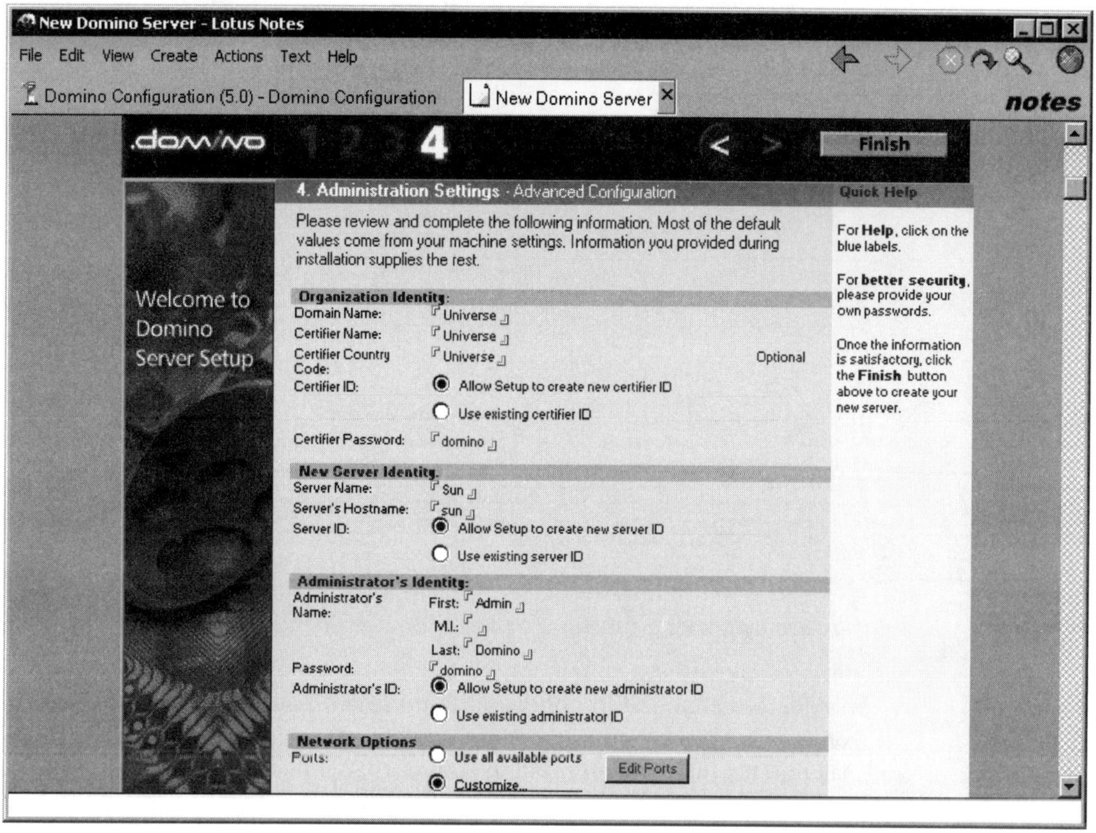

Figure 17. The first Domino server configuration

Note that we have opted to configure the ports manually. This is done so that all the unwanted protocols will be disabled.

6. To configure the ports during the initial configuration, select **Customize...** in the Network Options section and click **Edit Ports**. The Port Setup window is displayed.
7. Disable all but TCP/IP and verify that the settings for the port are correct, then click **OK**. The Port Setup window for the example setup configuration is shown in Figure 18:

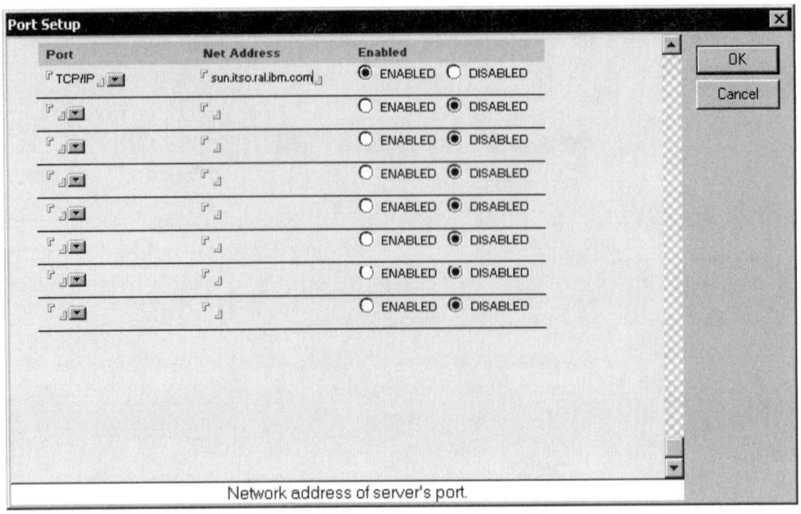

Figure 18. Modifying the port settings

8. After filling in the required configuration information, complete the setup process by clicking **Finish** (Figure 17).
9. After completing the Notes configuration, it is recommended that two settings are changed to optimize the Windows 2000 environment for the Domino server:
   - Select **Start -> Settings -> Control Panel -> System Properties -> Advanced** tab. Click **Performance Options** and select **Background services** as shown in Figure 19:

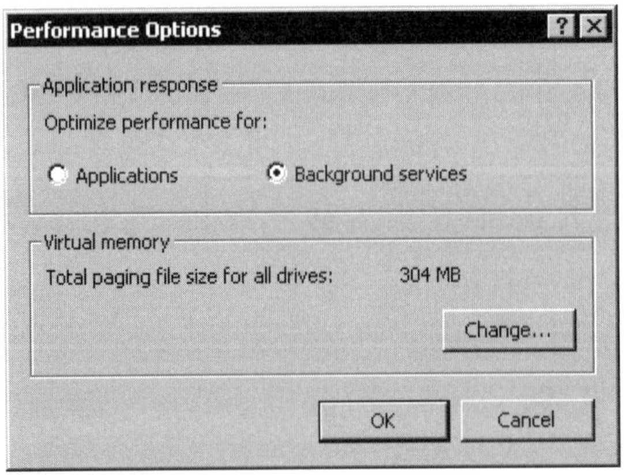

Figure 19. Changing Windows 2000 performance options

Click **OK** to close the dialog box.

Informational message

Using Windows NT 4.0, this setting eliminates the following message, displayed in the Domino console during startup:

```
Informational: The registry value
HKEY_LOCAL_MACHINE\System\CurrentControlSet\Control\PriorityControl\
Win32PrioritySeparation is currently set to 2. For better server
performance, change the setting to 0
```

Using Windows 2000, the setting changes the value from 38 to 24 and the message is still displayed. It can safely be ignored.

- Select **Start -> Settings -> Network and Dial-up Connections**.
- Double-click the icon for the network adapter being used by the Domino server, and click **Properties** in the Status window that appears.
- Select **File and Printer Sharing for Microsoft Networks**. Click **Properties** and select **Maximize data throughput for network applications** as shown below:

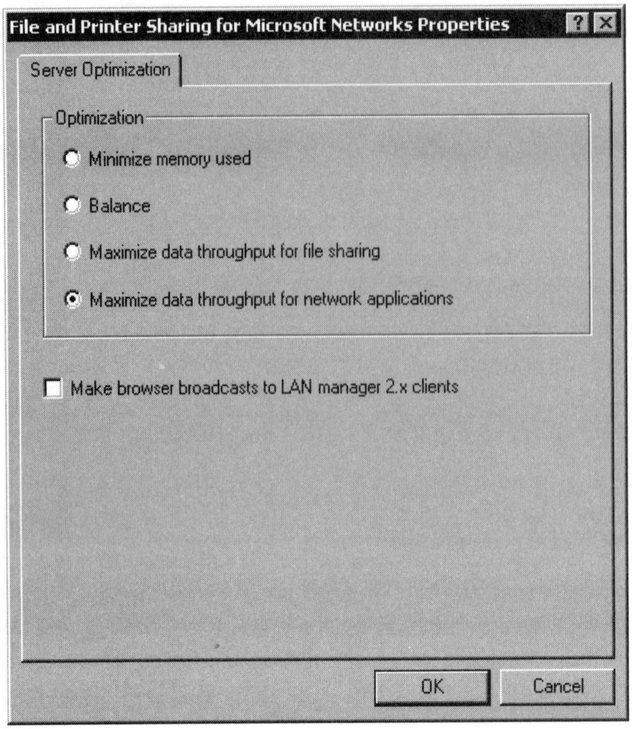

Figure 20. Maximizing server throughput

4.3.2.2 Port and named network configuration on the first server

We have emphasized the benefits of using a private network for cluster traffic several times. In our lab environment we used a token-ring network for client traffic and Ethernet for the private cluster network.

In the initial Domino server configuration we enabled the TCPIP port for client traffic. Now we have to set up another port to handle the cluster traffic. These are the steps we used:

1. From the Domino Administrator, select the **Server** tab.
2. Choose the server from the Servers pane.
3. From the Tools pane, choose **Server -> Setup Port**.
4. In the Communications Ports box, click **New** to create a new port name. We chose TCPCLUST. Do not use spaces in the name.
5. Select the TCP driver.
6. Select the **Port Enabled** check box. You should now have the following information displayed in the Port Setup dialog box:

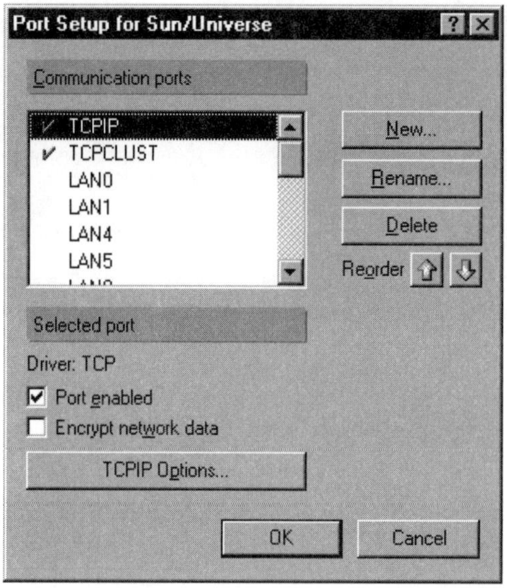

Figure 21. Creating a new port for cluster replication

Click **OK** to confirm your choices and close the dialog box.

7. From the **Configuration** tab, open the appropriate Server document in edit mode.

Select the **Ports -> Notes Network Ports** tab, and enter values for the new port as shown below:

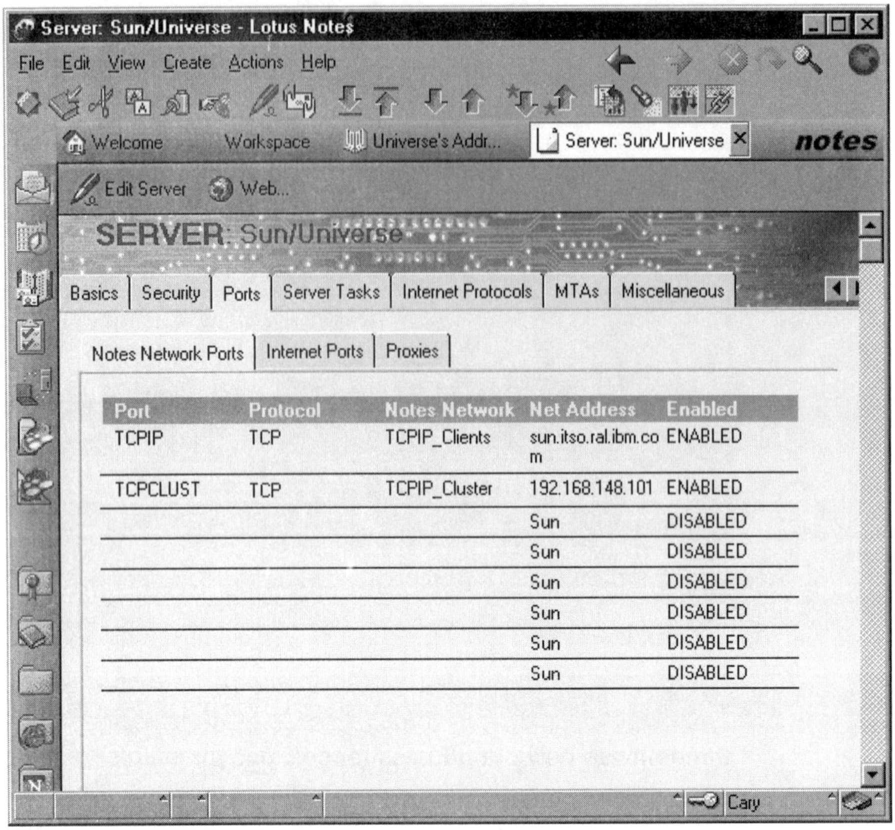

Figure 22. Defining a port for cluster traffic

Host name or static IP address?

If you are using host names instead of static IP addresses, make sure that the IP address can be resolved using DNS. If you are in any doubt about the reliability of DNS, use either static addresses or resolve the name in the server's hosts file. The hosts file is located in the \WINNT\system32\drivers\etc directory on Windows 2000 server and in the \etc directory on the Linux server.

8. Save and close.
9. Finally, you should modify the NOTES.INI file to assign IP addresses to these ports. You will add TCP/IP address parameters for each port:

```
<TCPIP PortName>_TCPIPAddress=0,IP,port
```

Parameters are described in the following table:

Table 8. Setting TCP/IP port parameters

Parameter	Description
PortName	Port name as defined on the Ports tab in Figure 22.
IP	TCP/IP address for that port. Verify that it is the same address as defined in the Windows 2000 network configuration.
port	TCP/IP port number on which the Domino server listens. This value should be set to zero or to the default Domino TCP/IP port 1352.

Here is example of settings that we added to NOTES.INI file on one of our Domino servers in the cluster:

```
TCPIP_TCPIPAddress=0,9.24.104.198,0
TCPCLUST_TCPIPAddress=0,192.168.148.101,0
```

In our lab cluster, the `TCPIP` port was used for client connections and it used a real, registered TCP/IP address. `TCPCLUST` was the port we defined to provide a dedicated connection between servers in the cluster, our private LAN. We recommend that you use addresses from the TCP/IP address space reserved for private networks. According to the TCP/IP standard (RFC 1597), there are three private network address ranges, one for each address class:

- 10.0.0.0 to 10.255.255.255 (class A)
- 172.16.0.0 to 172.31.255.255 (class B)
- 192.168.0.0 to 192.168.255.255 (class C)

4.3.3 Preparing additional cluster servers

The next step is to create server IDs for the remaining servers to be added to the cluster.

4.3.3.1 Creating the Certification Log

Before creating IDs for additional servers or users, you need to create a Certification Log for your Domino domain. Select **File -> Database -> New...** to invoke the New Database dialog box as shown in Figure 23:

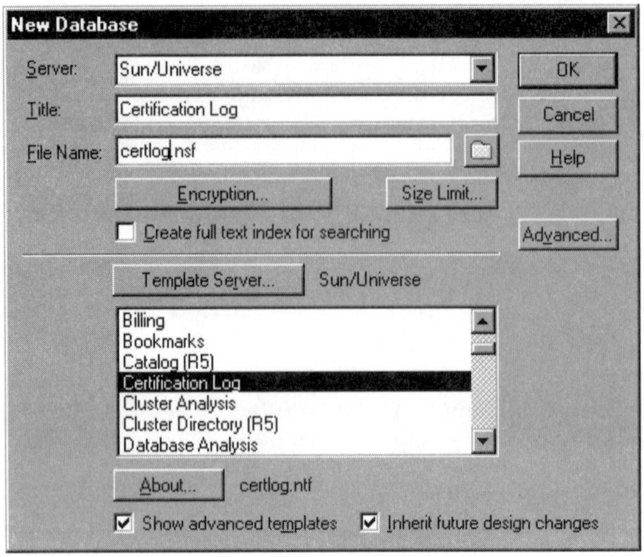

Figure 23. Creating the Certification Log database

The database name has to be CERTLOG.NSF. Also, remember that you need to select the administration server from the server list rather than the local server. Click **OK** to create the database.

4.3.3.2 Registering additional servers

Before you install additional servers, you must register them. In effect, registering a server adds the server to the domain. The server registration process creates both a Server document for the server in the Domino Directory and a server ID.

To complete this process, the following prerequisites must be in place:

- The registration server, that is the one from which you register other servers, must be up and running.
- You must have access to the registration server and have at least Author access with the ServerCreator role in the Domino Directory's ACL.
- You must have access to the certifier ID and its password.

To register each additional Domino server, follow the steps below:

1. From the Domino Administrator, click the **Configuration** tab.
2. From the Tools pane, click **Registration -> Server**.
3. Enter the certifier ID password and click **OK**.

Domino uses either the certifier ID specified in Administration Preferences or the ID specified in the CertifierIDFile setting of NOTES.INI. If you want to switch from one to the other, click **Certifier ID** and make your selection.

4. Choose the Administration server as your registration server by using the **Registration Server...** button.
5. Select the security type and enter the expiration date of the server certificate.
6. Click **Continue**.

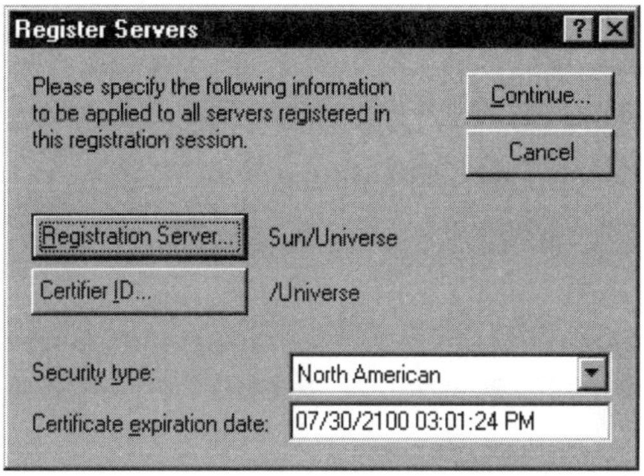

Figure 24. Registering an additional Domino server

7. In the **Basics** window, enter values for the Domino server name, Password, Domino domain and Administrator.

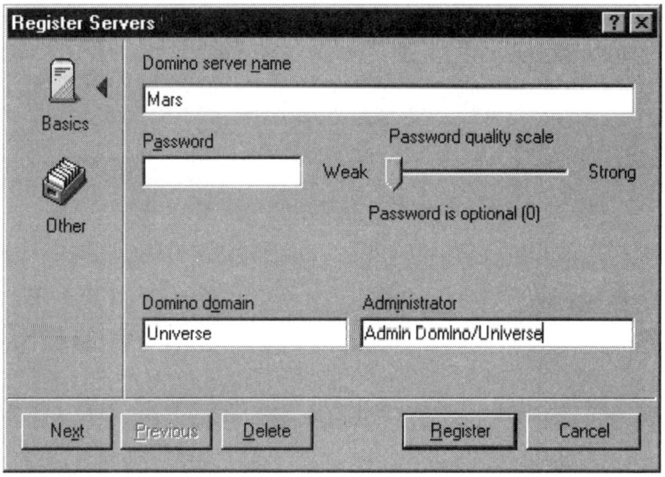

Figure 25. Setting the server's name

8. Select the **Other** icon and enter values for Server title, Network, and Local administrator.
9. By default Domino stores the server ID file in the Server document of the Domino Directory. Instead of storing it in the Server document, you can store the ID in another location. To select another location, click **Set ID file** and select the name and path for the file. Click **Save**.
10. Finish the server registration by clicking the **Register** button.

Repeat the above steps for each server that you intend to add to the cluster. At the end of this step, all members of the cluster will be registered.

4.3.4 Installing and configuring additional cluster servers

This step includes information on how to install and configure the remaining Domino servers. Repeat the following process for each additional server.

4.3.4.1 Installation

Install the Domino server software in the same way as you did when installing the first Domino server. You must install Domino Enterprise Server on each server that will be added to the cluster.

4.3.4.2 Server configuration

After the Domino code installation phase is complete, the server must be configured. To configure the server follow the steps below:

1. Select **Start -> Programs -> Lotus Applications -> Domino Server**. The Domino setup client will be launched.
2. Select the **Additional Domino Server** radio button in setup window 1.
3. Select **Advanced setup** in setup window 2.
4. Select the additional services that you want to run on the New Domino Server in setup window 3.
5. The New Domino Server setup window 4 is shown in Figure 26:

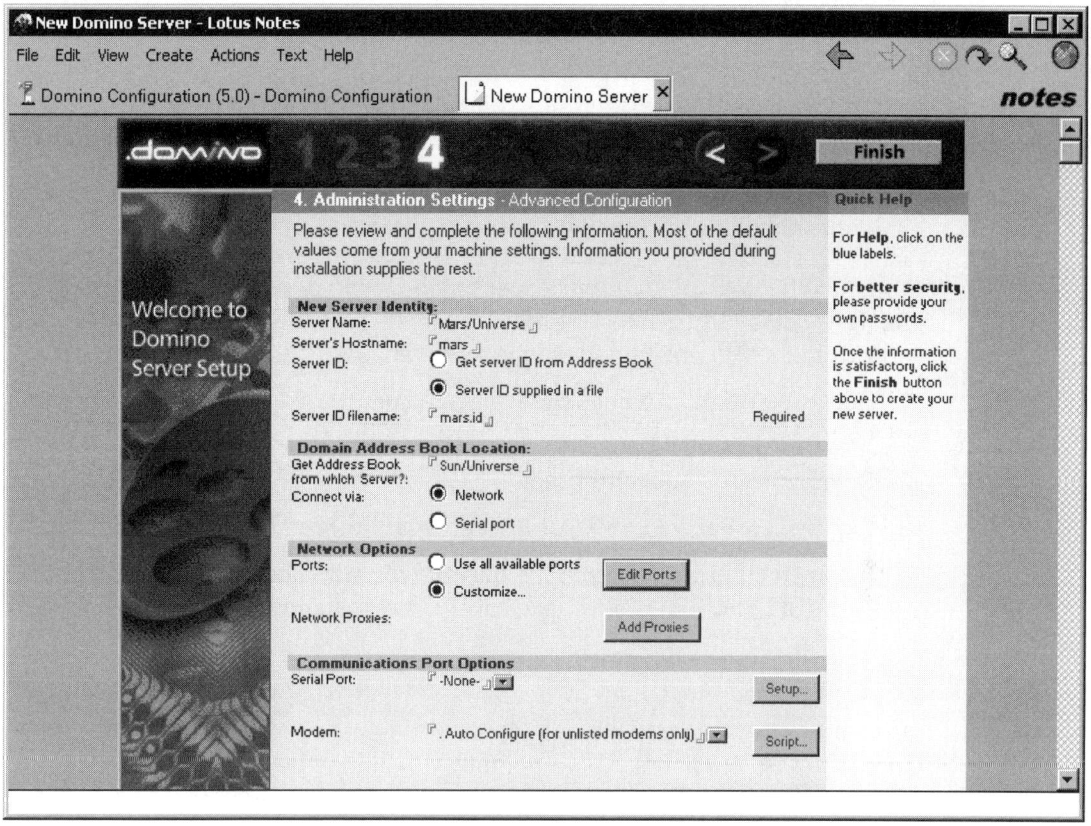

Figure 26. Using the ID file created earlier for the new server identity

6. In the New Server Identity section, select **Server ID supplied in a file**.
7. As with the first server, disable all ports except for TCP/IP.
8. Finish the configuration by clicking **Finish**. Accept the offer to copy the server ID file to the Domino data directory when prompted.

4.3.4.3 Port and named network configuration

After configuring the server, you need to set up an additional port for cluster communication if you decided to use a dedicated port for cluster traffic.

The second port is set up in exactly the same way as we did for the first Domino server (see 4.3.2.2, “Port and named network configuration on the first server” on page 90).

The above installation and configuration has to be completed for each server that is going to join the cluster.

4.3.5 Creating a cluster

Now that all of the servers that you have planned to be members of the cluster have been installed and configured, it is time to add them to the cluster.

4.3.5.1 Adding servers to a cluster

When you add Domino servers to a cluster, use the administration server. The administration server does not have to be part of the cluster.

You must have at least Author access with Delete document rights and the ServerModifier and ServerCreator roles in the Domino Directory, and Author access in the Administration Requests database.

1. Using the Domino Administrator, make sure the administration server is current.
2. Select the **Configuration** tab.
3. Expand **Server** and click **All Server Documents**.
4. In the Results pane, select the servers you want to add to the cluster and click **Add to Cluster**. Figure 27 shows the resulting dialog box:

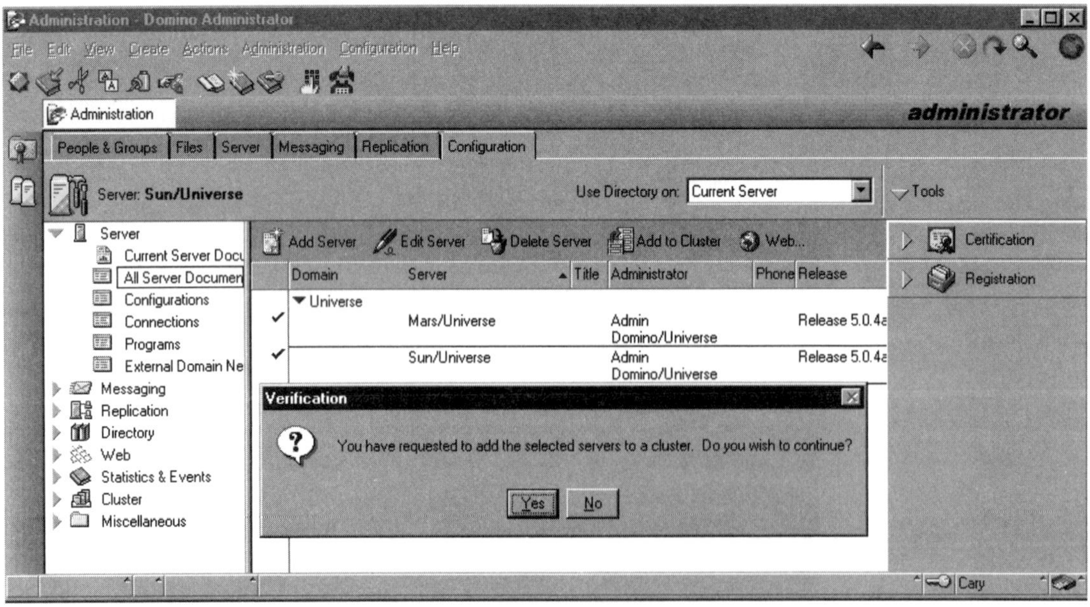

Figure 27. Adding servers to a cluster

5. You are prompted to confirm the addition of selected servers to the cluster. Click **Yes**.

6. The Cluster Name window is displayed. You can select either an existing cluster or, as in this case, select ***Create New Cluster** and click **OK**. You will be prompted to enter the name of the new cluster.

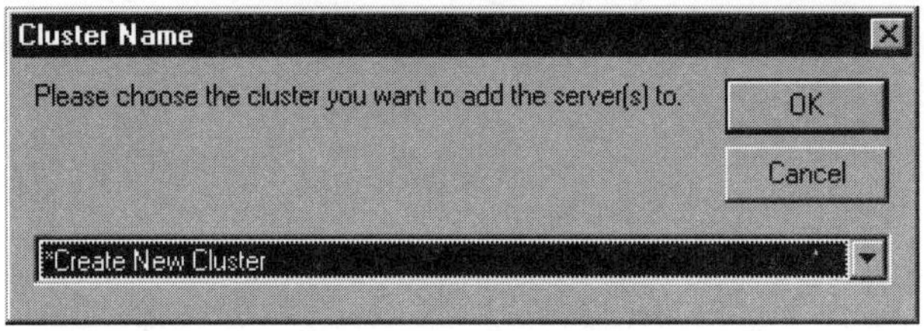

Figure 28. Entering name of the new cluster

7. Enter a name of your choosing and click **OK**.
8. In the next dialog box, you can click **Yes** to add your servers to the cluster immediately or **No** to submit a request to the Administration Process to add the server to the cluster.

   We recommend that you select **Yes** to add your servers to the cluster immediately. Their Server documents will be modified and, as soon as these changes in the Domino Directory are replicated to your new clustered servers, Domino clustering tasks will be initiated. The clustering tasks are Cluster Manager, Cluster Administrator, Cluster Database Directory Manager (CLDBDIR) and Cluster Replicator (CLREPL). Cluster Administrator adds task names CLDBDIR and CLREPL to the ServerTasks setting in NOTES.INI for each server so that these tasks start each time you start the server.

When you add servers to a cluster, there can be an initial performance impact due to the amount of replication that must take place to create the cluster replicas. Depending on the types of databases on the server and the number of replicas you create, adding a server can affect CPU performance, input/output and network traffic. Therefore, it may be a good idea to add only one or two servers at a time to a cluster, depending on the spare capacity of the systems in the cluster. If you set up a private LAN for cluster traffic, adding multiple servers at the same time will not be such a concern because it will not affect your primary network.

4.3.5.2 Dedicating the private port to cluster traffic

You should configure the TCP/IP port on the private LAN to be dedicated for the backbone communication between servers participating in the cluster. You can set it up either by editing NOTES.INI manually or by using a Server

Configuration document to update the NOTES.INI file on all servers in the cluster.

The following NOTES.INI entry controls the cluster traffic destination port:

```
Server_Cluster_Default_Port=PortName
```

where `PortName` is the port name defined in the Domino Directory. In our setup we added the line as shown:

```
Server_Cluster_Default_Port=TCPCLUST
```

You should also set the default port for cluster server probing. This port is used between the servers in the cluster to exchange information about cluster server status. The following NOTES.INI entry sets the probing port and should be added for all cluster members:

```
Server_Cluster_Probe_Port=PortName
```

where `PortName` is the name of the port to be used for server probing. Only a TCP/IP port should be used for server probing. This parameter is especially useful if the servers in the cluster are configured to run protocols other than TCP/IP. Using this parameter you can be sure that probing occurs on the TCP/IP port only.

To set the port for probing, we added the following setting on each Domino server in our cluster:

```
Server_Cluster_Probe_Port=TCPCLUST
```

After saving the changes to NOTES.INI, you should restart each Domino server.

4.3.5.3 Cluster Database Directory

The Cluster Database Directory (CLDBDIR.NSF) resides on every server in a cluster. The Cluster Database Directory contains a document about each database and replica in the cluster. This document contains such information as the database name, server, path, replica ID and database status.

The Cluster Database Directory and its replicas are kept up to date automatically by cluster replication. The quickest way to get an overall view of which databases are clustered and which servers are carrying replicas is to open the Cluster Database Directory and use the Databases by replica ID view as shown in Figure 29:

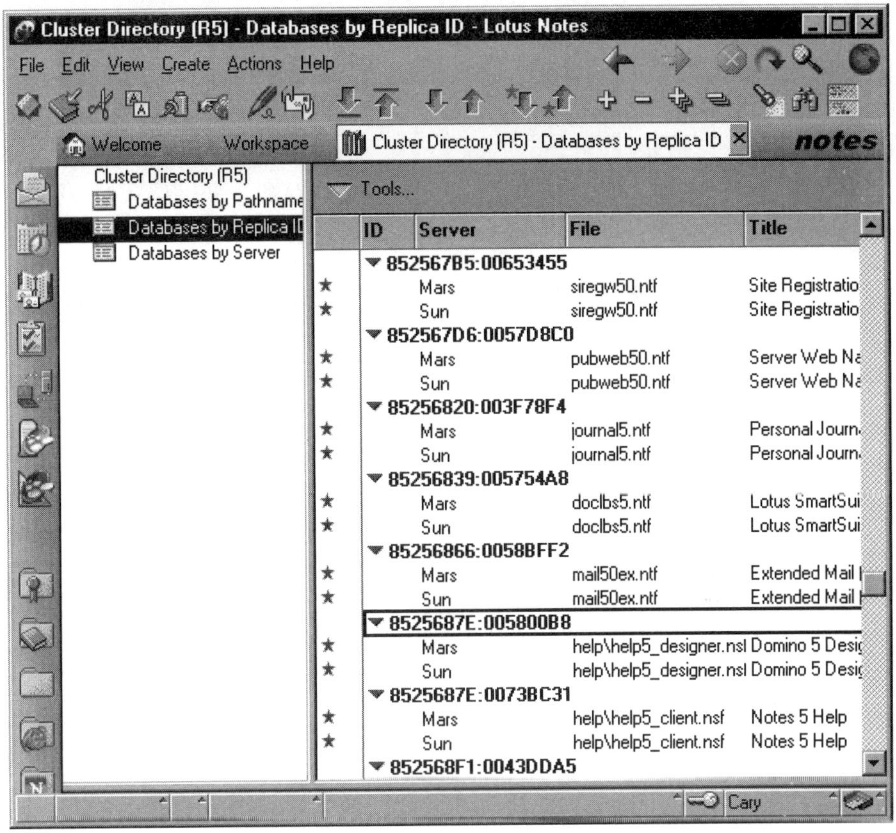

Figure 29. Cluster Database Directory

Because the Cluster Database Directory is so essential for the cluster's operation, make sure that database replication was successful by comparing the replica IDs on all the servers in the cluster. The replica IDs should be the same.

4.3.5.4 Configuring replication in a cluster

Both scheduled and cluster replication are necessary within a cluster. Cluster replication is used as the primary means of keeping database replicas up to date in a cluster and scheduled replication is used as a backup to cluster replication within a cluster, as well as to synchronize database replicas outside the cluster.

Because of the dynamic nature of cluster replication, and the fact that database updates are stored in memory, there is a possibility that database updates may be missing in the event of hardware or network failure. For this reason, it is recommended that scheduled replication is configured across the servers in a cluster. A suitable scheduled replication repeat interval will depend on both the number and the sizes of the databases on your servers.

Traditional scheduled replication relies on administrator-defined Connection documents in the Domino Directory. An example of how to configure a Connection document between clustered Domino servers is shown in Figure 30:

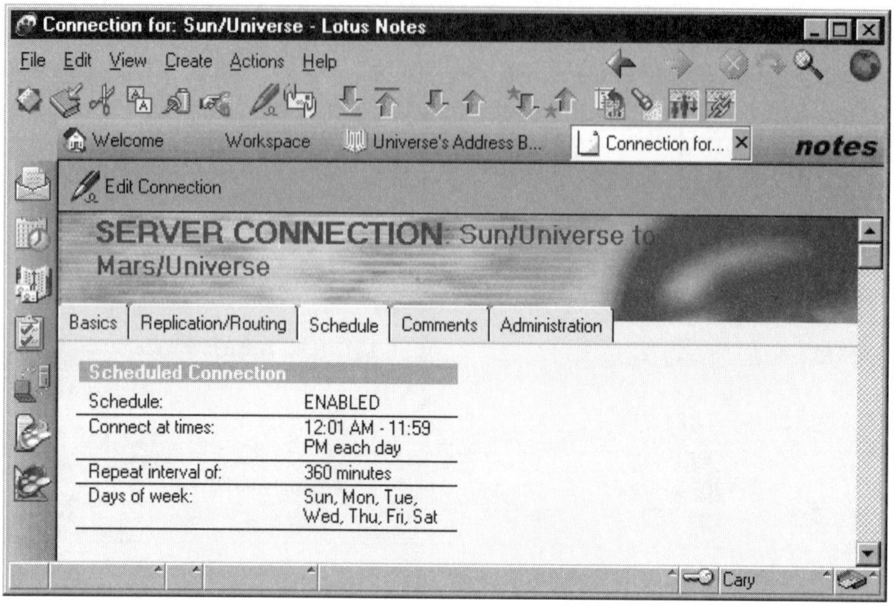

Figure 30. Connection document for scheduled replication

Remember that for each clustered server you *must* create a Connection document.

To ensure that all the replicated databases are up to date when the server starts, you can define replication to take place at startup by defining a new Program document in the Domino Directory. Refer to 5.6.4, "Setting up scheduled replication at server startup" on page 154 for more details.

In contrast to the predictable nature of scheduled replication, cluster replication is event driven. Whenever a change occurs to a database in the cluster, the Cluster Replicator immediately pushes the change to the other replicas in the cluster. This ensures that each time users access a database, they see the most up-to-date version. The Cluster Replicator also replicates changes to private folders that are stored in a database.

Each server in a cluster runs one Cluster Replicator by default. This configuration is adequate if only a few moderately sized databases exist in a cluster consisting of two or three Domino servers. In typical high-volume clustered environments, we recommend that you should configure as many Cluster Replicator tasks on each server as there are total number of servers defined in the cluster, less one. This guideline suggests, for example, five Cluster Replicator tasks for a cluster composed of six servers. In this way, there will always be at least one CLREPL task available to handle replication requests to another server in the cluster.

To configure multiple Cluster Replicator tasks, append additional CLREPL instances to the ServerTasks parameter in NOTES.INI, as shown below:

```
ServerTasks=Router,Updall,Replica,AdminP,CLDBDIR,CLREPL,CLREPL,CLREPL
```

Make sure all CLREPL tasks are listed after the CLDBDIR task. The Cluster Replicator relies on information provided by the Cluster Database Directory Manager.

For more details about cluster replication, see Chapter 5, “Administering Domino clusters” on page 119.

4.3.6 Changing cluster membership

A server can easily be moved from one cluster to another, or removed from a cluster to be a standard Domino server.

To move a server from one cluster to another, you simply add the server to the new cluster. Domino automatically removes the server from the old cluster. For more information, see 4.3.5.1, “Adding servers to a cluster” on page 98.

You can remove a server from a cluster using the Administration Client.

1. Open the Domino Directory on the server specified as the Administration server for domain.
2. Select the **Configuration** tab.
3. Expand the Cluster section in the left pane.
4. Click **Clusters**.
5. Select the server(s) that will be removed from the cluster.
6. Click **Remove from Cluster**. This can be seen in Figure 31:

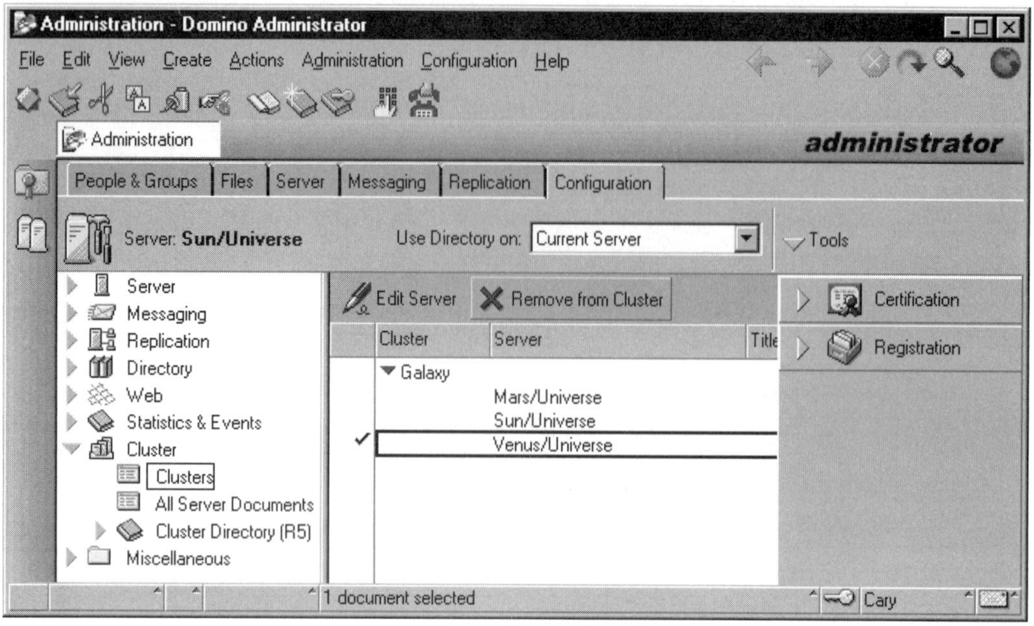

Figure 31. Removing a Domino server from a cluster

7. Confirm that removal should continue by clicking **Yes** in the Verification dialog box.
8. Decide if the server should be removed immediately or through the Administration Process and click the appropriate button as shown in Figure 32:

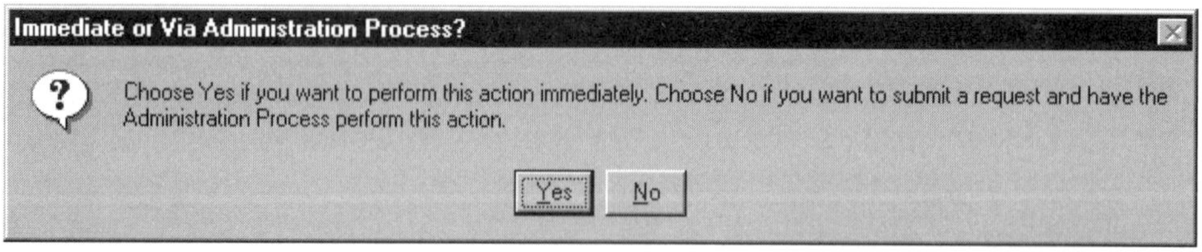

Figure 32. Choosing when to remove the server

9. If your choice in step 8 was **Yes**, then a confirmation dialog box will be displayed. Click **OK**.
10. If your choice in step 8 was **No** then the request will be submitted to the Administration Process.

11. The cluster processes CLREPL and CLDBDIR will be stopped on the server, and the relevant entries removed from the ServerTasks setting in NOTES.INI.

12. Entries relating to databases hosted by the server being removed will be purged from the replica copy of the Cluster Database Directory on the least busy of the remaining cluster servers.

13. The local Cluster Database Directory will be deleted from the server that is being removed from the cluster.

14. Schedule Manager deletes the clustered Free Time database (CLUBUSY.NSF) and creates the Free Time database (BUSYTIME.NSF).

4.3.7 Joining a cluster

Follow the steps below to upgrade a standard Domino server to a clustered server:

1. Upgrade the Lotus Domino software to Domino R4.61 or later, or if you are already running R4.61, install Lotus Advanced Services. If you are running Domino R4.62 and later or Domino R5 you need to install Domino Enterprise Server. The installation steps are described in 4.3.1, "Installing the first Domino server" on page 84.

2. Verify the Domino port configuration. You need to define at least one TCP/IP port for cluster traffic. The client traffic can either run on the same port or on another port, which can be running any protocol that Domino supports. If you are using only one port, then you *must* run TCP/IP on that port.

   The cluster traffic does not require a separate network link but, as stated previously, we recommend this due to the increased network traffic created by event-driven cluster replication.

   You can find details on how to define ports in 4.3.2.2, "Port and named network configuration on the first server" on page 90.

3. Edit the NOTES.INI file or create a Configuration document to make bindings between the port names and TCP/IP addresses as described in 4.3.5.2, "Dedicating the private port to cluster traffic" on page 99.

4. Now you are ready to add your server to a cluster. See 4.3.5.1, "Adding servers to a cluster" on page 98.

4.4 Installing Domino R5 for Linux on IBM Netfinity servers

In this section we discuss those Domino installation and configuration steps that are specific to Linux. In particular, we examine:

- Linux patch requirements for Domino R5
- Preparing Linux for Domino installation
- Disabling services on Linux
- Installing Domino on Linux
- Configuring Domino on Linux
- Starting and stopping Domino on Linux

4.4.1 Linux patch requirements for Domino

Identifying the required patches for Linux is difficult because there is no single defined Linux distribution. The various distributions, Red Hat, SuSE, Caldera, TurboLinux, and so on, are at different levels, with different combinations of code packages included and available. By setting requirements based on kernel and library levels, however, and then evaluating each distribution based on this, a set of requirements can be determined.

By certifying and supporting distributions, a certain set of patches is guaranteed. At the lowest level, Linux kernel 2.2.5 or greater is required, along with glibc 2.1.1 or greater, and libstdc++ 2.9.0 or greater. Each of the supported/certified distributions contains these levels or higher.

There is one exception to this rule: the version of glibc/libstdc++ installed must contain the libstdc++-libc6 naming convention. If it does not, you must make the appropriate link yourself. For example, in Red Hat 6.0, the file is /usr/lib/libstdc++-libc6.1-1.so.2. In Caldera 2.2, this naming convention is not used and therefore you must link /usr/lib/libstdc++-libc6.1-1.so.2 to the file /usr/lib/libstdc++.so.2.9.0 , which is the appropriate library. A distribution that meets these requirements should be able to accommodate the Domino server.

The upgrade from Red Hat 6.0 to Red Hat 6.1 contains patches to the Linux kernel that allow larger process/thread limits and increased file descriptor limits for greater utilization of server resources. Other distributions may offer similar changes from release to release.

4.4.2 Preparing Linux for Domino installation

Before you can install Lotus Domino for Linux you must ensure that the Linux server is correctly configured and ready for the installation. To run Domino for Linux you must create Linux user and group accounts to own and run the Domino server on Linux. To create a user account you must run the configuration utility for your distribution of Linux. For convenience, these are listed in Table 9:

Table 9. Linux configuration utilities

Distribution	Utility
Caldera	coastool
Red Hat	linuxconf
SuSE	YaST, command-line utilities and files
TurboLinux	turboservice

Select a user account name and a group account name that will be unique to your company. As a security precaution, we recommend that you do not use obvious names such as “notes”, “domino”, “lotus” or variations of these.

4.4.3 Disabling Linux services

Most Linux distributions enable services for the following by default: NNTP, SMTP, IMAP, POP3, and HTTP. In order to use the versions of these services provided by the Domino server, you must disable the corresponding Linux services. For IMAP and POP3, this is most easily done by editing the /etc/inetd.conf file and commenting out the entries for POP3 and IMAP. To disable SMTP, NNTP, and HTTP, you must use the appropriate utility for your particular Linux distribution.

For more details on how to disable or modify services, see the IBM Redbook *Lotus Domino R5 for Linux on IBM Netfinity Servers*, SG24-5968.

4.4.4 Installing Domino

Now that your Linux server is prepared, you need to obtain the Domino code for installation on the server. Lotus Domino for Linux can be obtained in two ways; you can download the code directly from the Web or purchase a CD-ROM from Lotus.

4.4.4.1 Domino code downloaded from the Web

You can download Domino for Linux from the World Wide Web at:

`http://www.notes.net`

The code you download is in the form of a .tar file. .tar files are Tape ARchive files and are similar to .zip files in that they contain a collection of other files and information about the directories that they reside in. They differ from .zip files in that the contained files are not compressed.

To be able to install Domino, you need to unpack the .tar file and place the files in their appropriate directories. This process is performed by the Linux utility called `tar`. From the command line enter the following command:

```
tar -xvf filename.tar
```

Upon completion of this command, a new subdirectory, named linux, will have been created in the current directory and the files from the .tar archive will have been extracted to it. Change directories to the linux directory by using the cd command:

```
cd linux
```

Then type:

```
./install
```

to invoke the text-based installation script for Domino.

4.4.4.2 Domino code on a CD

If you have the CD-ROM version of Domino for Linux, you will need to mount the CD-ROM and run the install script from there.

To mount the CD-ROM, insert the Domino for Linux CD-ROM and enter the following command:

```
mount /dev/cdrom
```

Once the CD-ROM is mounted, you install Domino for Linux by issuing the following command:

```
/mnt/cdrom/linux/install
```

Do not change directories to the CD-ROM device. Issue the command from a directory on the hard-disk drive.

The `install` command will invoke the text-based installation script for Domino.

4.4.4.3 Installation

Follow the on-screen instructions to install the Domino software to the Linux server. The same steps are used regardless of the distribution of Linux that you are using.

Make sure that you choose the Domino Enterprise Server option during the installation process, if you plan to add this server to a cluster.

If you need more detailed information to help you install Domino for Linux, we recommend the IBM Redbook *Lotus Domino R5 for Linux on IBM Netfinity Servers*, SG24-5968.

4.4.5 Configuring Domino

So far you have prepared the Linux server and installed the Domino software. As there is no Notes client for Linux and the configuration requires local access, a Web browser is used to configure the server.

You can use a browser locally on the Linux server, or use a browser from another computer that can connect to the Linux server using TCP/IP over the network. You must use a Web browser that supports graphics and Java.

To configure Domino, you will use the Lotus Domino Web server in initial configuration mode. The Web server is started from the Linux command line. First change directories to the Domino data directory:

```
cd /data
```

Then issue the following command:

```
/opt/lotus/bin/http httpsetup
```

This will launch the Web server and use the SETUPWEB.NSF database to complete the configuration. The Web server listens on port 8081 and will only provide access to the setup configuration database.

Using a Web browser, enter the following URL:

```
http://<server>:8081
```

where <server> is the TCP/IP address or DNS name of the Linux server. When your browser loads the page returned by the server, you will see the familiar windows that are used to configure the Domino server. Just as in all other Domino server platforms, you need to fill in the appropriate information for your Domino installation. This will be similar to any other additional Domino server installation. The installation process was explained earlier, in 4.3.4.2, “Server configuration” on page 96.

4.4.6 Starting and stopping Domino

To start the Domino server for the first time, issue the following command from the command line:

```
/opt/lotus/bin/server
```

For additional flexibility and security reasons, we recommend that you start the Domino server from a script. Some examples of Domino startup scripts can be found in the IBM Redbook *Lotus Domino R5 for Linux on IBM Netfinity Servers*, SG24-5968.

After starting the server, the Domino console appears and is identical to that found on all other supported platforms. You can now issue commands from the console as you would from any Domino server, or you can connect from another system by using the Windows Domino R5 Administration client.

There are several ways to stop your Domino server on Linux:

- From the foreground server console:

  Type `exit` or `quit` to shut the server down.

- From the Domino Administrator client, follow these steps:

  a. Open the Domino Administrator client.
  b. Click **Server -> Status**.
  c. Choose the server you wish to shut down and select **Tools -> Server -> Shutdown** from the Tools pane, or **Server -> Server -> Shutdown** from the menu bar.
  d. You will be prompted to confirm the shutdown. Click **Yes**.
  e. The Domino Administrator will confirm that the server has stopped by indicating that it no longer responds.

- From the Linux command line:

  To shut down the Domino server from the Linux command line, make sure you are logged in with the user account you created for running the Domino server. Type `server -q` to shut down the server. The directory containing the installation binaries, /opt/lotus/bin, must be in the user's PATH statement.

- With a stop script:

  You might decide to create a script file to stop a Domino server. An example of a Domino stop script can be found in *Lotus Domino R5 for Linux on IBM Netfinity Servers*, SG24-5968.

4.5 Setting up calendaring and scheduling

A Domino server that is not clustered contains a database that includes scheduling information for all users who use that system as their mail server. This database is named BUSYTIME.NSF and is known as the free time database. In a cluster, there is a single free time database for everyone whose mail server is a member of the cluster. This database is named CLUBUSY.NSF and it contains all the information that was in the individual free time databases of all the servers that became cluster members. Each server in the cluster contains a replica of this database.

When you add a server to the cluster, the Schedule Manager deletes the server's BUSYTIME.NSF database and creates its replica of CLUBUSY.NSF, which is synchronized with the other replicas in the cluster. When a user in the cluster requests free time information, the server looks in its own CLUBUSY.NSF first to find information for every user in the cluster. For users whose mail servers are outside the cluster, requests are sent to those servers for the free time information. Whenever there is a change to the CLUBUSY.NSF on any server in the cluster, the Cluster Replicator updates the other replicas in the cluster.

When you remove a server from a cluster, the Schedule Manager deletes CLUBUSY.NSF from that server and recreates BUSYTIME.NSF. The Schedule Manager on each server in the cluster removes the deleted information from its replica of CLUBUSY.NSF.

If there are Domino R4.x servers in a cluster, they maintain their BUSYTIME.NSF databases. These databases are not converted to CLUBUSY.NSF. Calendaring for these servers works the same as in a non-clustered environment.

If one of the clustered servers is unavailable, mail users will fail over to another server in the cluster that has a replica copy of their mail files. These users will then be able to continue using their mail as they usually do. In this situation, we discovered that free time search and group calendar-related operations are either not available or appear to be working but present incomplete information based on data entered by the user prior to the failover.

In our lab we were able to reproduce these problems with calendaring and scheduling in a clustered Domino R5 environment.

1. For example, user A has a home mail server (Server A) that is clustered. When his home server becomes unavailable, he fails over to the other server in the cluster that has a replica copy of his mail database (Server B). User A continues to work with his mail and schedules several meetings. User B now wishes to book a meeting with user A, and so wants to check user A's schedule. A free time search in this case returns incorrect information. It shows that user A is free for any time slot that he has filled since the failover. This occurs for all entries user A added to his calendar after his home server became unavailable. It appears that the Scheduler task on Server B does not update information in CLUBUSY.NSF for those users that have Server A as their home mail server.

   Once Server A becomes available, the Scheduler task on Server A updates Server A's copy of CLUBUSY.NSF, which is then cluster replicated to Server B.

   Figure 33 shows an inaccurate result from a free time search made while the user's home mail server was not reachable, and both chair and invitees had their mail databases on Domino servers in the same cluster.

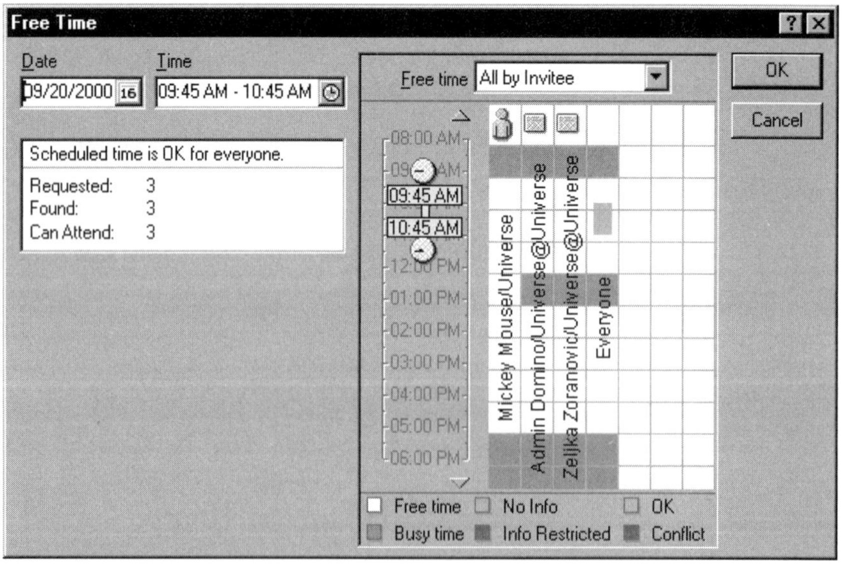

Figure 33. Free Time search in a clustered environment

   Even though meetings were booked in the requested time slots, the free time search shows them as available.

2. User A has a clustered server as his home mail server, which we stopped. When user B (who is using another Domino server in the cluster as his home mail server) opens his/her own mail database and tries to open user A's calendar by selecting **Tools -> Calendar Tools -> Open Another Calendar**, failover does not occur. User B will get a `Server Not Responding` error message.

   This shows that the formula corresponding to the Open Another Calendar menu option, @Command([OpenCalendar]), does not support cluster failover.

3. When a user retrieves a group calendar for a group that has members whose home mail server is clustered and unavailable, he receives incomplete calendar data for these users. Information entered by group members prior to their home mail server failure is shown properly. Any schedule data entered after their home mail server failure is shown as free time. Also, when a user tries to display the calendar for a user whose home mail server was clustered but unavailable, clicking user B's name produces the following error message:

   `Unable to open user's mail database.`

4. When user A, whose home mail server resides outside the cluster, makes a request for free time information about user B, whose home mail server is a cluster member that is unavailable in the cluster, the request does not fail over. Free time information is shown as No Info.

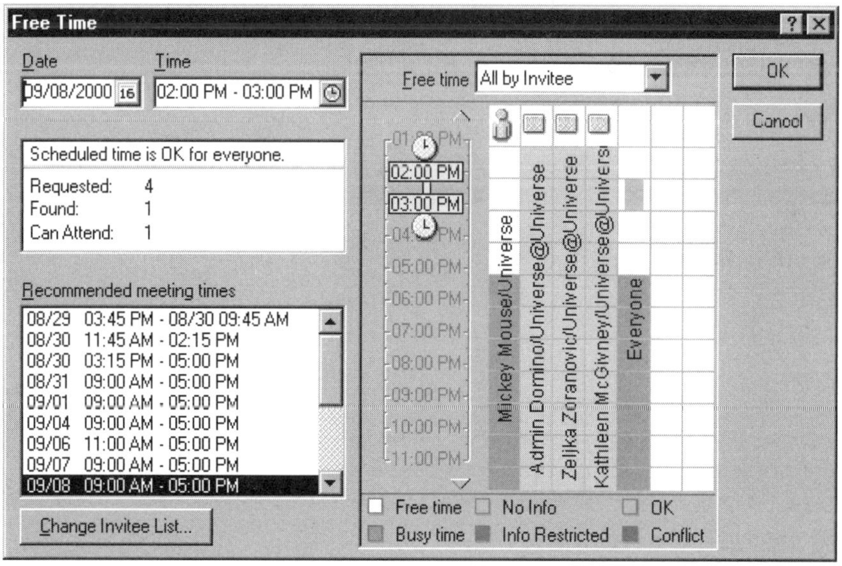

Figure 34. When Free Time search does not work

We have no firm information to indicate that this behavior will be modified, but Lotus is aware of the problem and we anticipate that correct operation will be incorporated into Domino in a future update.

4.6 Configuring Internet Cluster Manager

An Internet Cluster Manager (ICM) is dedicated to a single cluster. So, if you have two clusters, you must have at least one ICM for each cluster. The ICM needs to be in the same domain as the Domino cluster because the ICM always uses the local copy of Domino Directory.

The ICM is a Domino server task that ships as part of Domino R5 clustering. To install the ICM, you must install the Domino Enterprise Server. The ICM is automatically installed as a part of the Domino clustering support that ships with R5 Domino Enterprise Server.

> **Note**
>
> Be sure to include the ICM configuration information on every server on which you run the ICM, as well as on every Web server in the cluster.

You can configure the ICM settings on one server and have more than one server accessing these settings.

4.6.1 Setting up ICM

To configure the ICM, you make entries in the Internet Cluster Manager section of the Server document in the Domino Directory.

1. From the Domino Administrator, select the **Configuration** tab.
2. Expand Server and click **All Server Documents**.
3. In the Results pane, select the Server document for the server on which you want to run the ICM; then click **Edit Server**.
4. Select the **Server Tasks -> Internet Cluster Manager** tab and complete the following fields:

Table 10. Entering the ICM settings

Section	Field name	Description
Basics	Cluster name	The name of the cluster the ICM will service. If this field is blank, Domino uses the name of the cluster that contains this server.
	ICM Notes port	The name of the Notes port the ICM will use to communicate with HTTP clients. This field is blank by default, so that ICM can use any Notes port.
	ICM SSL keyfile	The name of the SSL key file that contains certificates to identify the ICM when communicating with HTTP clients.
	Allow users to browse databases in the cluster over HTTP	Allows HTTP clients to view a list of all databases in a cluster.
Configuration	Get configuration from	You can specify a different Server document from which to get the configuration data.
	Obtain ICM configuration from	This field appears when you select **another server document** in the field Get configuration from:
	ICM hostname	This is the fully qualified name of the host that clients should use to communicate with ICM.
ICM HTTP Port Settings	TCP/IP port number	The port number that ICM will use. If you run the ICM on the same server as the Web server, you must avoid address and port conflicts.
	TCP/IP port status	Choose **Enabled** to allow HTTP communication with the ICM.
	SSL port number	Enter the port number to use for SSL.
	SSL port status	Choose **Enabled** to allow HTTPS communication with the ICM.

If the ICM runs on the same system as the Domino HTTP server, you can configure either the ICM or the HTTP task to run on separate ports or to run with different TCP/IP addresses in order to avoid conflicts. We recommend that you assign the ICM its own TCP/IP address.

The Host name(s): field in the HTTP section of the Server document must match the entry found in the Fully qualified Internet host name: field on the Basics tab in the same document. The ICM fails if they do not match.

4.6.2 Starting ICM

If you want to start the ICM every time you start the server, append ICM to the `ServerTasks` setting in NOTES.INI:

```
ServerTasks=Router,Replica,AdminP,HTTP,ICM
```

If you want to start the ICM manually while the server is already running, use the following command at the server console:

```
load icm
```

4.7 Hints and tips for installation problems

The following sections include hints and tips to help you if you are experiencing problems with installing Domino clustering.

4.7.1 Check NOTES.INI

Check the `ServerTasks` and the `Server_Cluster_On` settings. The `ServerTasks` line in NOTES.INI should include the tasks CLDBDIR and CLREPL.

Make sure that CLDBDIR is listed on the `ServerTasks` line before the CLREPL command. The CLDBDIR is responsible for building and maintaining the Cluster Database Directory, CLDBDI.NSF. The Cluster Database Directory must exist for the cluster replicator to load.

Also make sure that the cluster is enabled with the following entry:

```
Server_Cluster_On=1
```

4.7.2 Cluster Database Directory

The Cluster Database Directory (CLUBUSY.NSF) contains an entry for each database within the cluster. Look in this database to make sure all databases within your cluster are listed. For example, if a database within your cluster is not pushing changes to a cluster member that contains a replica copy of this database, you can investigate by making sure the entry for each replica exists in the Cluster Database Directory.

A missing database entry within the Cluster Database Directory is usually due to the Cluster Manager failing to initially replicate with other cluster members during that server's addition to the cluster. Forcing a replication with a cluster member rectifies this issue.

To help ensure that the Cluster Database Directory is kept up to date, you should also use a standard replication task as a backup to cluster replication.

4.7.3 Using the Server Web Navigator in a cluster

If you use the Server Web Navigator in a cluster, make sure that the Web database (WEB.NSF) on the cluster servers are replicas. Since the Web database is generated automatically when you start the Server Web Navigator task, it is a common error for the clustered servers to contain Web databases that are not replicas of each other. Therefore, these databases do not fail over to each other.

To be sure that the Web databases are replicas, start the Server Web Navigator on only one of the clustered servers. Then replicate the Web database to the other cluster servers before starting the Server Web Navigator on those servers.

4.7.4 Choosing a time zone on a Linux server

Linux uses GMT (Greenwich Mean Time) internally. All internal Linux operations are done using this one time setting. For example, file time stamps are stored based on GMT. Displaying times in "local time" is a user interface issue. This strategy allows meaningful data exchange over a WAN (over the Internet being an obvious example).

To show the time correctly, Linux must be told which time zone applies to the server's location, that is the difference between local time and GMT.

To change the time zone, you will need to run the configuration utility for your Linux distribution. The zone field allows you to select the zone/country code that reflect how the time is managed at your location. This selection also influences the deviation from normal time used in some countries (winter time versus summer time).

In the Domino environment, a setting called TimeZone is defined during the Notes workstation or Domino server setup procedure. Time zones begin at Greenwich and move westward around the world. For example, TimeZone=5 represents the US Eastern Standard Time (EST) while TimeZone=0 represents Greenwich Mean Time. This setting is held in the Local time zone field in a Location document for workstations and the Local time zone field in the Server document on a server.

Confusion can arise if you choose "numeric" selection while configuring time zones during a Domino for Linux installation. We made this error ourselves, so felt it worth pointing out. When we first configured the time zone on our Linux server we chose the following value:

```
GMT-5
```

This was because our location, Raleigh, is in the US EST time zone which is five hours *behind* (hence "-") GMT. Our Linux Domino server interpreted this as ZE5 (five hours east of GMT). So, we changed our Linux setting to a non-numeric value to avoid this confusion:

```
US/Eastern
```

Our Domino server then correctly reported its time and time zone.

Chapter 5. Administering Domino clusters

Now that your Domino cluster is installed and configured, you can take advantage of the additional capabilities of failover and workload balancing to achieve greater database availability.

From making sure that database replicas are distributed to ensure that workload remains balanced in the event of server failure, to optimizing workload balancing, administering your cluster appropriately will maximize the return on your investment.

There are several considerations to take into account when you configure a cluster environment. In this chapter, we explain how to administer a Domino cluster. We discuss how to provide failover and workload balancing facilities, the cluster administration tools that are available, and how to use them.

5.1 Cluster failover and workload balancing strategies

There are several different strategies for optimizing database and server access:

- High failover

  Consider configuring the cluster to fail over servers where high availability of their databases is a requirement, and where workload balancing is not so much of an issue. For example, mail databases should be highly available, but only one person uses a personal mail database. You can make a database highly available by creating a replica on another server in a cluster. In this way, the user will be switched over to the replica when the database on the primary server is not available.

- Active workload balancing

  In a cluster, the distribution of users and databases is very important. If you have a large amount of user activity on your system, you should aim to distribute your databases evenly across the cluster so that no single server has a significantly larger number of client sessions than any other server.

- High failover and active workload balancing

  A combination of the previous two approaches, this strategy is often employed where you have a database that users access continuously, such as an active discussion database. Not only do you need high availability, but you also need to distribute the heavy workload created by users accessing the database within the cluster.

© Copyright IBM Corp. 1998, 2000

5.2 Setting up failover

Failover redirects users to another server in the cluster when they attempt to access a database on a server that is unavailable. Automatic failover may occur because they cannot access either the server or the database itself. It is also possible to trigger a failover manually if you wish. In the following sections we discuss how to tailor the failover settings to suit your environment.

5.2.1 Triggering failover

There are several instances where failover may occur. In the following sections you will learn how to set up the parameters that trigger failover, and how to implement and monitor failover activities in a cluster. We discuss the parameters that are involved and how to set them.

5.2.1.1 Server unavailable

A server is considered unavailable when any one of the following conditions are present:

- Server unreachable

  The server is down or otherwise unreachable by the user. You could decide to shut down the server or disconnect it from the network, or the server may be unreachable because of any number of hardware, software, or network failures. Any time there is a situation that would prevent the Notes or browser client from communicating with the Domino server, the server is considered unavailable.

- Server restricted

  You can set the server to be restricted. In a restricted state, the server will deny any new database open requests. The administrator can enable this situation using the `Server_Restricted` NOTES.INI parameter. Remember that `Server_Restricted` does not affect local database access.

  You can update this parameter from the server console by typing the following command at the server console:

  ```
  set config Server_Restricted=n
  ```

  where n = [0 | 1 | 2].

  If n is set to 0, the server is unrestricted. Any other valid value (that is, 1 or 2) places the server in the restricted state. If set to 1, once the server is rebooted this variable is reset to 0 and the server will no longer be restricted, but if set to 2 the server will remain restricted until this variable is manually modified.

A server in the restricted state cannot accept new database open requests. Existing connections to a database, however, will not be terminated.

If you want to force all users off the server, you can set the server to be restricted, and then issue the DROP ALL command to terminate all user sessions. When the client attempts to re-establish the session with an already opened database, it will receive the following message:

```
Server error: Access to the server has been restricted by the administrator.
```

The user will be forced to close and re-open the database, which will then fail over to another server in the cluster.

- Server in the MaxUsers state

  A server is in the MaxUsers state when it reaches the maximum number of client sessions allowed. You can restrict the workload that will be placed on a server by setting the maximum number of active client sessions that a server will accept. The maximum number of client sessions allowed is specified by modifying the Server_MaxUsers entry in NOTES.INI.

  You can update this parameter from the server console by typing the server console command:

  ```
  set config Server_MaxUsers=maximum number of active users
  ```

  The Cluster Manager monitors this setting and, if the number of active users reaches the maximum number, the server state changes to the MaxUsers state. A server in the MaxUsers state will not allow any additional user sessions to be established on the server. Users attempting to access a server that has reached its maximum number of active users will fail over to a replica on another server in the cluster.

  There are two user implications that you should be aware of:

  - A server in the MaxUsers state will allow new database open requests from a client that has just opened a session.
  - If a server reaches the MaxUsers state, it will not allow any new client sessions and if failover does not occur the user will receive the following error message:

    ```
    Server error: Access to the server is restricted due to maximum number of users.
    ```

There is another NOTES.INI parameter related to the maximum number of sessions on a server: the Server_MaxSessions parameter. It is strongly recommended that you do not use the Server_MaxSessions parameter to set up clustering features, because this restricts server sessions in addition to client sessions.

5.2.1.2 Database unavailable

A database is considered unavailable when any of the following conditions are present:

- The database is marked out of service

  When you mark a database out of service, users cannot open the database. Domino maintains all existing connections to the database, however, and allows replication updates from other replicas to continue. If a user closes an out of service database and then tries to re-open it, the request is sent to another replica on an available server. This means that the database is gradually brought to an out of service state without disruption to users who are actively using it.

- The database is marked pending delete

  In order to minimize disruption to users, you can set a database to be deleted only after all active users have finished using the database. When you mark a database for deletion, no new database open requests are accepted. After all users have terminated their connections to the database, changes are pushed to another replica and the database is deleted.

You can set up these conditions using the database cluster management tools, and check the database attributes in each database document within the CLDBDIR.NSF database. Use this setting when you need to move or delete a database from a server, or perform other maintenance operations.

If failover does not occur, the user trying to access a databases marked as pending delete or out of service will receive the following message:

Figure 35. Database restricted message

For more details about making a database out of service or pending delete, see 5.5.2, "Database cluster management tool" on page 143.

5.2.2 Setting up mail routing failover

If users have replicas of mail files located on multiple servers, you have to set the `MailClusterFailover` variable in the NOTES.INI file of all Release 4.x servers in the domain to let users receive mail from servers within and outside the cluster when their home servers are down.

You can update this parameter from the server console by typing the server console command:

```
set config MailClusterFailover=n
```

where n = [0 | 1].

If set to 0, Mail Router request failover is disabled. If set to 1, Mail Router request failover is enabled.

We recommend that you use the Domino Configuration document in the Public Address Book (NAMES.NSF), as shown in Figure 36:

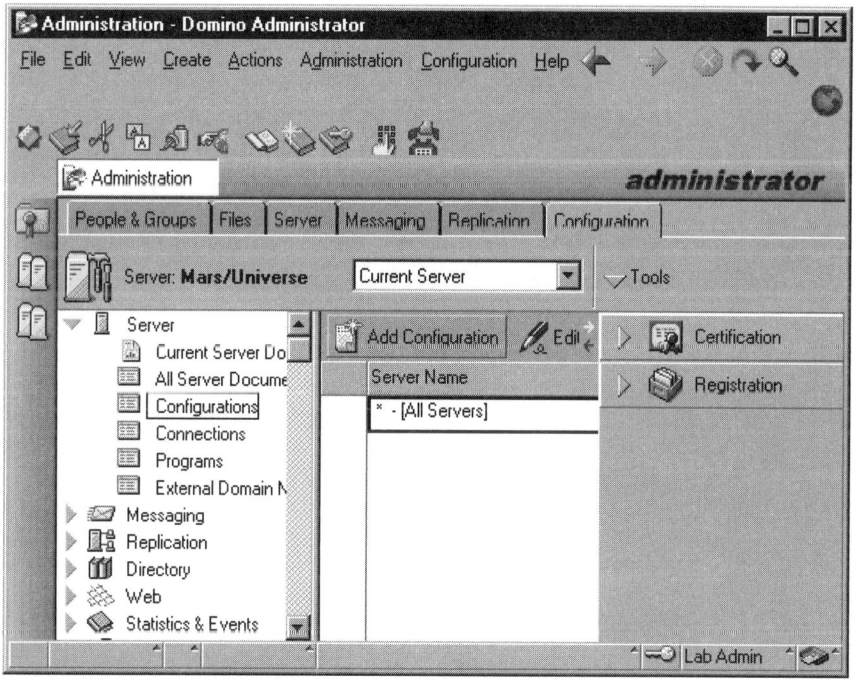

Figure 36. Server configurations view

To change the configuration settings for your servers, do the following:

1. Go to the Configuration tab in the Administrator client and select the **Configurations** view as shown in Figure 36.
2. Click **Add Configuration.**
3. Go to the Basics tab as shown in Figure 37, and check **Yes** in the **Use these settings as the default setting for all servers:** checkbox:

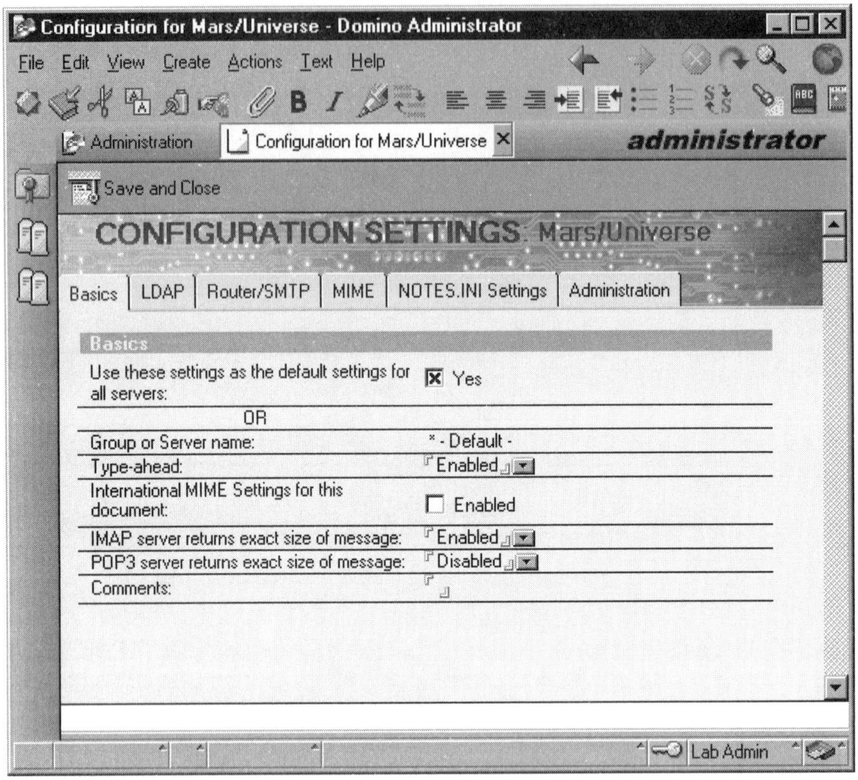

Figure 37. Basics tab of Configuration Settings document

4. Go to the NOTES.INI Settings tab and click **Set/Modify Parameters.**
5. Select a parameter from the list; in this case, select **MAILCLUSTERFAILOVER** as shown in Figure 38:

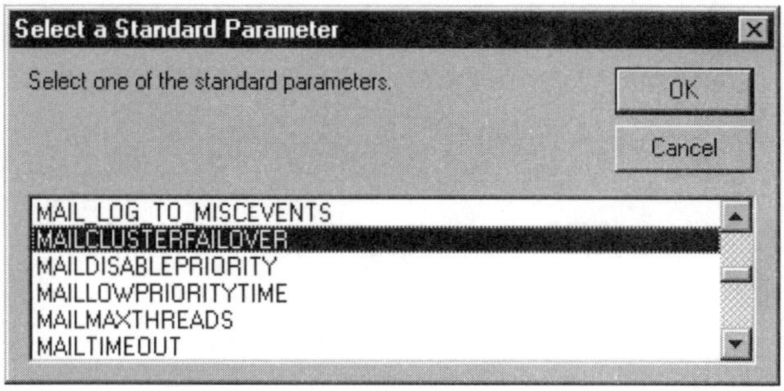

Figure 38. Modifying NOTES.INI parameters

You will then see the dialog box in Figure 39, which allows you to set the value for the selected parameter:

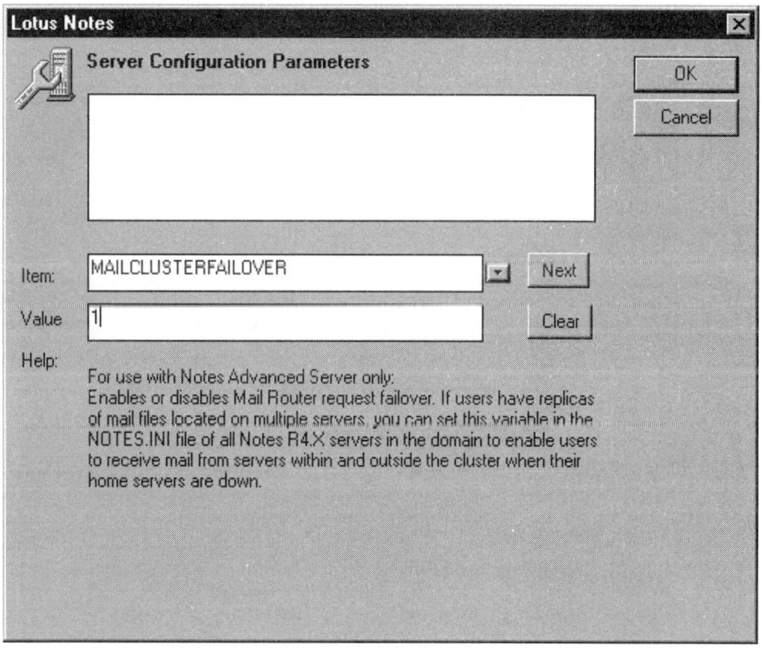

Figure 39. Server configuration parameters dialog box

6. Enter a value in the Value field. In this case, we are setting the value to 1 to enable mail cluster failover.
7. Click **Next.** The variable will then be transferred to the parameters box, indicating that you have successfully set the parameter, as shown in Figure 40:

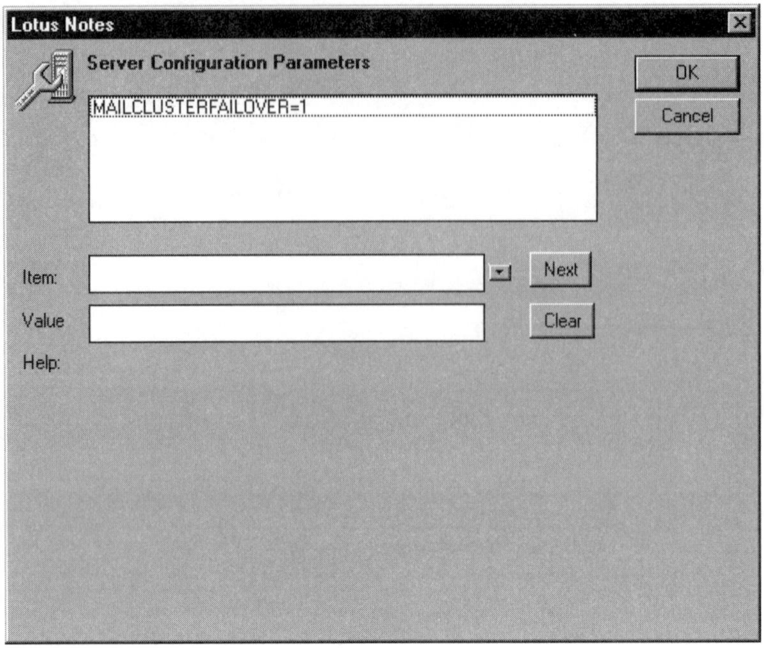

Figure 40. Setting configuration parameters

8. Click **OK** to complete the change and return to the Configuration Settings document.
9. Click **Save and Close** to save the Configuration Settings document. The NOTES.INI tab should appear as shown in Figure 41 when you have successfully completed these steps:

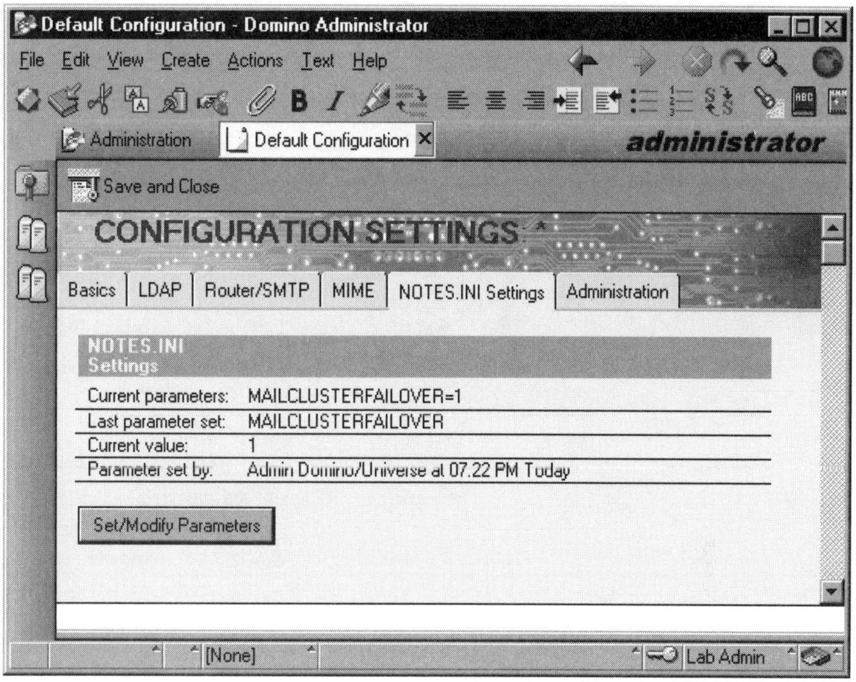

Figure 41. NOTES.INI settings

Now that you have set the servers to enable mail routing failover, users will receive mail even when their home server is unreachable if they are connected to a clustered server storing the mail database replicas (the secondary mail server).

5.2.2.1 Mail failover across a domain

By default, mail routing fails over for the last hop of the delivery route only, that is the hop to the recipient's mail server. You can, however, configure mail routing to fail over on any hop in the delivery route, or you can disable mail routing failover altogether.

To change the default mail routing failover setting, follow these steps to edit the Configuration document for every Domino R5 server in a domain that can route mail:

1. From the Domino Administrator, click the **Configuration** tab and expand the **Messaging** section.
2. Select **Configurations**.

3. Select the Configuration document for the server or servers you want, and click **Edit Configuration**.
4. If you do not have Configuration documents for this server or group of servers, you can create one by clicking **Add Configuration**.
5. Select the **Router/SMTP -> Advanced -> Controls** tabs as shown in Figure 42.

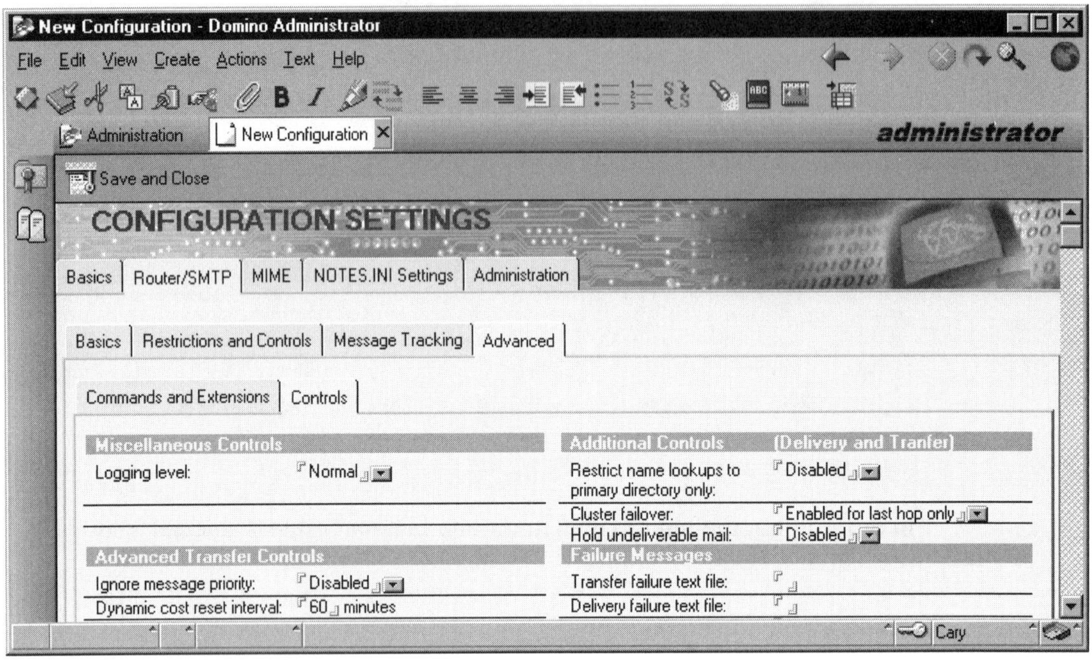

Figure 42. Changing the mail routing failover setting

6. In the Cluster failover field, choose one of the following:
   - Disabled
   - Enabled for last hop only (the default)
   - Enabled for all transfers in this domain
7. Save and close the Configuration document.

If you have Domino R4.x servers in your domain, you should enable mail cluster failover on them as well. You can enable mail cluster failover on any Domino R4.x server by setting the `MailClusterFailover` parameter in the server's NOTES.INI file:

```
MailClusterFailover=1
```

If you upgrade an existing Domino R4 server to Domino R5, and the server has a `MailClusterFailover` setting in NOTES.INI, it will warn you that `MailClusterFailover` is controlled by Configuration document the first time you start Domino R5 server. You can therefore delete this setting from NOTES.INI prior to upgrading the server.

> **Secondary mail server**
>
> To ensure users have access to all mail functions while failed over, we suggest you set up clients' workstations with a "backup" location for the secondary mail server. When a client fails over to the secondary mail server, the client needs to switch to a location with parameters that relate to the secondary mail server in order to provide the client with mail functions such as replying to a note, enabling scheduled replication for a local mail replica, and so on.

5.2.3 Setting up shared mail in a cluster

The shared mail feature (or single copy object store) is supported on clustered servers. In 3.3.2, “Shared mail” on page 55 you can find general information about shared mail and how it works in a clustered environment. In this section we explain how to set up shared mail between two clustered servers.

In order to get the shared mail feature to fully integrate with cluster replication, you have to enable shared mail for mail database replicas by executing the following server console command on each server that is hosting mail database replicas:

```
LOAD OBJECT SET -ALWAYS USERNAME.NSF SHARED.NSF
```

where `USERNAME.NSF` is the name of a mail database replica or a directory of mail databases replicas and `SHARED.NSF` is the name of the shared mail file linked to the mail databases replicas.

Note: You do not have to replicate the shared mail database; each shared mail database has a different replica ID.

Once you have executed the above command, regardless of which server the router task delivers a message to, the cluster replicator task distributes it to all other replicas using the shared mail database on each server.

5.2.3.1 Example: two clustered servers and shared mail

Figure 43 shows an example of one way to set up shared mail in a simple cluster configuration:

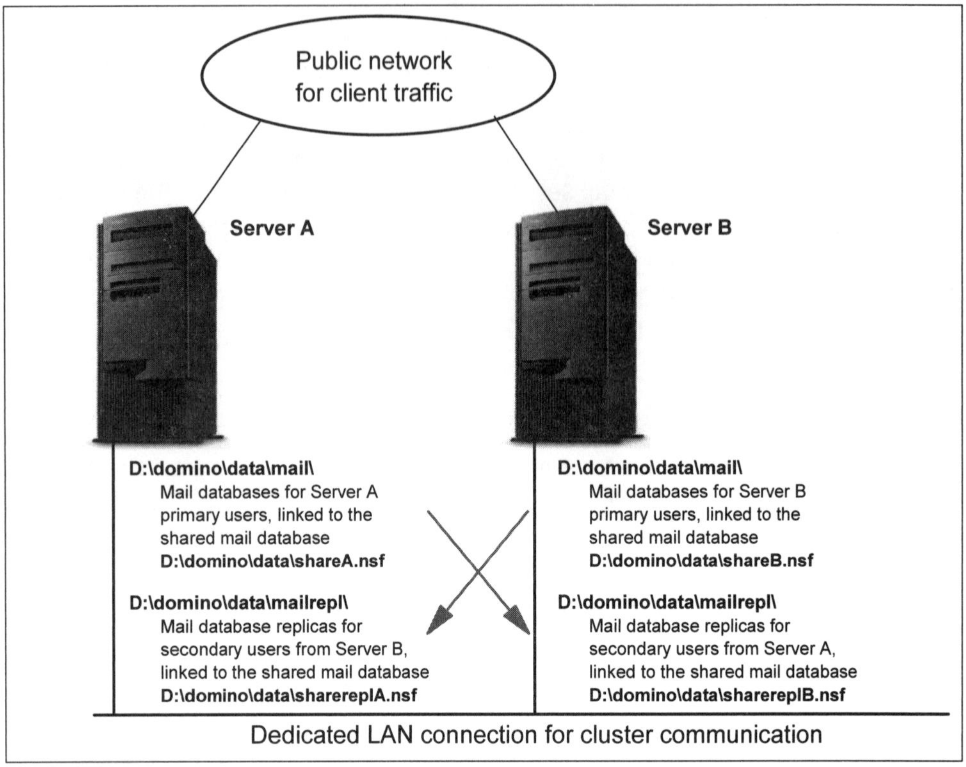

Figure 43. Clustering with shared mail databases

The figure shows two clustered servers (Server A and Server B) and the way their mail databases and replicas are distributed. Each server is a primary mail server for 100 users and a secondary mail server for 100 other users. The mail databases are located in subdirectories of the Domino data directory. Those for each server's primary users are stored in the mail\ subdirectory, while the database replicas are stored in the mailrepl\ subdirectory on each secondary server.

The following method can be used to set up this configuration. To avoid confusion, we have indicated which server is being worked on for each step:

1. ***Both servers:*** Before setting up shared mail you should make sure that the mail router task is running on both servers.
2. ***Server A:*** Register Server A's users and create their mail databases.

3. ***Server A:*** Create Server A's shared mail database and enable it using the following command:

   ```
   TELL ROUTER USE ShareA.nsf
   ```

   SHAREA.NSF is created automatically and the NOTES.INI parameter `Shared_Mail` is set equal to 2.

4. ***Server B:*** Next, register Server B's users and create their mail databases.

5. ***Server B:*** Create Server B's shared mail database and enable it using the following command:

   ```
   TELL ROUTER USE shareb.nsf
   ```

   SHAREB.NSF is created automatically and the NOTES.INI parameter `Shared_Mail` is set equal to 2.

6. ***Server A:*** Create an additional shared mail database by executing the command:

   ```
   LOAD OBJECT CREATE sharerepla.nsf
   ```

7. ***Server A:*** Create replicas of the Server B users' mail databases in the subdirectory mailrepl\ on Server A (from the subdirectory mail\ on Server B).

8. ***Server A:*** Link all databases stored in mailrepl\ to the shared mail database for the replicas from Server B by issuing the following command:

   ```
   LOAD OBJECT LINK mailrepl sharerepla.nsf
   ```

9. ***Server A:*** Enable shared mail for these mail database replicas so that the content of messages is placed in the SHAREREPLA.NSF database as messages are replicated from the original mail file, using the server command:

   ```
   LOAD OBJECT SET -ALWAYS mailrepl sharerepla.nsf
   ```

10. ***Server B:*** Create an additional shared mail database by executing the command:

    ```
    LOAD OBJECT CREATE shareren1b.nsf
    ```

11. ***Server B:*** Create replicas of the Server A users' mail databases in the subdirectory mailrepl\ on Server B (from the subdirectory mail\ on Server A).

12. ***Server B:*** Link all databases stored in mailrepl\ to the shared mail database for the replicas from Server A by issuing the following command:

    ```
    LOAD OBJECT LINK mailrepl sharerepla.nsf
    ```

13. ***Server B:*** Enable shared mail for these mail database replicas so that the content of messages is placed in the SHAREREPLB.NSF database as

messages are replicated from the original mail file, using the server command:

```
LOAD OBJECT SET -ALWAYS mailrepl sharereplb.nsf
```

For more information about setting up Shared Mail, refer to *Domino Administration Help - Shared Mail* in the product help files, shipped with Domino.

5.2.4 Logging and monitoring failover

When failover occurs on a server, Domino generates a failover event in the log file. An example is shown below:

```
09/11/00 12:29:06 PM Failing over from Mars/Universe!!test.nsf for replica id
862565BB:0061BF4A, directing open to Saturn/Universe
```

You can check if any failover events have occurred by looking at the statistics parameters on each server, which can be checked by using the `SHOW STAT` command at the server console for each server. The information that will be returned is:

- The number of times that the server was or was not able to redirect a client to another cluster member (by replica ID or by path)
- The number of times that a client attempted to open a database that has been marked as out of service on this cluster member
- The number of times that a client has attempted to open a database on this server when the server was MaxUsers or Restricted

For more details, see 5.5, “Cluster administration tools” on page 137 and Appendix B, “Tuning Domino clusters” on page 217.

Note: These statistics parameters are cumulative since the server was started or since they were reset to zero using the `Set Statistics` command.

5.3 Setting up workload balancing

Workload balancing is used to redirect new user sessions to another server in the cluster in order to distribute workload to the available servers in a way that maximizes the utilization of cluster resources. This feature lets you distribute user workloads across multiple clustered servers by utilizing replicas of heavily used databases. Workload balancing is invoked when a server is available but it has been determined that it is too busy to take on any more user or server sessions.

When running as part of a cluster, a Domino server constantly monitors its own workload. The Cluster Manager Process computes the server's availability index statistic automatically each minute.

All servers in a cluster are kept informed about the availability of all other servers in the cluster. Using this facility enables a Domino server to monitor the workload of the other servers in the cluster. The server state (Busy or Available) is determined by the server availability threshold value, which by default is zero, and so has to be set by the administrator, and is representative of the response time experienced by users accessing the server.

This section describes how to implement workload balancing in a cluster. We discuss the parameters that are involved and how to set them.

5.3.1 Triggering workload balancing

As the cluster administrator, you should closely monitor your system for usage patterns during peak periods and adjust cluster resources accordingly. You can provide failover and workload balancing for databases by creating replicas on two or more servers.

Depending on server performance, you have to set the maximum level of workload that your server can handle. There are two different ways to provide load balancing:

- Setting the server availability threshold as described in the following section.
- Setting the maximum number of users, which we discussed in 5.2.1, "Triggering failover" on page 120.

5.3.1.1 Definition of server Busy

By setting the server availability threshold you decide when your server becomes Busy. When the server enters the Busy state, it load balances new users' requests to another server in the cluster.

A server is in the Busy state if the server availability index drops below the server availability threshold. The server availability index is a server.cluster statistic, while the server availability threshold is a NOTES.INI parameter.

- Server availability index

  Each server in a cluster periodically determines its own workload, based on the average response time of client requests recently processed by the server. The workload on the server is expressed as the server availability index, which is a value between 0 and 100, where 100 indicates a lightly loaded server (fast response times), and 0 indicates that the server is heavily loaded (slow response times).

The server availability index is closely related to a common performance metric called the *expansion factor*. The expansion factor is simply the ratio of the response time for a function under the current load to the response time for this same function in an optimum (light load) condition.

To compute the server availability index, the Domino server computes the expansion factor for a representative set of Notes remote procedure call (RPC) transactions over a recent time interval (approximately the previous minute). The server availability index is then set to 100 minus this expansion factor.

Remember that the server availability index only considers the response time as measured at the server, which is typically only a small portion of the overall response time as seen by clients. In particular, the network time between the client and server often accounts for a significant portion of client response time. So a server availability index of 90 does not indicate that the response time as seen by clients is 10 times the optimal value, only that the server processing of this request took 10 times longer than the optimal value.

- Server availability threshold

  To set up workload balancing and distribute workload, use the `Server_Availability_Threshold` NOTES.INI entry. You can update this parameter from the server console by typing the server console command:

  ```
  set config Server_Availability_Threshold=n
  ```

  where n is in the range of 0 to 100.

  It is up to you, the Domino Administrator, to decide the appropriate value to set for this threshold, that is, when a server should load balance users to another server in the cluster. You can monitor the server availability index during periods of normal to heavy load to help in determining what the threshold should be set to. The parameter can be found using the `SHOW CLUSTER` console command (see 5.5.1, “Domino server console” on page 138), in the STATREP.NSF database or by viewing the server statistics with the Domino Administrator client (see Appendix B, “Tuning Domino clusters” on page 217 for more information). Another good reason to check the server availability index is if your user community reports unfavorable response times.

Server availability threshold

You can set a different `Server_Availability_Threshold` value on each server in the cluster.

There is no rule to determine the right `Server_Availability_Threshold` value. You could start by using a value such as 80, then monitor your server, and increase or decrease the `Server_Availability_Threshold` value as you begin to understand the overall performance levels. For example, if the server availability index is at 80 when the users report unfavorable response times, the administrator can set the server availability threshold to 85. Alternatively, you can set it equal to 70 if you realize that with `Server_Availability_Index=80` the server is performing well.

If you want to check the server state in the cluster, see the related statistics parameter in the STATREP.NSF database:

```
Server.Cluster.Member.<ServerName>.Index
```

For more information on statistics parameters see Appendix B, “Tuning Domino clusters” on page 217.

5.3.1.2 Using Server_MaxUsers for workload balancing

Limiting or restricting the user connections that a server will support is another way to distribute the workload around the cluster. To do this you can use the following NOTES.INI parameter:

```
Server_MaxUsers
```

For more information on this setting, see 5.2.1.1, “Server unavailable” on page 120.

Busy compared with MaxUsers and Restricted

Neither the MaxUsers state or the Restricted state allows a user to access the server under any circumstances, whereas a server in the Busy state does allow users to access the server if the users cannot successfully be routed elsewhere.

5.3.2 Logging and monitoring workload balancing

As with failover, each time a redirection occurs on a server, Domino generates an event in the log file.

```
09/11/00 12:29:06 PM Failing over from Mars/Universe!!test.nsf for replica id
862565BB:0061BF4A, directing open to Saturn/Universe
```

You can check workload balancing events in the statistics parameters on each server by viewing the Cluster Report document in the STATREP.NSF or by typing the `SHOW STAT` command at the server console on each server. This will show you:

- The number of times that the server was in the Busy state or was not able to redirect a client to another cluster member (by replica ID or by path).
- The number of times that a client had attempted to open a database when the server was Busy.
- The number of times a client attempted to open a database when all the servers in the cluster were Busy.

Domino allows administrators to set up several ways to provide notification of monitored events. For example, one notification method is to send a note that includes information about events to a specific user such as the system administrator. Events can also be reported in the log and reported to another server.

See 5.5, “Cluster administration tools” on page 137 and Appendix B, “Tuning Domino clusters” on page 217 for more information.

5.4 Setting up failover and workload balancing working together

As a cluster administrator, you can optimize failover and workload balancing for different purposes. As explained before, you provide failover for databases by creating replicas on two or more servers. Then you should closely monitor your system for usage patterns during peak periods and adjust the cluster resources accordingly. You can balance server workloads by adjusting the availability thresholds step by step, but you can also use some workload balancing and failover features for particular administration operations. Some examples are:

- You can force a server to be 100% busy so that failover occurs from the secondary server back to the primary server once the primary system comes back up. By setting the secondary server to Busy and keeping it in that state, it will then only accept open requests when the primary is down.

  You can set the secondary server to a Busy state by typing the following command at the server console:

  ```
  set config Server_Availability_Threshold=100
  ```

or by using the Configuration document in the Name and Address Book. This operation takes a few seconds to run and can be performed without shutting the server down. The next time a user attempts to open the same database (a new session) he will be directed back to the original server because the destination server is now in the Busy state.

- If you plan to migrate a server from one machine to another, clustering features can help you make the migration less disruptive to your users. You should first create the new server as a clustered server, create the appropriate replicas, then use the workload balancing and failover settings to move the users from the original server to the new one.
- If you are planning to upgrade a production server, you can use the clustering and workload balancing settings to temporarily move users from one server to another server in the cluster. Once all of the users have been moved off the server to be upgraded, it can be taken out of service and then brought back online when the upgrade is complete.

5.5 Cluster administration tools

This section describes how to use the cluster administration tools to help you to optimize your cluster's operation and to manage its day-to-day functioning. Almost all of the operations in this section can be implemented using the Domino Administration Client from your workstation.

The Domino Administration Client is a new feature in Release 5. It allows administrators to manage their Domino servers with a graphical interface. Many of the tasks that required remote server console commands or switching back and forth between the administration panel and the Public Address Book can now be handled within the Administrator client with ease.

The Domino Administration client can be opened in several ways:

1. Select **File -> Tools -> Server Administration** from the Notes client
2. Click the **Domino Administrator** bookmark on the left side of your Notes client as shown in Figure 44:

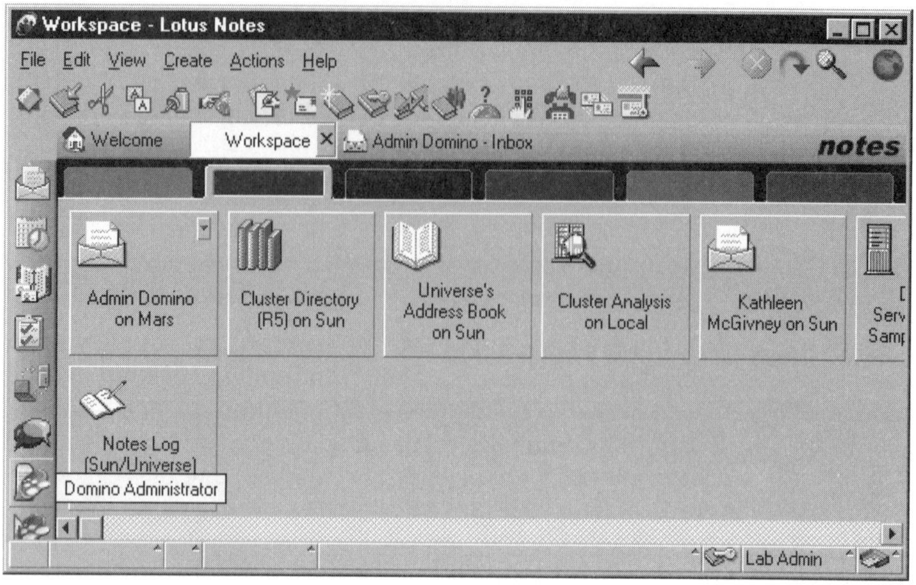

Figure 44. Launching the Domino Administrator from the Notes client

After you have launched the Domino Administrator client, select **Administration -> Server -> Status** to get to the server status display.

5.5.1 Domino server console

Viewing the Domino server console is an immediate means of determining the status of the cluster. It allows you to display all cluster-related processes that are currently running as well as their statuses. Cluster processes include the Cluster Manager, Cluster Replicator and the Cluster Database Directory manager tasks. From the remote console panel you can start and stop cluster processes while troubleshooting or tuning the cluster's performance.

To see a list of all the servers in your domain, click the server icon for your domain. In this example, we are administering the Universe domain. If you are administering only one domain, you will see only one icon. Select the server that you wish to access from the left pane of the Administrator client as shown in Figure 45:

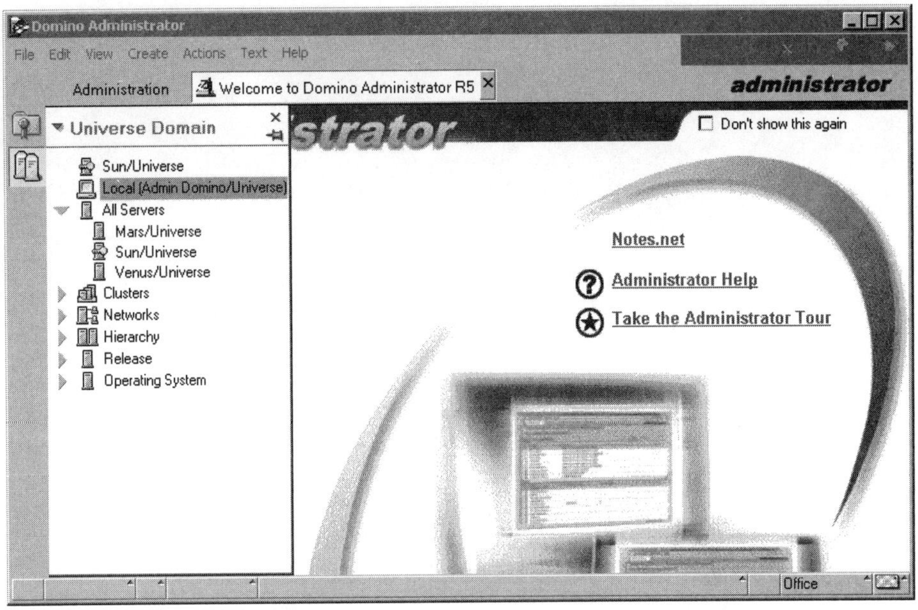

Figure 45. Select a server to administer.

The server icon that is overlaid with a key is the administration server for the domain. Once you have chosen a server to administer, you will see the following window:

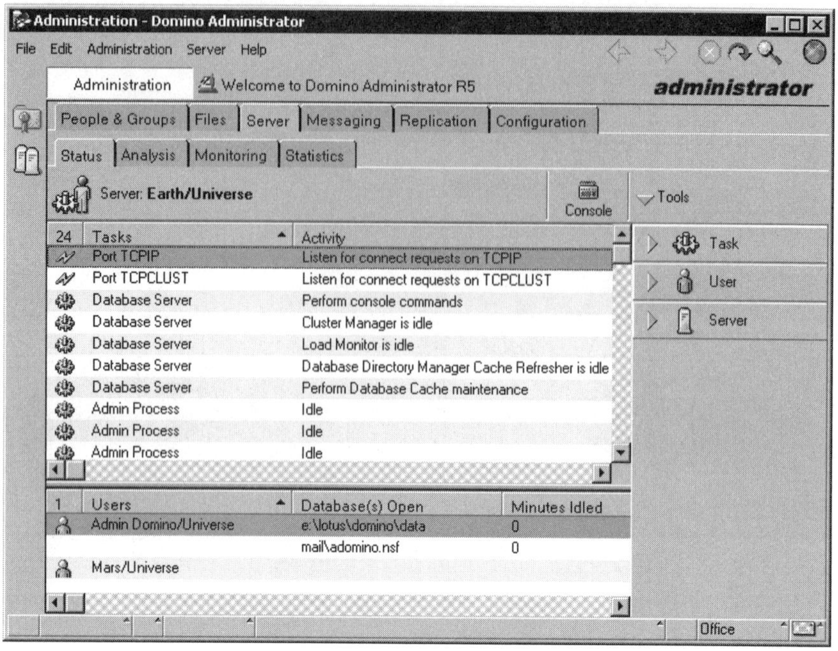

Figure 46. Server status display

Click **Console** (in Figure 46) to view the remote server console. Then click **Live** to open a live remote server console session.

We now describe some of the cluster-related console commands:

- `Show Cluster`

  This command lists all the cluster members and provides information as shown in Figure 47:

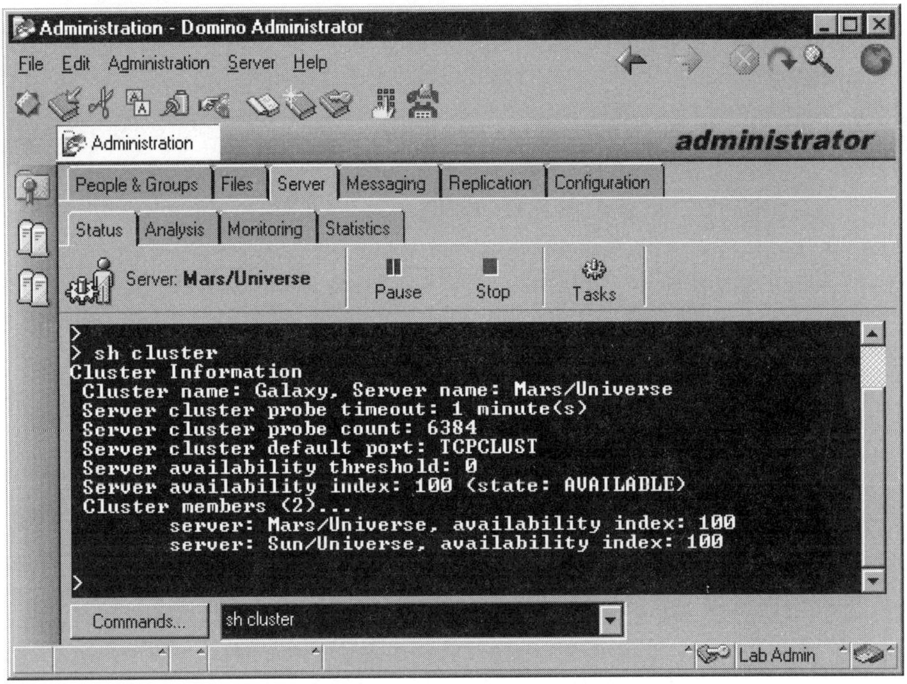

Figure 47. Show Cluster command

The Show Cluster command allows you to view most of the NOTES.INI settings for your cluster:

- Cluster name.
- Probe timeout.
- Cluster port name.
- Cluster availability index and threshold.
- Number of cluster members.
- The availability index of all the servers in the cluster (if the servers are in an Available state) or the availability information when a server is unreachable from the server on which you are working.

For more details about these parameters, please refer to Appendix C, "NOTES.INI variables" on page 229.

- `Load Cladmin`

This command loads the Cluster Administration task, which oversees the correct operation of all components in a cluster. The Cluster Administration task starts automatically unless you remove it from the NOTES.INI startup list, but you may need to manually restart it if you shut it down. This may be necessary while troubleshooting, for example.

- `Load Cldbdir`

  This command starts the Cluster Database Directory Manager add-in task, which keeps the Cluster Database Directory (CLDBDIR.NSF) up to date with the most current database information. It also manages databases with cluster-specific attributes, such as databases marked out of service or pending delete.

  This task is used by the Cluster Administration and the Cluster Replicator task processes to determine which servers in the cluster have replicas of each database. Please refer to Chapter 3, "Designing a Domino cluster" on page 39, for more information about cluster components.

- `Load Clrepl`

  This command starts one Cluster Replicator task. You can use this command to start additional Cluster Replicator tasks in the active session. If you want to add a Cluster Replicator task that will be automatically started, use the NOTES.INI `ServerTasks` parameter as discussed in 4.3.5.4, "Configuring replication in a cluster" on page 101 and also in 5.6, "Configuring replication within the cluster" on page 149.

  You should make sure that the CLREPL tasks are started after the CLDBDIR task, because the Cluster Replicator relies on information provided by the Cluster Directory Manager.

- `Tell Clrepl Quit`

  This command instructs *all* instances of the Cluster Replicator to terminate. Use this command if you want to disable cluster replication.

- `Tell Clrepl Log`

  This command instructs the Cluster Replicator to generate a log record immediately for activity performed since the last log, rather than wait for the next log interval. Normally, the Cluster Replicator generates log records only once each hour.

  This command can be useful for troubleshooting suspected cluster replication errors. After executing this command you can view the current set of errors in the Replication Event log records.

  You can also control these tasks using the Domino Administrator client. Using the Stop or Start options in the Domino Administration Client for server tasks is the equivalent of typing the commands directly into the server console. An example is shown in Figure 48:

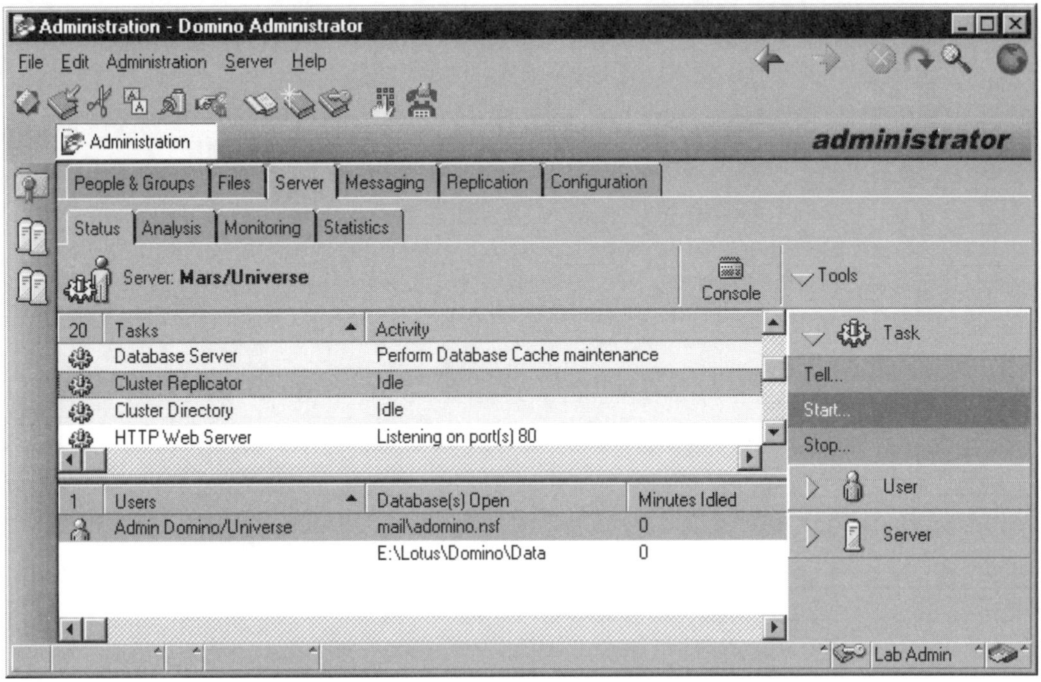

Figure 48. Starting an additional Cluster Replicator task

5.5.2 Database cluster management tool

The database cluster management tool allows you to manage the attributes of databases in your cluster. You can change a database's availability status, change its cluster replication status, and move databases within the cluster.

From the Domino Administrator client, select **Administration -> Files** or select the **Files** tab as shown in Figure 49:

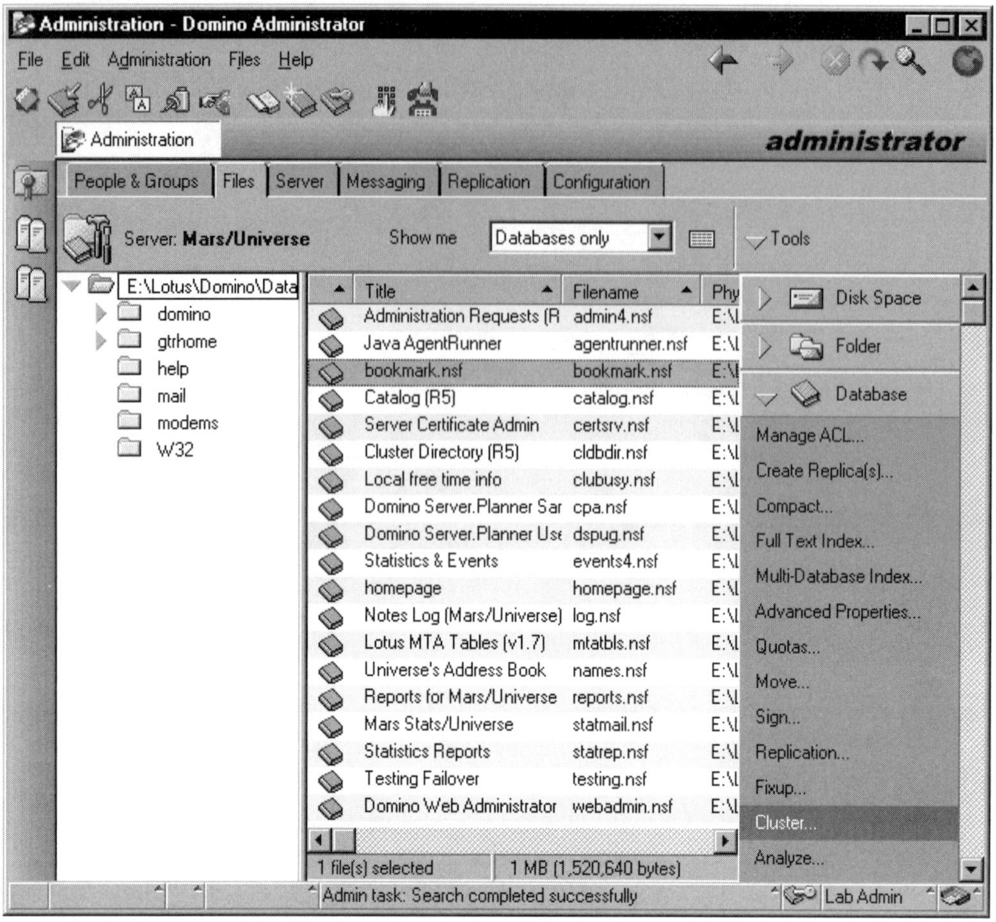

Figure 49. Files tab in the Domino Administrator client

To manage the cluster attributes of a database:

1. Select the database(s) you want to manage from the list of files.
2. Click the **Database** drop-down on the right side of the Administrator client.
3. Click **Cluster**.
4. Select the attributes you wish to assign to the database and click **OK**. Figure 50 shows the available attributes:

Figure 50. Manage Clusters dialog box

The different attributes you can select are:

- Out of service

  When you mark a database out of service, users cannot open the database. If there is a replica of the database on another server in the cluster, users attempting to access the database will be automatically redirected to an available replica. If there is no other replica available in the cluster, users attempting to access the database will receive the following message: `Access to the database has been restricted by the administrator`. Domino will maintain all existing connections to the database, however, and will also allow replication updates from other replicas.

- In service

  This option will make a database that was previously marked out of service fully available to users again.

- Pending delete

  In order to minimize disruption to users, you can set a database to be deleted only after all active users have finished using the database. Databases that have been marked for deletion will not accept new database open requests. However, the database will not be deleted until all users connections to it have been terminated. Any changes will be pushed to replicas before the database is deleted.

5.5.3 Create database replica tool

The create database replica tool allows you easily to create one or more replicas of databases in your cluster. Using the Domino Administrator client, you can make replicas of several databases at the same time.

From the Domino Administrator client, select **Administration -> Files** or select the **Files** tab as shown in Figure 51:

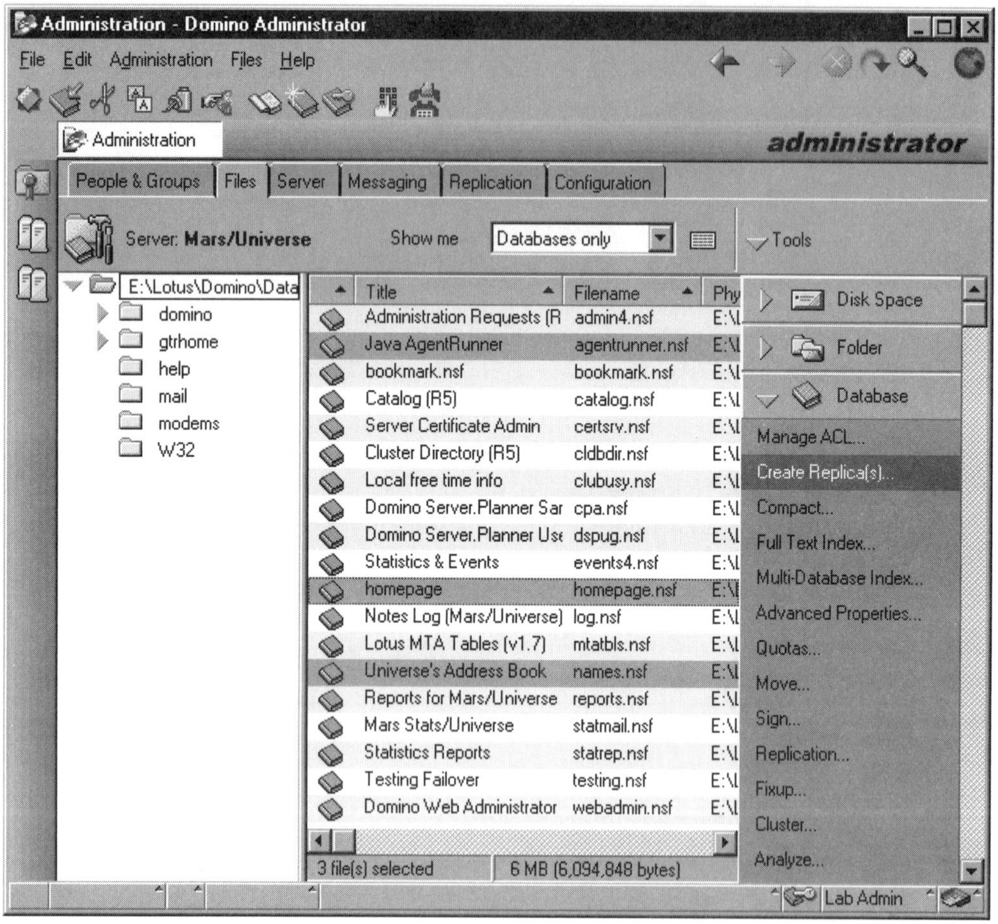

Figure 51. Create database replica tool

To create replicas of databases:

1. From the Files tab in the Administrator client, find and select the databases that you wish to create replicas of. To select multiple databases, press the **Ctrl** key while clicking each database.
2. Click **Create Replica(s)**.
3. Select one or more servers on which you wish to create the replicas, as shown in Figure 52:

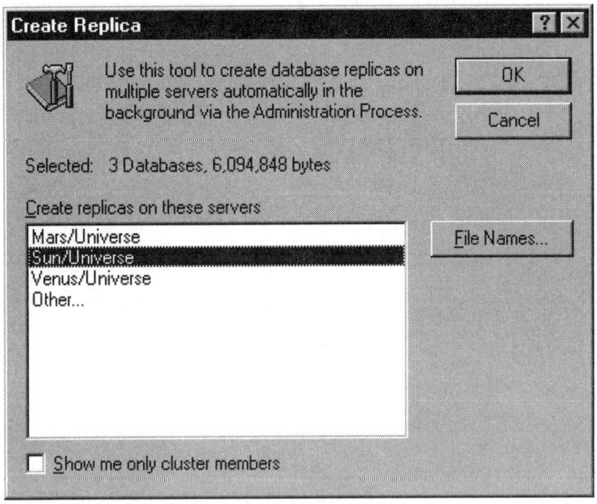

Figure 52. Create Replica dialog box

4. Click **OK** to create the replicas. The Administration Process will complete the creation and initialization of the new replicas.

5.5.4 Move database replica tool

The move database replica tool allows you easily to move databases to different servers within the cluster. You can move multiple databases at once using the Domino Administrator client.

From the Domino Administrator client, select **Administration -> Files** or select the **Files** tab as shown in Figure 53:

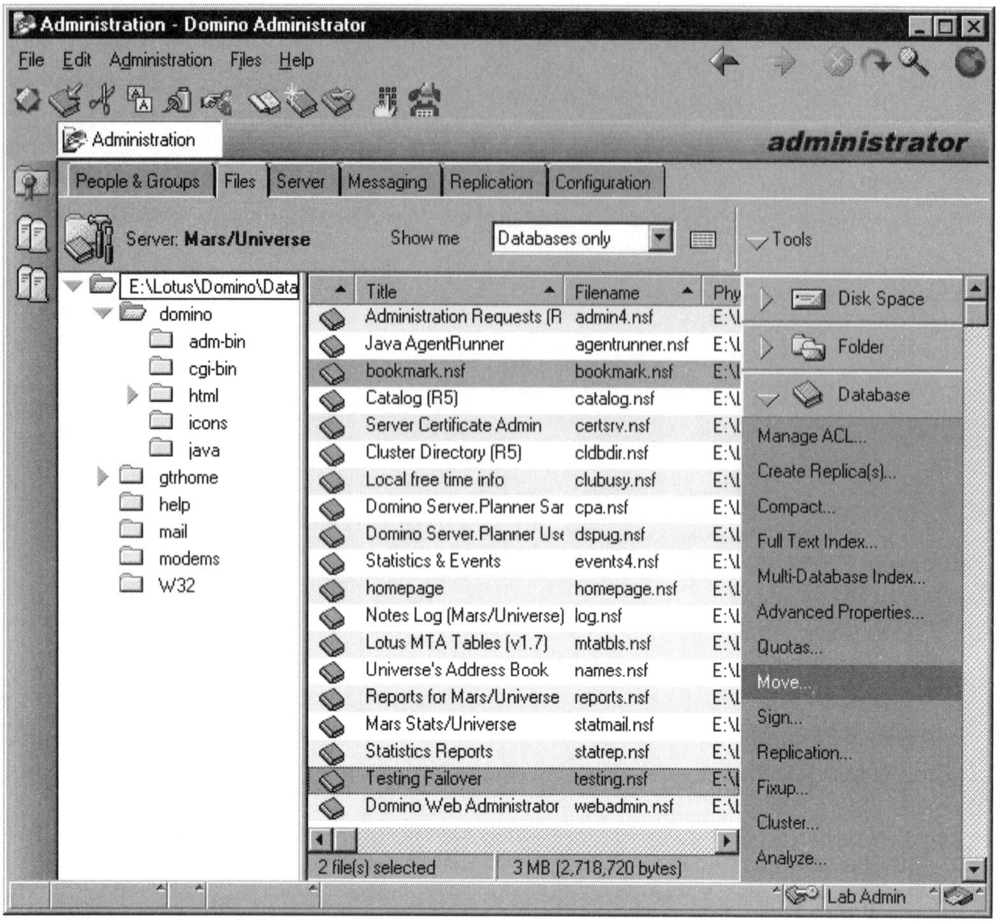

Figure 53. Move database replica tool

To move databases within your cluster:

1. From the Files tab in the Administrator client, select the database(s) you wish to move. To select multiple databases, press the **Ctrl** key while clicking each database.
2. Click **Move...**
3. Select the server(s) to which you would like to move the database(s), as shown in Figure 54:

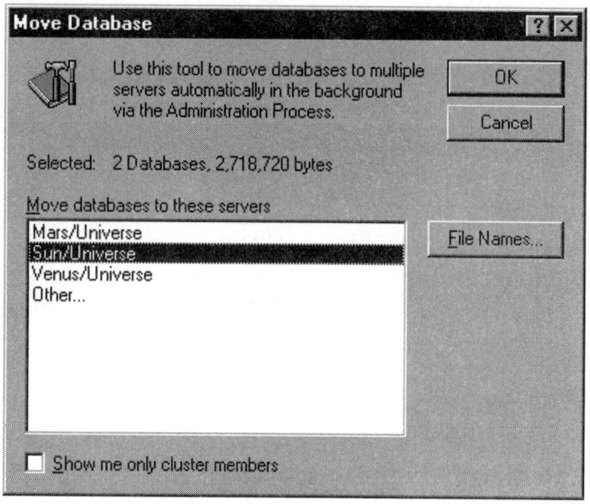

Figure 54. Move database dialog box

4. Click **OK**. The Administration Process will complete the database move.

5.6 Configuring replication within the cluster

In contrast to the predictable nature of scheduled replication, cluster replication is event driven. Traditional scheduled replication relies on administrator-defined connection records between Domino servers to initiate a periodic exchange of data. Both types of replication are necessary within a cluster, as explained in the following section.

5.6.1 Setting up cluster replicators

Database replicas within a cluster are primarily synchronized by the Cluster Replicator task (CLREPL). Changes made to any replica of a particular database in a cluster are detected by the Cluster Replicator and immediately pushed out to all other replicas of that database residing in the cluster. The Cluster Replicator obtains information about clustered databases from the Cluster Database Directory and maintains replication tables for the entire cluster in memory.

When clustering is installed on a server, a single Cluster Replicator task is configured by default. This configuration is adequate if only a few moderate databases will exist on a cluster consisting of two or three servers. However, if many small or, perhaps, a few large and very active databases are to be maintained in a cluster, then several instances of the Cluster Replicator should be executed on each Domino server in the cluster. This is particularly true as the number of servers in the cluster approaches the maximum of six.

Multiple Cluster Replicators executing on a single Domino server cooperate with each other to update database replicas in a cluster. That is, cluster replication workload is spread evenly across all configured Cluster Replicators on a server. In typical, high-volume clustered environments, we recommend that you configure as many cluster replicas on each server as there are total servers defined in the cluster, minus one. This means, for example, five Cluster Replicator tasks for a cluster composed of six servers. In this way, there will always be at least one CLREPL task available to handle replication requests to another server in the cluster.

When multiple Cluster Replicators are enabled on a server, they work in parallel to replicate changes to other servers. If one Cluster Replicator is busy replicating changes to one database, a second Cluster Replicator can begin replicating changes to another database. By sharing replication workloads, multiple Cluster Replicators ensure that data updates are made quickly and stay tightly synchronized. Cluster replication, like all other Domino server tasks, will take advantage of symmetric multiprocessing hardware where available.

To configure multiple Cluster Replicators, append additional CLREPL statements to the `ServerTasks` parameter in NOTES.INI, as shown below:

```
ServerTasks=Router,Updall,Adminp,CLDBDIR,CLREPL,CLREPL
```

Make sure all CLREPL tasks are listed after the CLDBDIR task. The Cluster Replicator relies on information provided by the Cluster Directory Manager.

5.6.2 Disabling cluster replication for specific databases

You can disable cluster replication for individual databases by editing the database document for that database in the Cluster Database Directory (CLDBDIR.NSF), or you can disable it using the Domino Administrator client. Each method is discussed below:

To disable cluster replication for a specific database using the Cluster Database Directory:

1. Open the Cluster Database Directory (CLDBDIR.NSF) on one of the servers in the cluster.
2. Select the database(s) for which you wish to disable cluster replication.
3. Select **Tools -> Disable Cluster Replication on Selected Databases**, as shown in Figure 55:

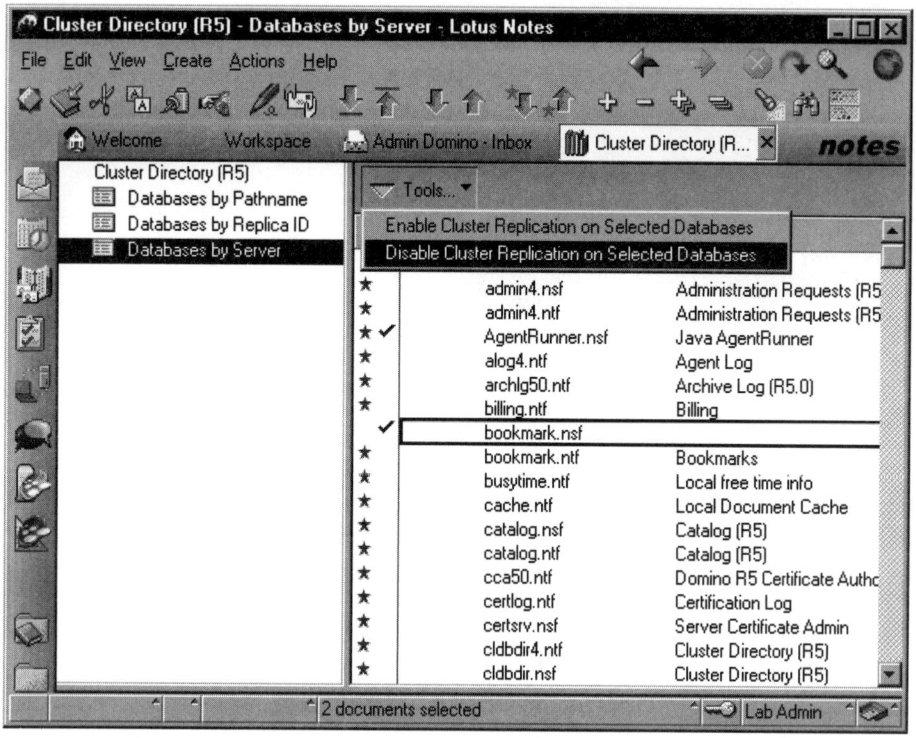

Figure 55. Disabling cluster replication for specific databases

To disable cluster replication for a specific database using the Administrator client:

1. From the Domino Administrator client, select **Administration -> Files** or select the **Files** tab.
2. Select the files for which you wish to disable cluster replication and click **Cluster**.
3. In the Manage Clusters dialog box, select **Disable cluster replication**, as shown in Figure 56:

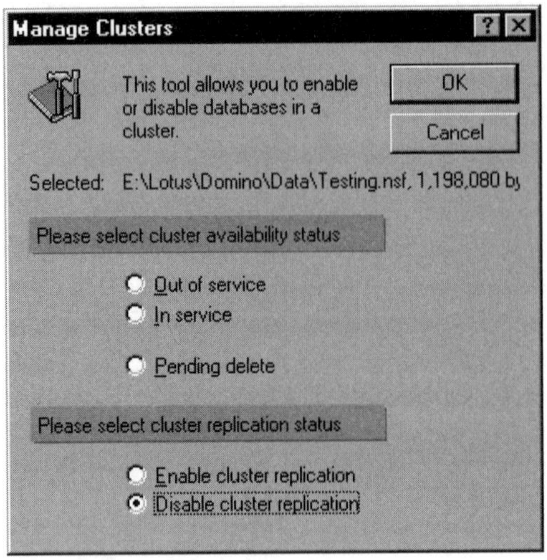

Figure 56. Disabling replication using the Administrator client

4. Click **OK** to complete the change.

5.6.3 Setting up scheduled replication

Since cluster replication is event-driven, and database updates are stored in memory, there is a small chance that some database updates may be lost in the event of a network or hardware failure. This problem can be helped by enabling transaction logging, which is described in 1.3.4, "Transaction logging" on page 6. However, Lotus recommends that you configure scheduled replication within clusters at least once a day as a backup to cluster replication.

An example of a scheduled replication document is shown in Figure 57:

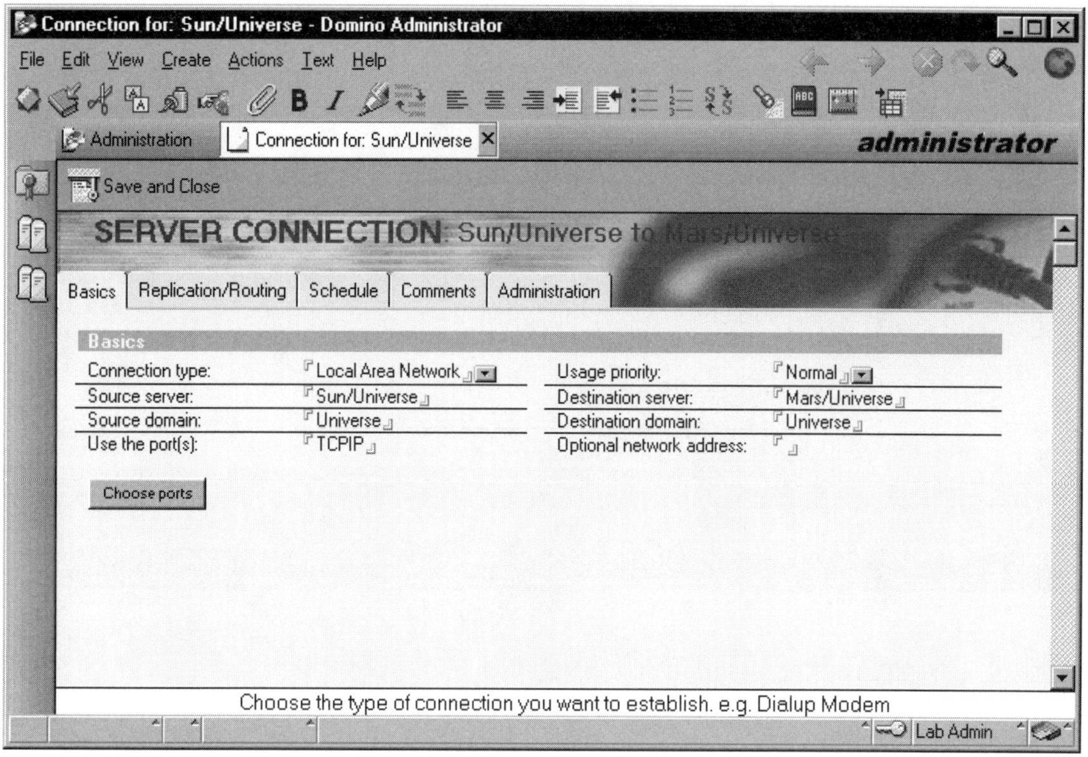

Figure 57. Basics tab of Server Connection document

The Schedule tab of the above connection document is where you establish a replication schedule and is shown in Figure 58:

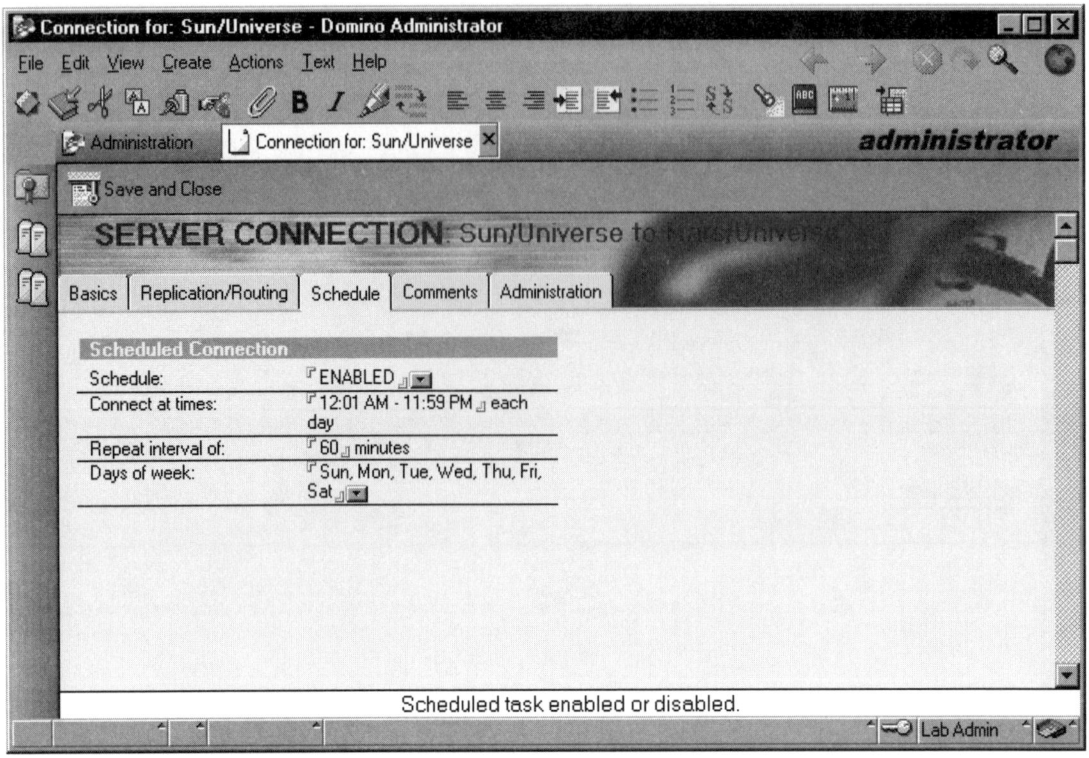

Figure 58. Schedule tab of Server Connection document

As you can see, the fields on the Schedule tab allow you to:

- Enable or disable scheduled replication for this connection.
- Set the range of times during which replication will take place.
- Set the interval between replications.
- Select which days of the week you wish to allow replication to take place.

Using these fields, you can set up an appropriate schedule for each connection you have in your Domino network.

5.6.4 Setting up scheduled replication at server startup

You can schedule replication to begin at server startup. This is achieved by adding `replica` to the ServerTasks entry in NOTES.INI, or you can set up a program document. An example of a configured program document is shown in Figure 59:

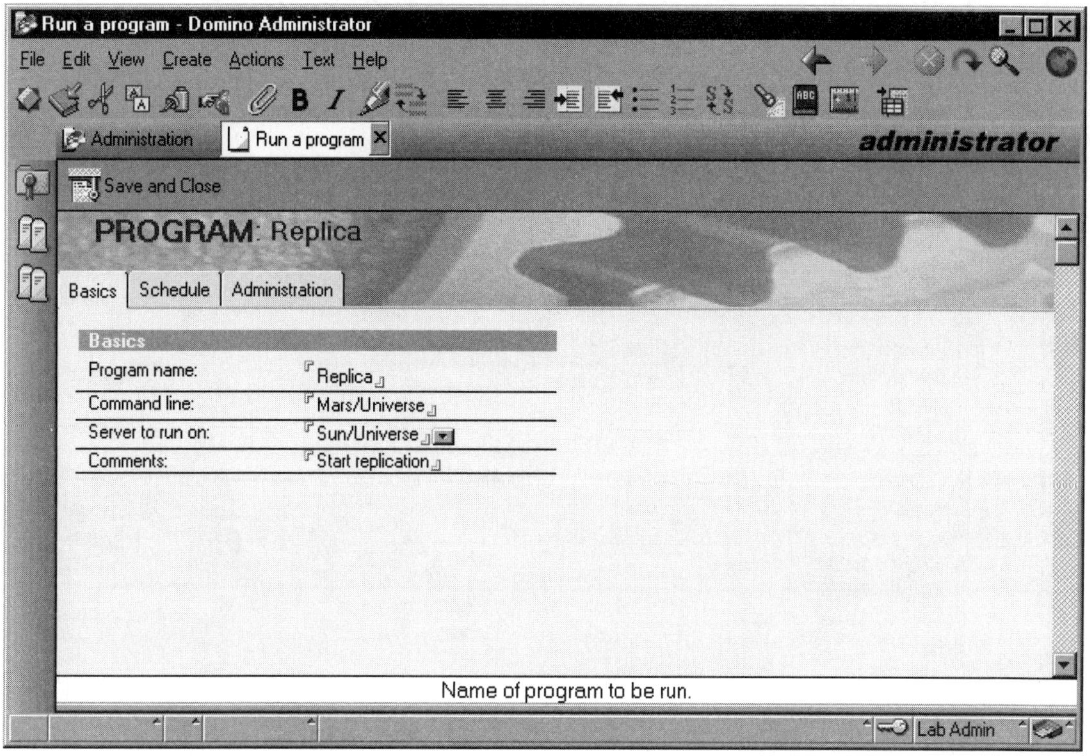

Figure 59. Sample Program document

To create a Program document from the Domino Administrator client, follow these steps:

1. Select **Server -> Programs** on the Configuration tab as shown in Figure 60:

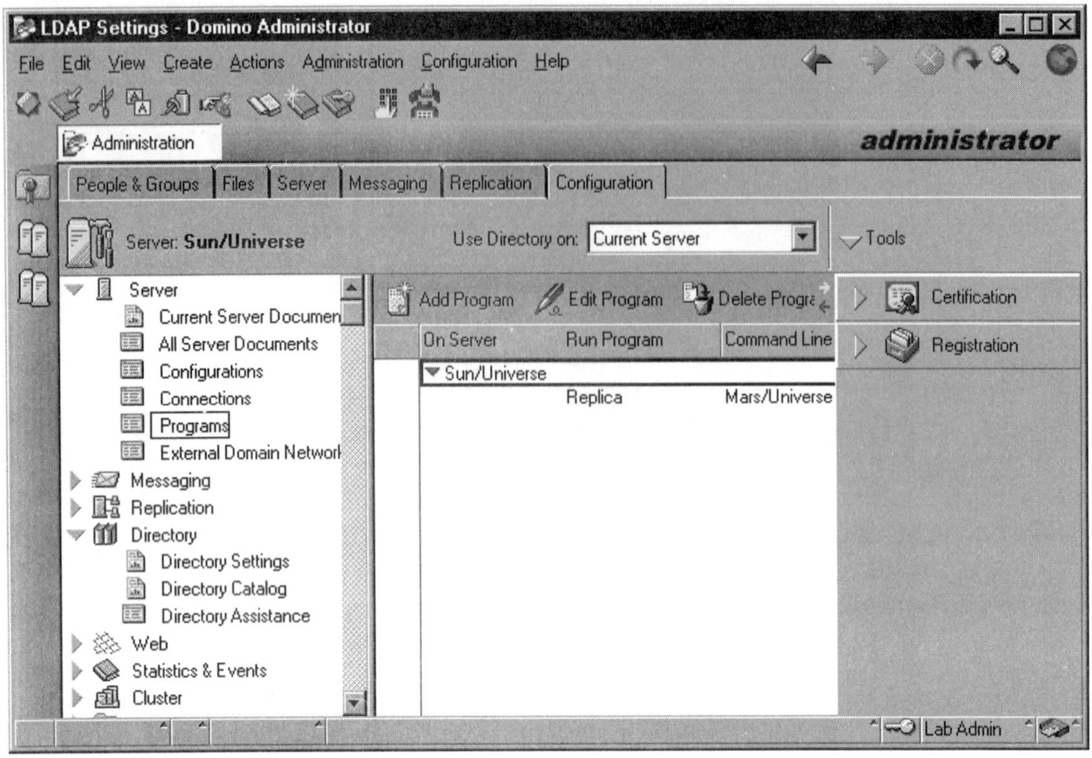

Figure 60. Programs view in configuration tab

2. Click **Add Program**.
3. On the Basics tab, enter the following:
   Program name: REPLICA
   Command line: Destination server
   Server to run on: The server that you want to initiate replication
4. On the Schedule tab, select **Startup Only.**
5. Select **Save and Close** to save your changes.

5.6.5 Logging replication

The Cluster Replicator generates Replication Event log records once an hour and writes information about all replications performed during that hour. Each Replication Event record provides information about database replications and any currently outstanding errors. The Cluster Replicator generates one Replication Event document for each server with which it replicates.

You can force the cluster replicator to generate a log record immediately, by typing the following command at the server console:

```
TELL CLREPL LOG
```

The log file records all replication events since the last replication record.

To enable the Domino server to log replication events and open session events at the server console, you must set the following NOTES.INI entries:

- `Log_Sessions=1`

  This entry specifies whether individual sessions are recorded in LOG.NSF and displayed on the server console. If set to 0, it is disabled; if set to 1, it is enabled.

- `Log_Replication=n`

  This entry specifies whether the start and end of the replication session are recorded in LOG.NSF and displayed on the server console. There are six different values for this parameter. You have to choose between:

  0: Do not log replication events
  1: Log server replication events
  2: Log replication activity at the database level
  3: Log replication activity at the level of database elements (view, document, and so on)
  4: Log replication activity at the field level
  5: Log summary information.

5.6.5.1 Logging Cluster Replicator activity

If you want to monitor Cluster Replicator activity, you can do so by setting the `RTR_Logging` entry in NOTES.INI. You can update this parameter from the server console by typing the server console command:

```
set config RTR_logging=n
```

where n = [0 I 1].

If set to 0, this parameter disables monitoring of the Cluster Replicator, and if set to 1, monitoring is enabled.

5.7 Cluster analysis tool

There is a cluster analysis tool that you can use to examine how your clustered databases are performing. This tool allows you to create detailed reports about specific aspects of a cluster. You should be aware that, on busy servers, cluster analysis can take several hours. If you do not have a dedicated server to perform the analysis, you should schedule detailed database analysis to be performed during off-peak hours unless you are troubleshooting existing problems.

To run the cluster analysis tool, follow these steps:

1. From the Domino Administrator client, select the **Server -> Analysis** tabs as shown in Figure 61:

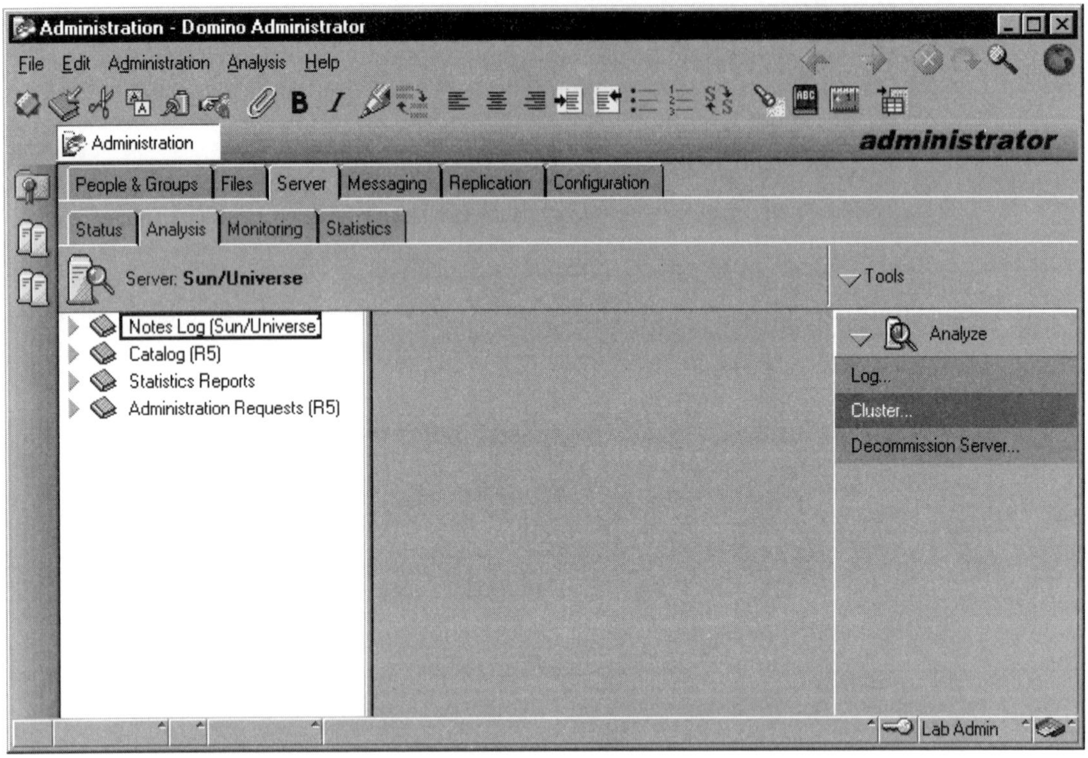

Figure 61. Server-Analysis tab in Domino Administrator

2. Select **Tools -> Analyze -> Cluster** in the Tools pane on the right side of the Administrator client. You will be presented with the dialog box shown in Figure 62:

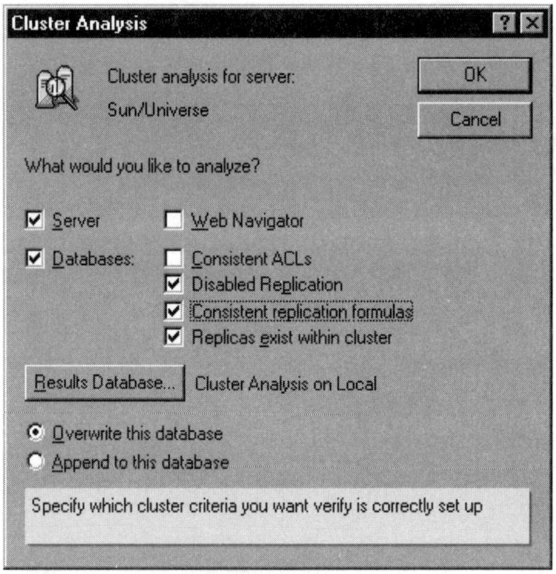

Figure 62. Cluster Analysis dialog box

3. The cluster analysis tool will set the cluster analysis database on the local machine as the default results database. If you want to change this, click **Results Database...** and specify the database you wish to use.
4. If a cluster analysis database already exists, and you want to append the new results to the existing database, click the **Append to this database** radio button. By default, the cluster analysis tool will overwrite the existing database.
5. Select the types of reports you would like to generate. You can select multiple types or just a single type by checking the appropriate boxes: **Server**, **Databases**, or **Web Navigator**.
6. If you selected **Databases** in Step 5, select the level of detail you want to include in the report. You can select multiple items or a single item: **Consistent ACLs**, **Disabled replication**, **Consistent replication formulas**, or **Replicas exist within cluster**. These are especially helpful when troubleshooting replication problems within the cluster.
7. Click **OK** to run the analysis and open the results database.

Once the cluster analysis is complete, you can view the results in the cluster analysis database (or the database you specified in Step 3, if you changed the default setting). The results can be seen in different views that are sorted according to the data that was collected. The views are:

- By Cluster
- By Date
- By Test

For example, if you are running an analysis on multiple clusters, and want to view results separately for each cluster, you would use the By Cluster view to obtain the information. If you are attempting to troubleshoot a problem that occurred on a specific date, the By Date view would be more useful. Finally, if you are troubleshooting a specific problem such as cluster replication, you would check the By Test view and look for anomalies in the tests that pertain to replication, such as Consistent ACLs or Replicas Exist within Cluster.

An example of the output, using the By Cluster view, is shown in Figure 63:

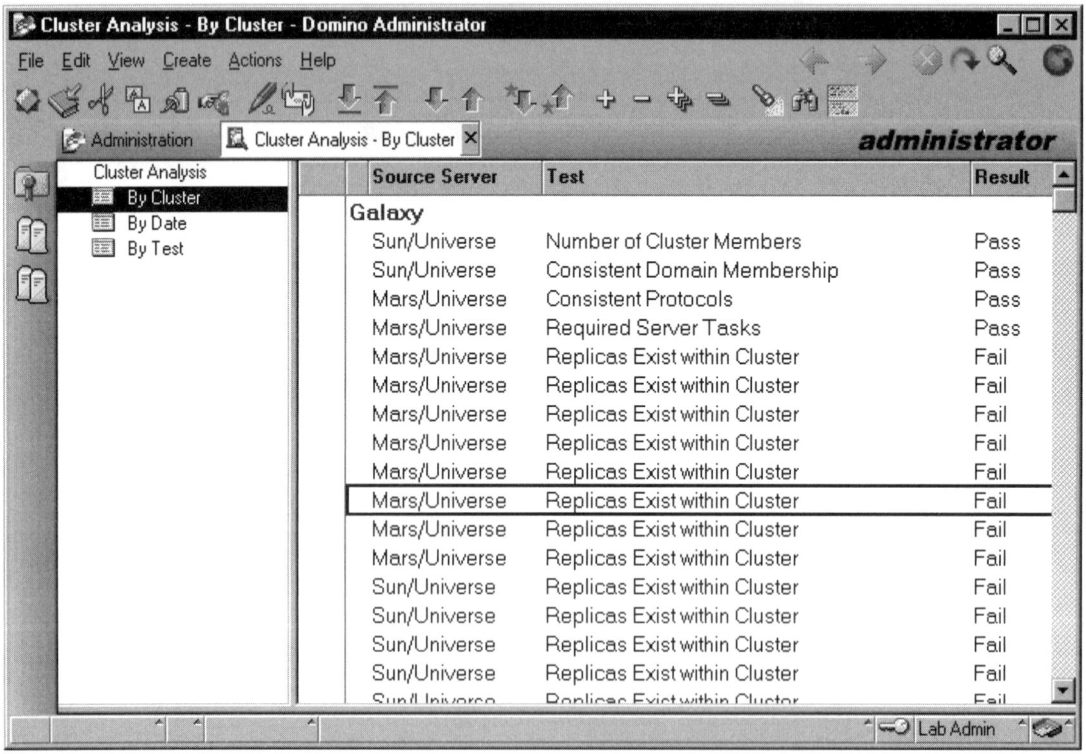

Figure 63. Cluster Analysis results

5.8 Administering Internet Cluster Manager

Internet Cluster Manager administration is essentially no different from administering cluster administration as we have already discussed. The only difference is the ICM specific statistics and events available for examination. In this section, we look at some of these. For more information on this topic, please review the Administration Help supplied with Domino.

5.8.1 Viewing ICM events

The ICM records significant events, such as not being able to find a database, in the Miscellaneous Events view in the log file. To view ICM events in the log file, do one of the following:

From the Domino Administrator:

1. Click the **Servers-Analysis** tab.
2. Expand **Notes Log**, and then click **Miscellaneous Events**.
3. In the Results pane, open the Log Entry document you want to view.

From the Domino server log file:

1. Open the Domino server log file.
2. Open the **Miscellaneous Events** view.
3. Open the document you want to look at.

5.8.2 Viewing ICM statistics

The ICM generates statistics that indicate how the cluster and the ICM are performing. To view these statistics, you can do one of the following:

From the Domino Administrator:

1. Click the **Server - Statistics** tab.
2. In the All Statistics list, click **ICM**.

From the server console:

Type `show stat icm`

You can use these statistics in conjunction with the standard cluster statistics to determine which servers in the cluster are the busiest so you can better balance the workload in the cluster.

Chapter 6. Domino and Windows 2000 clustering

Microsoft offers two clustering technologies that are provided as extensions to the base Windows 2000 operating systems. They are Microsoft Cluster Services (MSCS) and Network Load Balancing, which are included as standard with Microsoft Windows 2000 Advanced Server. In this chapter we discuss the key features of MSCS and how it complements the Lotus Domino clustering technology. We also explain how to install and configure Domino on a Windows 2000 cluster.

6.1 Introducing Microsoft Cluster Services

When referring to MSCS in this chapter, we specifically discuss clusters running on Windows 2000 Advanced Server. Microsoft's Windows 2000 Datacenter Server also provides clustering support, but that product is not generally available for purchase. It is, instead, normally bought as part of a package that includes services such as design, planning, installation, training, and so on, and is subject to much more rigorous control in order to ensure the highest levels of availability.

Microsoft Cluster Services (MSCS) is an operating system-based clustering technology for Intel CPU-based servers. It supports both uniprocessor and symmetrical multiprocessing (SMP) servers. This means that you will be able to take full advantage of Windows 2000 Advanced Server's support for up to eight processors and 8 GB of random access memory (RAM).

The servers that comprise an MSCS cluster are referred to as nodes. Windows 2000 Advanced Server supports two-node, active-active, failover clusters. A cluster's resources are distributed between the two nodes and made available to network users. Resources includes mundane items such as file shares and IP addresses, but may also include applications, such as Domino. If one of the nodes in a cluster fails, the resources it was supporting are transferred to the surviving node and made available to the network again.

MSCS is a collection of software components that execute on each node and perform cluster-specific tasks. These include managing the cluster's resources and the way that they are interrelated, in addition to performing the failover function when required.

There are various approaches to cluster implementations, each of which has its own characteristics. Windows clustering is based on a *shared nothing* clustering model. In this model, each node owns and manages its local

© Copyright IBM Corp. 1998, 2000

devices. External devices common to the cluster, such as disks in a common disk subsystem, are selectively owned and managed by a single server at any given time. Controlling ownership of common resources is an important function of the clustering software.

MSCS supports a variety of different media for the external common disk subsystem that is accessible by both servers in the cluster. These include the IBM SCSI, Serial Storage Architecture, and Fibre Channel subsystems. For the purposes of this book, we created a two-node server cluster in our lab, using a SCSI disk subsystem.

For more information about MSCS and other clustering technologies, see the redbook, *IBM @server xSeries Clustering Planning Guide*, SG24-5845.

6.2 Domino and MSCS clustering comparison

Domino offers an application-level clustering approach, while MSCS is an operating system-level clustering approach. Can you use both clustering models at the same time? When should you select the MSCS clustering model to gain high availability instead of Domino clustering? The answer to the first question is simple: Yes, Microsoft Cluster Services on Windows 2000 Advanced Server can be combined with Lotus Domino clustering. Answering the second question is not so easy, but the following section should give you a better understanding of the two clustering methods, and provide some guidelines to enable you to decide if operating system clustering is needed or not.

6.2.1 Functional differences from a server perspective

As Domino clustering and Microsoft clustering are implemented in very different ways and from different premises, straightforward comparison would not be fair to either of the products. So we will introduce the main features of both products, and then discuss scenarios where these two clustering methods can be used. Table 11 illustrates and compares the key characteristics of Domino clustering and Microsoft Cluster Services:

Table 11. Domino and MSCS feature comparison

Feature	Domino cluster server	Microsoft Cluster Services
Provides fault tolerance	Yes	Yes
Provides workload balancing	Yes	No[1]
Special hardware required	No	Yes
Requires separate software license	Included with Domino Enterprise Server	Included with Microsoft Windows 2000 Advanced Server
Maximum number of nodes in cluster	6[2]	2
Supported protocols	TCP/IP, SPX/IPX, NetBEUI/NetBIOS, AppleTalk, VINES [3]	TCP/IP
Supported platforms	Windows 2000 (Intel, Alpha), AS/400, S/390, AIX, HP-UP, Sun Solaris, Linux	Windows 2000 (Intel, Alpha)
Option to cluster servers running on different operating systems	Yes	No
Requires a dedicated link between the servers in the cluster	No	Yes
Supports WAN connections between the nodes in the cluster	Yes[4]	No
Requires identical server hardware in the cluster	No	No
Requires a common disk subsystem	No	Yes
Supports remote administration of the cluster	Yes	Yes
Provides failover for Notes clients	Yes	Yes

Feature	Domino cluster server	Microsoft Cluster Services
Provides workload balancing for Notes clients	Yes	No
Provides failover for Domino tasks	No[5]	Yes
Provides failover for Web clients	Yes	Yes
Supports immediate failback	No[6]	Yes
Nodes must belong to the same domain	Yes (same Notes domain)	Yes (same NT domain)

Notes:

1 Microsoft offers Network Load Balancing, which provides workload balancing.
2 This is the maximum number of nodes supported on Windows 2000. Other platforms have different restrictions.
3 These protocols are supported for client-to-server access. TCP/IP is the only supported protocol between servers in the cluster.
4 This presumes LAN-speed WAN connections.
5 Domino tasks such as fax server, pager gateway or cc:Mail MTA cannot fail over in a Domino cluster. These tasks can be automatically restarted along with the Domino server with MSCS.
6 Failback can occur when the database is opened the next time.

It is easy to see, when browsing the table above, that these two systems are developed for different uses. Some of the items in Table 11 are worthy of further emphasis.

Microsoft Cluster Services offers a platform to provide fault tolerance for general application servers too, but does not offer workload balancing, unlike Domino clustering. Domino clusters also allow you to use protocols other than TCP/IP for client communications, although TCP/IP is the preferred protocol.

The Domino cluster implementation relies on database replication between the nodes in the cluster. This replication is event driven and assures the integrity of data in the databases within the cluster. MSCS is based on a common disk device model, which is discussed in detail later in this chapter.

Domino clustering requires no special hardware. Implementing MSCS clustering requires cluster-specific hardware in the form of the common disk subsystem, and hardware used in the cluster has to be specifically certified for MSCS. Microsoft maintains a hardware compatibility list at:

`http://www.microsoft.com/hcl`

IBM xSeries and Netfinity server operating system compatibility information, including clustering, can be found at:

`http://www.pc.ibm.com/us/compat/nos/ms.shtml`

Domino clustering has no enforced distance limit between nodes. This allows you to implement disaster recovery solutions without complex hardware. MSCS nodes cannot be separated by distances greater than those supported by the common disk subsystem. For SCSI subsystems this is a few meters, whereas more expensive solutions such as Fibre Channel can support distances up to 10 kilometers.

The Microsoft Cluster service limitation of two nodes in a cluster also makes Domino clusters more attractive in large environments where there may be several thousands of clients.

Depending on your precise requirements, you may find that, individually, either Domino or MSCS will meet all requirements. There are situations, however, where only a combination of the two will provide the level of availability you desire. In the remainder of this chapter we continue to explore the different features of the two cluster solutions and show how they can be effectively put into service alongside each other. Thus, the two products should not really be seen as being in competition, but rather as complementing each other's functions.

6.2.2 Functional differences from a Notes client perspective

The Notes client is Domino cluster-aware and maintains the cluster cache locally. The cluster cache provides a list of servers in the cluster. When the client tries to open a database on a Domino server that is unavailable, the client uses the cluster cache to find the next available server in the cluster. When that server receives the request from the client, its Cluster Manager redirects the request to a cluster member that is holding a replica of the requested database.

In practice this means that when the server that the client is connected to becomes unavailable, the client receives an error message saying that the server is not responding. If the client wants to continue working with the database, an `OpenDatabase` command must be issued again. Either the user has to explicitly reopen the database or the application must issue an `OpenDatabase` or `OpenDatabasewithFailover` API command. The user may then continue working with the database. This failover mechanism is described in more detail in 3.2, "Failover and load balancing in a cluster" on page 45.

The situation is somewhat different when the Domino server is running on a Windows 2000 MSCS cluster. When the MSCS cluster node hosting the Domino server fails, due to a hardware or software error, the other node takes over the Domino resources. That is, the Domino data files, hosted on the common disk subsystem, are transferred to the surviving server. It also adopts the IP address that was being used by the Domino server and then starts the Domino server. Since the Domino server continues running with the same IP address, your users may not even notice that the server failed and was restarted.

In some cases, depending on how many server tasks the Domino server was running and the TCP/IP time-out value, your Notes users may receive the following error message: `The requested network operation did not complete in reasonable amount of time. Retry the operation later.` Otherwise, the failover is totally transparent to the user. The typical failover time on a Windows 2000 server running MSCS is very short. Tests show failover times of between 30 seconds and a couple of minutes.

The Windows 2000 server running MSCS can be configured so that the users are dynamically reconnected to the original server when it becomes available.

6.3 Microsoft Cluster Services design

Microsoft released Microsoft Cluster Server in 1997, as part of the Microsoft Windows NT Server Enterprise Edition. This book was written not long after the release of Microsoft Windows 2000. In this operating system, the clustering function is provided by Microsoft Cluster Services, and is provided as standard with Windows 2000 Advanced Server and Datacenter Server.

Windows 2000 Advanced Server supports the connection of two nodes in a clustered configuration. Windows 2000 Datacenter Server is more specialized and supports up to four nodes. These nodes provide services and applications to users through LAN connections. A second network connection between the servers is dedicated to intra-cluster traffic. All traffic between nodes is directed over this network, which is required to ensure that failover will not take place inadvertently due, for example, to high network traffic on the public LAN.

The cluster can automatically detect and recover from different types of failures, including hardware, operating system, or application failures. If a failure occurs on one node, applications and services running on that node can be restarted on the other system. This is called failover and can be triggered automatically or manually. Manual failover can be useful for moving applications and services from one node to the other one if maintenance or an upgrade is necessary. After you bring the original node back online, its applications and services can be transferred back from the other node. This is called failback.

Resources running on the cluster are monitored at administrator-defined intervals. If a resource fails, the system tries to restart it. If the resource fails to restart after the retry count set for the resource is reached, the application or service is failed over to the other node.

The Microsoft Cluster Services implementation is based on the concept of a common disk subsystem. Both nodes in a cluster can access this subsystem, but only one node can own specific individual disk resources at any given time. In normal operation, each disk is accessed only by its owning node. A node can access a disk belonging to the other node only after MSCS has transferred ownership of the disk.

For more on Microsoft Cluster Service, components and how it works, see *IBM @server xSeries Clustering Planning Guide*, SG24-5845.

Figure 64 on page 170 shows the MSCS configuration we implemented on two Netfinity 7000 M10 servers in our lab, both of which were running Windows 2000 Advanced Server:

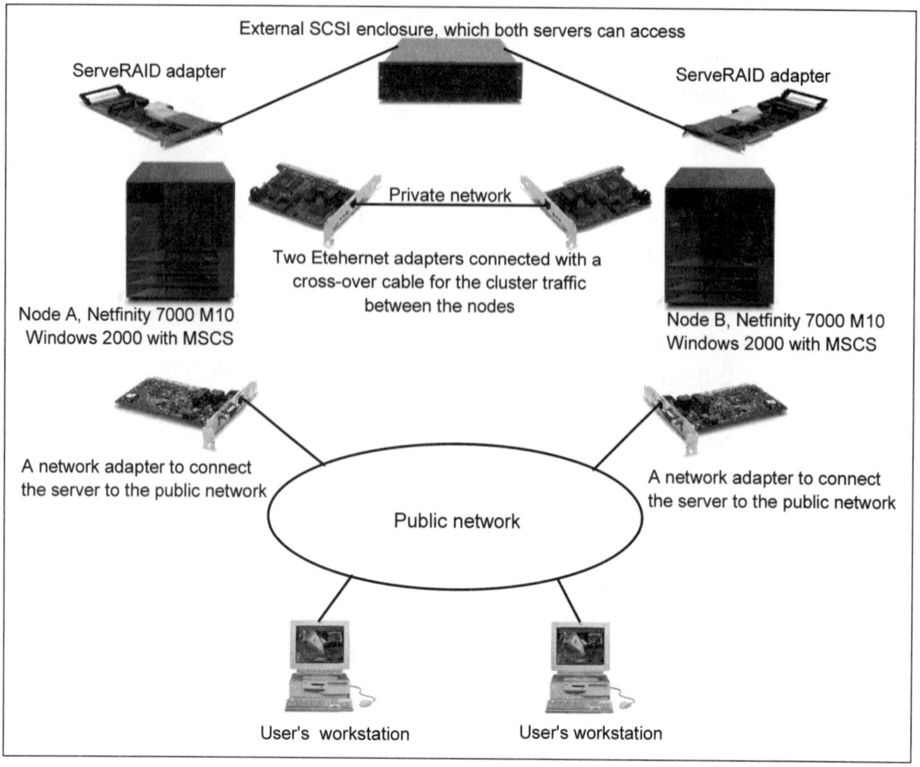

Figure 64. MSCS cluster: our lab configuration

Implementing MSCS clustering requires that the hardware used in the cluster is specifically certified for MSCS. Microsoft maintains a hardware compatibility list at:

`http://www.microsoft.com/hcl`

IBM xSeries and Netfinity server operating system compatibility information, including clustering, can be found at:

`http://www.pc.ibm.com/us/compat/nos/ms.shtml`

Heartbeat cable

Early versions of the IBM ServeRAID adapter required a direct SCSI connection between the RAID adapters in each machine when used to form an MSCS cluster. This was commonly referred to as the SCSI heartbeat cable. The cable is no longer required.

6.3.1 Active-passive configuration

An *active-passive* implementation of MSCS basically means that only one of the nodes in the cluster is actively providing services for clients. This kind of configuration is also known as a standby server. If the active server fails, all cluster resources are transferred to the standby machine. This has the advantage, assuming both servers in the node are equally powerful (which is usually the case), that response times provided to users do not change when a failover has occurred.

An active-passive configuration also has the advantage that it is easy to implement and does not require as much planning as an active-active configuration. The primary drawback to this implementation is the low utilization of the hardware. The possibility of the active node going down is relatively low, and as long as the primary node is operative, the standby node only exchanges status information.

Figure 65 illustrates a typical hardware setup for a Domino server running on a MSCS cluster in an active-passive configuration:

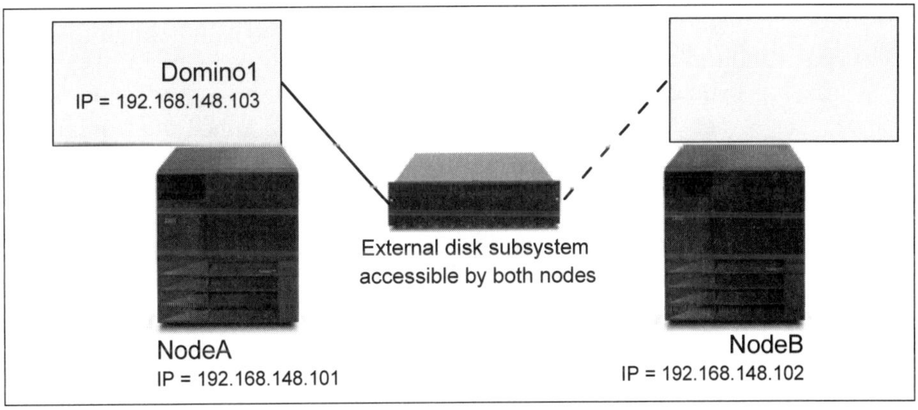

Figure 65. Domino running in an MSCS active-passive configuration

The Domino server is running on NodeA. Domino data files are installed on the external disk unit that both nodes can access. Each node has the Domino executables installed on its own local disks, usually in equivalent paths (D:\lotus\domino\, for example) to simplify administration. NodeA owns the cluster disk resource under normal operation. The Domino server has been assigned an IP address of its own.

When NodeA fails, NodeB takes ownership of the clustered disks and the Domino IP address and then starts Domino, as shown in Figure 66:

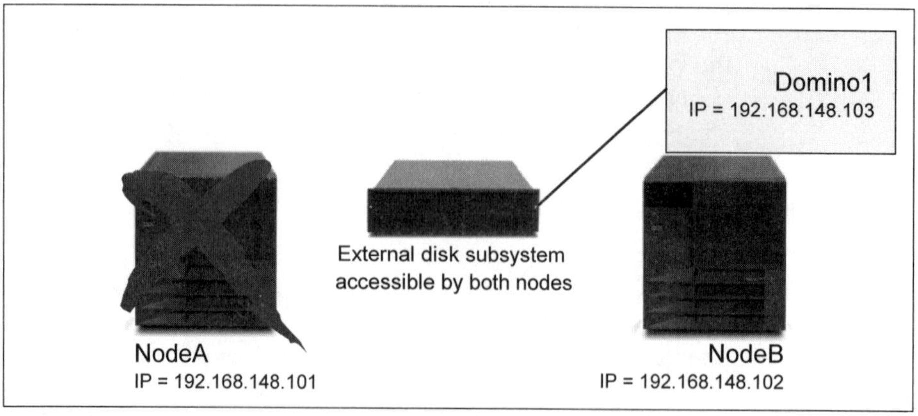

Figure 66. Domino failover in an active-passive MSCS configuration

Since Domino is using an IP address that belongs to the cluster, not to a local node, the clients are reconnected to the server, now running on the node named NodeB.

Once the problem that caused the primary node to fail has been solved, the primary node can join the cluster again. To minimize disruption to your users, you can choose that the primary server now adopts the role of the standby server, and the initial standby server becomes the primary server. Alternatively, you may choose to have Domino failback to the original primary server.

MSCS supports the concept of a preferred owner or, in other words, the primary platform for the resource. If the preferred owner is set to be NodeA, failback can be scheduled to take place automatically immediately after the preferred node comes back online, or failback can be scheduled to occur between certain hours.

6.3.2 Active-active configuration

An active-active configuration uses exactly the same basic hardware configuration as an active-passive configuration. It makes better use of the cluster hardware, however, in that both nodes provide services to your users. Now if one of the nodes fails, the other node takes over the failed node's resources and starts running them alongside its own resources.

The implication of this is that in normal operation, each server is underutilized to some extent, and both nodes must be capable of running all the services in the cluster with acceptable response times. Alternatively, you can choose to use somewhat less powerful servers and accept degraded performance on the relatively rare occasions that a failover has occurred.

Figure 67 illustrates how two Domino servers can be configured to run on a Windows 2000 servers configured with MSCS:

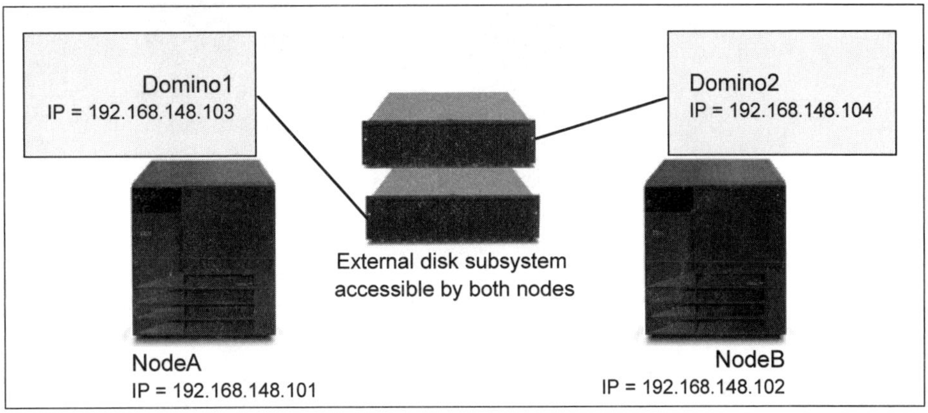

Figure 67. Domino servers running in an active-active MSCS configuration

The two Domino servers do not have to use the same Domino Directory; in other words, they do not have to be in the same Notes domain. Their data directories must be installed on a disk resource to which both nodes in the cluster have access, that is, in the clustered disk subsystem. Both Domino servers are assigned unique IP addresses. Now if one of the servers fails, the remaining node takes over, and starts the failed Domino server as shown in Figure 68:

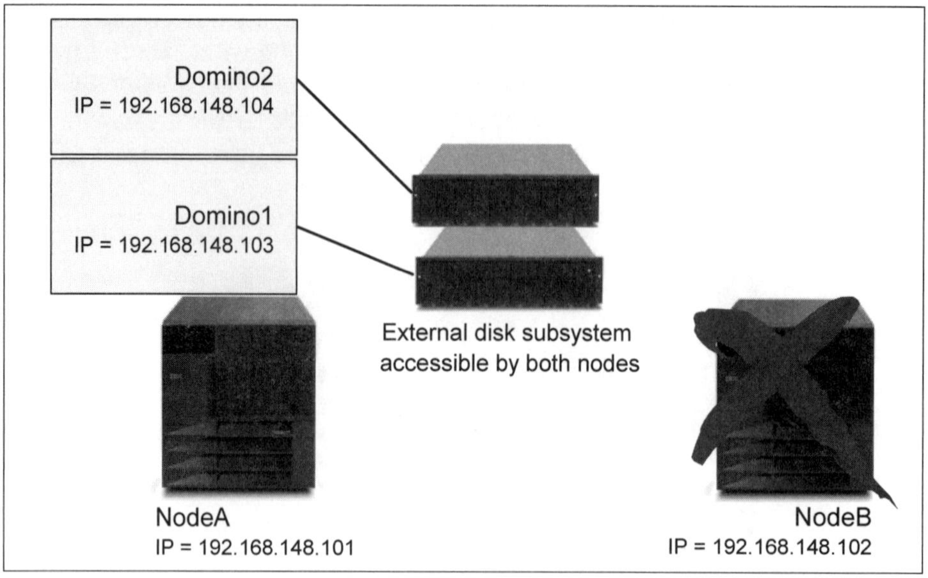

Figure 68. Domino server failover in an active-active MSCS configuration

After the cause of the failure has been found and corrected, and the server joins the cluster again, the system can be configured to move the second Domino server automatically from NodeA back to NodeB to equalize the workload between the Windows 2000 servers.

Active-active configuration does not have to mean that the application servers run the same products. In a small environment, where only one Domino server is sufficient, but when high availability is required, the nodes running in MSCS cluster can be configured to run Domino server on one node and, for example, SQL Server on the second node. Once again, the nodes have to be capable of running both the applications at the same time, if a failure occurs.

6.4 Installing Domino server on Windows 2000 cluster

This section explains how to install and configure Lotus Domino servers on Windows 2000 servers running Microsoft Cluster service. It is not intended to fully document a cluster installation, but to show how Domino can be installed on a cluster. We describe the installation steps required for a Domino server installation in a Windows 2000 cluster that is configured in active-passive mode, and then provide the additional steps to configure an active-active cluster.

To implement our MSCS cluster, we will use two identical IBM Netfinity 7000 M10 servers. The servers are connected using Ethernet adapters and a crossover cable to carry the cluster traffic and isolate it from the public network. These adapters are configured with private network IP addresses. The servers are connected to the public network with token-ring adapters that have public IP addresses. Both servers have internal disks for the operating system and Domino program files. The operating system is Windows 2000 Advanced Server with Service Pack 1, running MSCS. The Domino version used for this setup is Domino R5.0.4a.

The servers share external hard disks configured with drive letters E: and F:.

Attention

The actual drive letters used for installation are not important, but the same drive letters must be used on both nodes. That is, the files must be in the "same place" no matter which node owns the common disks.

The Microsoft Cluster Server quorum disk was configured to be drive Q:. Although we haven't mentioned this before, the quorum disk is an important component of the cluster. It is used to store dynamic information that is crucial to the cluster's operation. It must be defined as one of the disks in the common disk subsystem.

There is a SCSI ServeRAID disk controller installed in each server and both controllers are connected to the external disk enclosures.

We plan to run two Domino servers, named Wiley and Roadrunner, on the cluster. Each Domino server will have a unique IP address, linked to the server name in the network's DNS. In normal operation, one Domino server will reside on each node. This configuration is illustrated in Figure 69:

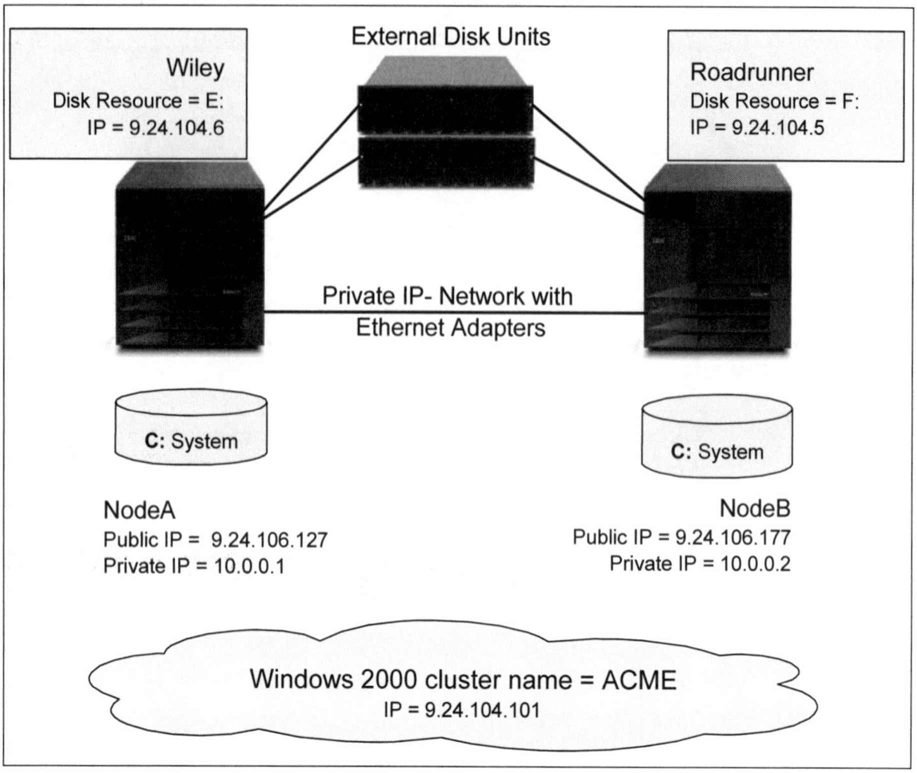

Figure 69. Windows 2000 cluster in our lab

6.4.1 Installation of Microsoft Cluster Services

Before you start installing the Lotus Domino server, you have to install and configure Microsoft Cluster Services. We will not describe the MSCS installation process, partly because it is hardware dependent, and partly because there are several other sources for this information. All of the main hardware vendors, including IBM, Compaq and Digital, for example, provide their own material for this purpose. Contact your hardware dealer or hardware manufacturer for details.

More material is also available from the following Microsoft Web pages:

`http://www.microsoft.com/technet/win2000/clustep.asp`

`http://www.microsoft.com/technet/win2000/win2ksrv/technote/clustsrv.asp`

And more about clustering on IBM servers on the following site:

`http://www.pc.ibm.com/ww/eserver/xseries/clustering/index.html`

6.4.2 Preparing Microsoft Cluster Services for Domino installation

This section describes the resource definitions that are required in Microsoft Cluster Services before installing the Lotus Domino server. You have to define a resource group, create a shared disk resource in the group, create an IP address in the group for the Domino server, and set up the failback behavior.

6.4.2.1 Creating the resource group

The first step to prepare MSCS for Domino is to create a resource group for the Domino server. A resource group defines a set of resources that are logically dependent on each other in some way. A dependency would be, for example, the relationship between a disk resource and a file share. The file share cannot exist before the disk resource is brought online and becomes accessible.

Microsoft Cluster Services administration is performed using the Cluster Administrator program, which installs automatically on both nodes in a Windows 2000 cluster. You can also install the administration utility on a non-clustered Windows 2000 server or on a Windows NT workstation. To start the administrator, select **Start -> Programs -> Administrative Tools -> Cluster Administration**.

Create the resource group for the Domino server to be installed in the Windows 2000 cluster by selecting **File -> New -> Group**. Enter the group name and an optional comment for the group as shown in Figure 70:

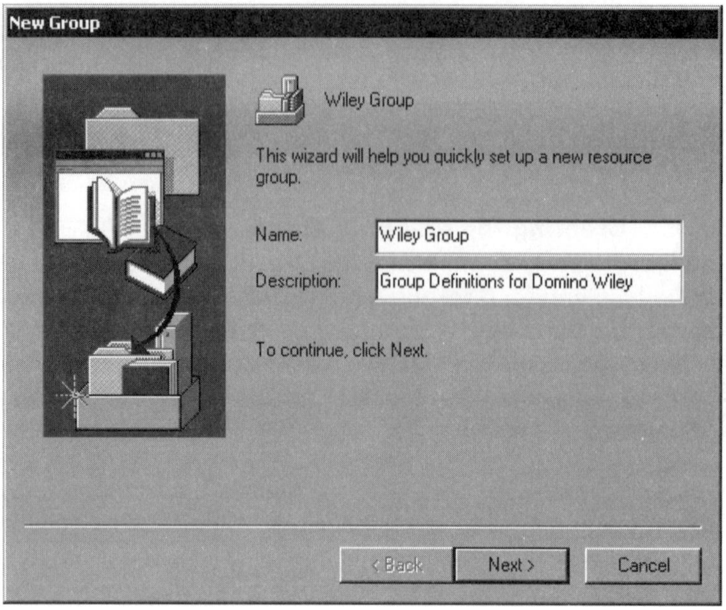

Figure 70. Create a new group for Domino server

It is good practice to use a naming convention, such as including the word "Group" in every group name, to make it easy to differentiate groups from other cluster resources.

6.4.2.2 Creating the disk resource

The next step after creating the resource group is to create a disk resource inside that group.

1. Create the disk resource from the Cluster Administrator by selecting **File -> New -> Resource**.
2. Enter the name for the disk resource as shown in Figure 71:

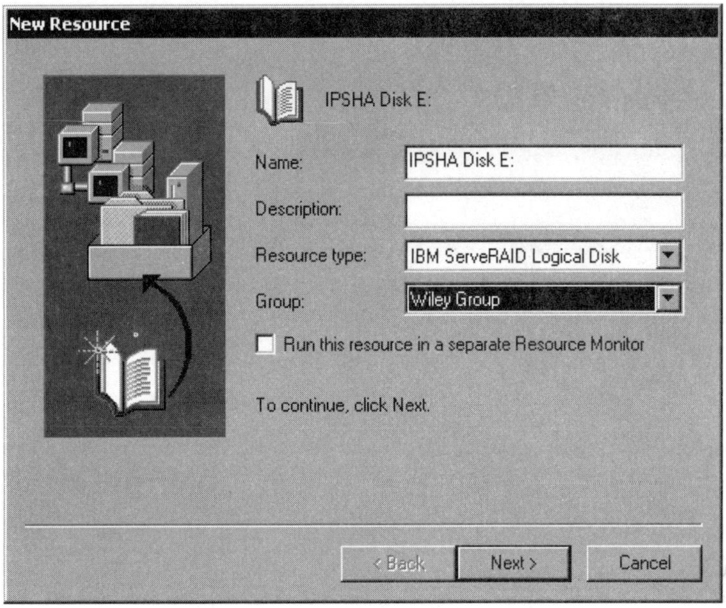

Figure 71. Defining the disk resource for the Domino server

As all the disk resources are assigned to a drive letter, a good naming practice could be, for example, Disk x:, where x: is the assigned drive letter. In our setup we used IPSHA Disk E:, to indicate that the resource is a disk connected to an IBM ServeRAID adapter, and the assigned drive letter in Windows 2000 server will be letter E.

3. Enter the description for the resource. This is optional and can be changed or added later if required.
4. Select the correct resource type from the drop-down list. The definition is either Physical Disk or a vendor-provided resource type if a RAID disk subsystem is being used, as in our case.

   We used IBM ServeRAID-3HB adapters in our system. Required drivers for the Microsoft Cluster Services must be installed in order to use RAID disks. Contact your hardware vendor or check their Web pages to get the latest version of the required drivers.
5. Select the group that will own the disk. Click **Next**.
6. To allow failover, both nodes have to be possible owners of the disk, so take the default and click **Next**.
7. It is not necessary to define dependencies for the disk, so click **Next** to complete the resource definition.

6.4.2.3 Creating the IP address

After the disk resource has been created, the IP address can be added to the group. Follow the steps below to complete the task.

1. Select **File -> New -> Resource** from the Cluster Administration tool.
2. Enter the name for the resource to be created as shown in Figure 72:

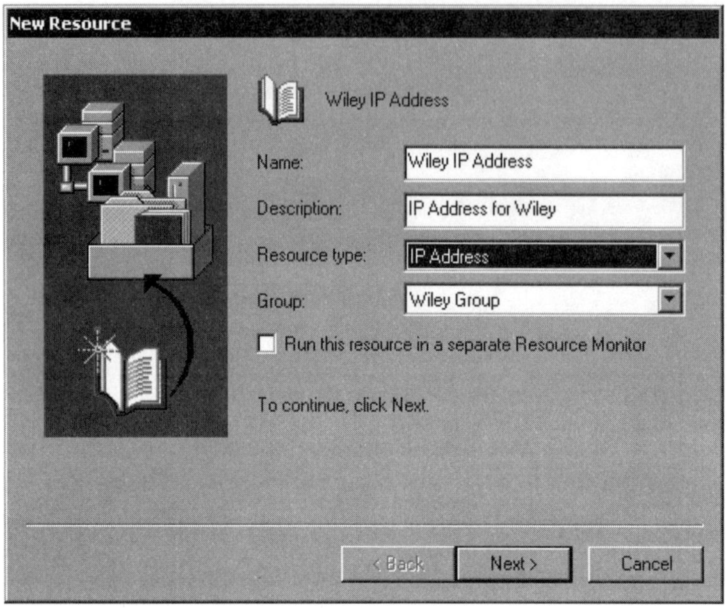

Figure 72. Creating an IP address as a resource

3. Choose IP Address as a Resource type.
4. Make sure you select the group name of the resource group that you previously created. Click **Next**.
5. Specify the possible owners for the IP address as shown in Figure 73. Once again, we specified both nodes as possible owners of this resource. Click **Next**.

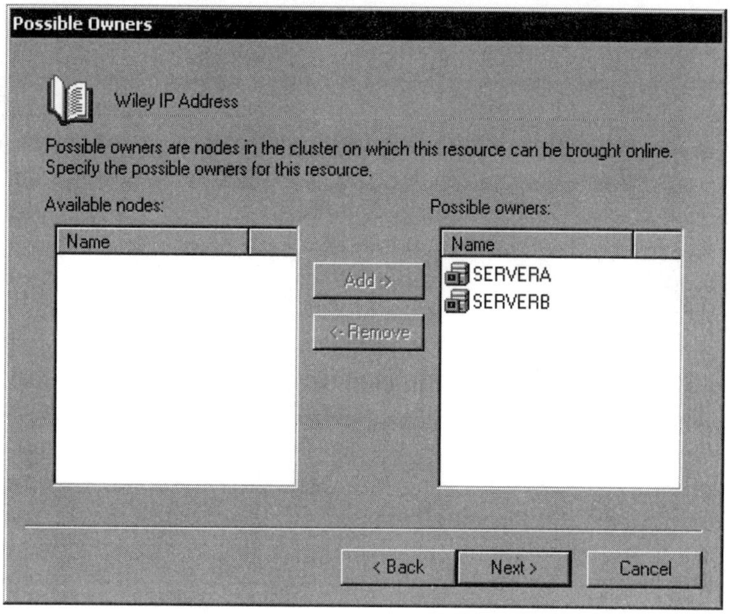

Figure 73. Assigning possible owners for the IP address

6. You are now prompted to specify dependencies for this resource (see Figure 74 on page 182). Dependencies define those other resources that must be brought online by the cluster service before the resource being created can be brought online. As this resource is an IP address, there is no need to create any dependencies for it. Click **Next**.

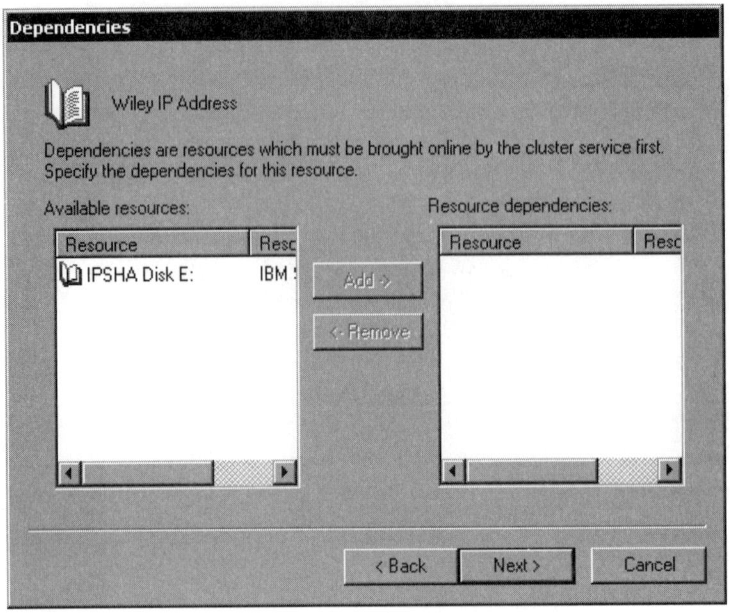

Figure 74. Defining dependencies for the IP address

7. Enter the IP address as shown in Figure 75. Users connect to Domino server via this address. Make sure that you choose the proper network for user access (not the private one). Click **Finish**.

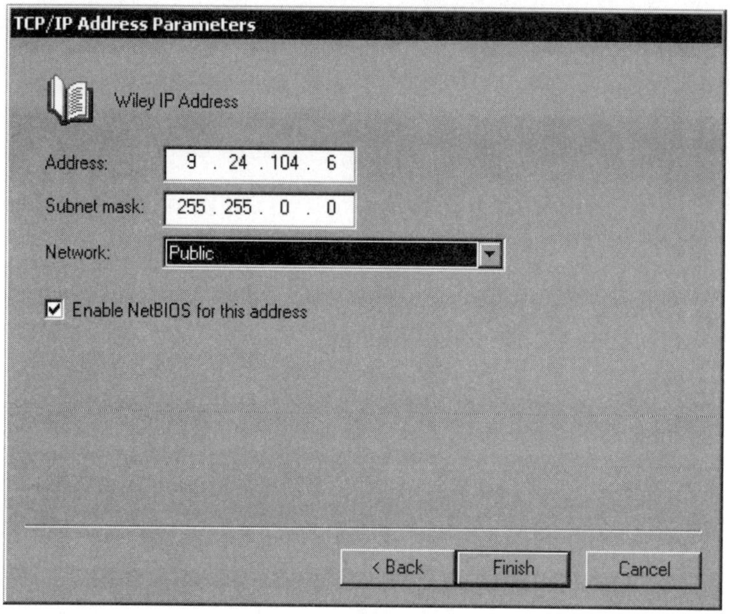

Figure 75. Configuring IP address as a resource

Microsoft Cluster Services supports only TCP/IP, although NetBIOS over TCP/IP can be used as well. Make sure that the IP address dedicated for Domino server usage can be resolved using DNS or another name resolution method.

A resource group with an IP address, and, perhaps, a network name, appears to be a normal server to network-attached clients. In fact, a named *virtual server* appears in a client's Network Neighborhood in Windows and is indistinguishable from a real, physical server. When failover occurs, the physical host of the virtual server changes, but the virtual server appears unchanged to the user.

To complete the Domino virtual server, we need to include the Domino application within the group, which is explained in 6.4.6, "Configuring Domino to run as a Generic Service" on page 189, but first we have to install the Domino code.

6.4.3 Domino installation steps for the first node

After creating the group, defining the disk resource and the IP address, you can continue with the Domino server code installation.

Make sure that the first node is the owner of the shared disk resource that you want to use for this installation. You can verify this by opening My Computer on the first node, which should allow you to access the shared drive.

Active-active configurations

The following discussion assumes an active-passive configuration is being installed. For active-active configurations, you have to install two Domino servers on each node. To do this you must specify partitioned server installation by checking **Partitioned Server Installation** in the dialog box following the License Agreement.

See Appendix A, “Partitioned Domino servers” on page 203 for more information.

1. Insert the Lotus Domino CD-ROM and start the server installation program as usual.
2. Read and accept the license terms.
3. Enter the user registration information.
4. In the Lotus Domino Installation window, select the program and data directories to be used for the Domino server.

   Domino program files should be installed on a non-shared drive. In our lab configuration, we installed them on drive C:. To allow the other node in the Windows 2000 cluster to access the data files when the Domino server fails over, the Domino data directory must be installed on a shared drive. In our example, the shared data drive for the Domino server is drive E: as shown in Figure 76:

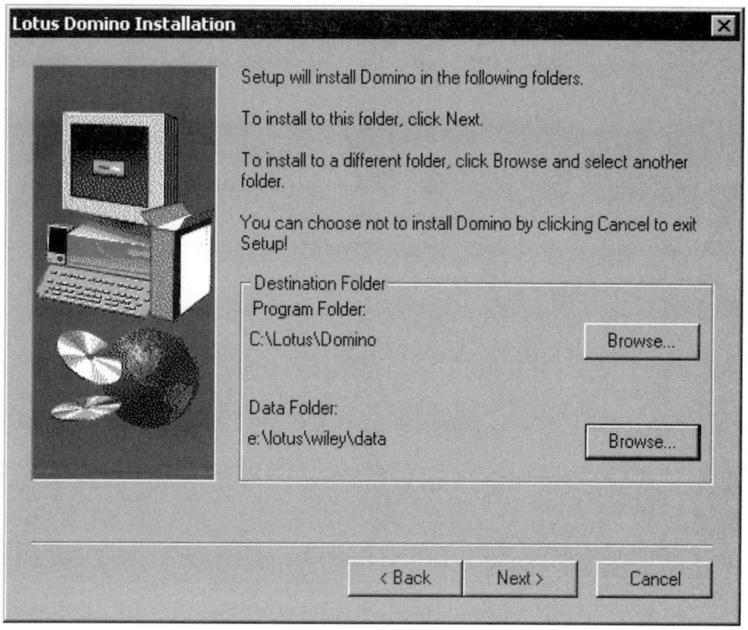

Figure 76. Select program and data directories for Domino installation

A good practice for data directory naming is to install the Domino data files in the directory \lotus\<virtual servername>\data, where <virtual servername> is the Domino server name. This makes it easier to track which server is the owner of the data.

Click **Next**.

5. Select the type of setup you want. Select either the **Domino Application Server** or the **Domino Mail Server** radio button. At this point we are not combining Domino clustering with MSCS, so we do not need to install Domino Enterprise Server. We discuss using both forms of clustering together in 6.5, "Combining Domino clusters with MSCS" on page 198.
6. Click **Customize**. Make sure you select **Domino as an NT Service** option as shown in Figure 77 on page 186. Click **Next**.

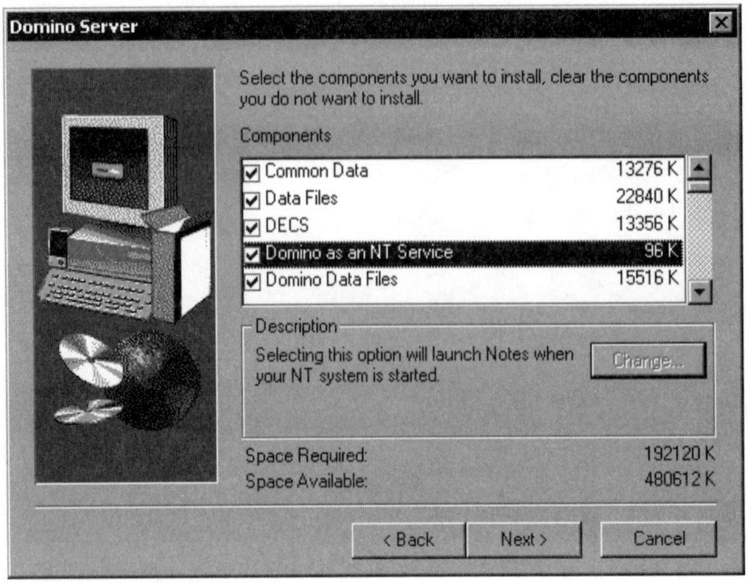

Figure 77. Customizing Domino installation

7. Installation will add program icons to the Lotus Applications folder by default. You may change that by typing a new folder name.
8. Click **Next** and the install process will begin.

6.4.4 Configuration steps for the first node

After you have successfully installed the Domino server code, you have to configure it. To complete this task, you should follow the steps in 4.3.2, "Configuring the first Domino server" on page 86 if this is the first server in your domain, or in 4.3.4, "Installing and configuring additional cluster servers" on page 96 if this is an additional Domino server in your domain. Remember to perform only the basic configuration steps; you are not setting up Domino clustering.

Make sure that you customize the port settings by disabling all ports other than TCPIP. Change the Net Address from the local machine host name to the host name registered for the Domino server in DNS. If the Domino server name is not registered in DNS, you can, instead, enter the explicit IP address created for the virtual Domino server using Cluster Administration. MSCS supports only the TCP/IP protocol for failover, so there is no need to define other protocols.

There are at least two IP addresses active on the Windows 2000 server that will run Domino. These are the server's public IP address and the virtual server's IP address, created as a cluster resource and reserved for Domino server usage. You have to identify the second one in NOTES.INI to avoid user connections through an incorrect IP address. If this step is not completed, and users connect to the Domino server through the local machines' IP address, those users cannot fail over to the other node should the physical server fail.

To identify the correct IP address, add the following setting in NOTES.INI:

```
TCPIP_TCPIPAddress=0,a.b.c.d,0
```

where `TCPIP` is the port name to be defined. The IP address is represented by a.b.c.d. The last parameter is the Notes IP port number, which should be left as zero, and equates to the default port, which is 1352. If you choose to set the port number to something other than 1352, you need to add the same definition to each and every Notes client that will connect to the server.

In our lab configuration, this setting is as follows:

```
TCPIP_TCPIPAddress=0,9.24.104.6,0
```

As both nodes in the cluster must have access to the same NOTES.INI file, you should move the NOTES.INI file from the Domino program directory on the local drive to the Domino data directory on the shared drive. You can use the following commands to do this:

```
c:\> copy c:\lotus\domino\notes.ini e:\lotus\wiley\data\notes.ini
c:\> del c:\lotus\domino\notes.ini
```

Also, you should update the Properties for the Lotus Domino Server icon in the Start menu. The icon is normally located by selecting **Start -> Programs -> Lotus Applications -> Lotus Domino Server**.

Add the following parameter after the executable name:

```
=<path>\notes.ini
```

For our lab configuration, therefore, the full command line is:

```
C:\Lotus\Domino\nserver.exe =e:\lotus\wiley\data\notes.ini
```

6.4.4.1 Verifying the server functionality

When you start Domino, you can check the server's port status by issuing the following command from the Domino server console:

```
show port tcpip
```

The response should be similar to the following screen:

```
>show port tcpip
TCP/IP Port Driver
Transport Provider: TCP


Notes Session Local Address Foreign Address
088200019.24.104.6:13529.24.106.246:1121
088300029.24.104.6:1352*:*
```

The output verifies that the Domino server is listening to the IP address 9.24.104.6, and has an active session on TCP port 1352 with foreign address 9.24.106.246, which in our case is the Domino administration workstation used to run remote commands. If the local address appears as *.*:1352, you need to check NOTES.INI and correct any errors.

6.4.5 Installation steps for the second cluster node

After you have verified the Domino server functionality on the first Windows 2000 cluster node, you need to install the Domino program files on the second cluster node. Follow the steps below to install the Domino server code on the second node:

1. Stop the Domino server you have just installed.
2. Move the resource group for the Domino server to the second node in the cluster using the Cluster Administration tool.
3. After moving the resource group including the disk and the IP address, switch to the second node, and install the Domino server code in exactly the same way as you did for the first node.

   Be sure to specify the same directories for the Domino program and Domino data directories as on the first server. If you fail to do so, the Domino server cannot fail over from one node to another.
4. Then you should delete NOTES.INI from the Domino program directory. Make sure that you modify the Domino server icon's Properties as described in 6.4.4, "Configuration steps for the first node" on page 186 so that the server uses NOTES.INI from the data directory.
5. Start the Domino server and test the functionality as described for the first node.

6.4.6 Configuring Domino to run as a Generic Service

The final step in setting up Domino server to run in a Windows 2000 cluster is to add the Domino server resource definition to the relevant resource group to complete the virtual server. Follow the steps below to accomplish this task:

1. Run the Cluster Administration tool and select **File -> New -> Resource** from the menu bar.
2. Enter a resource name for the Domino server that you want to run as a Generic Service in the Windows 2000 cluster. We used `Domino server Wiley` as you can see in Figure 78:

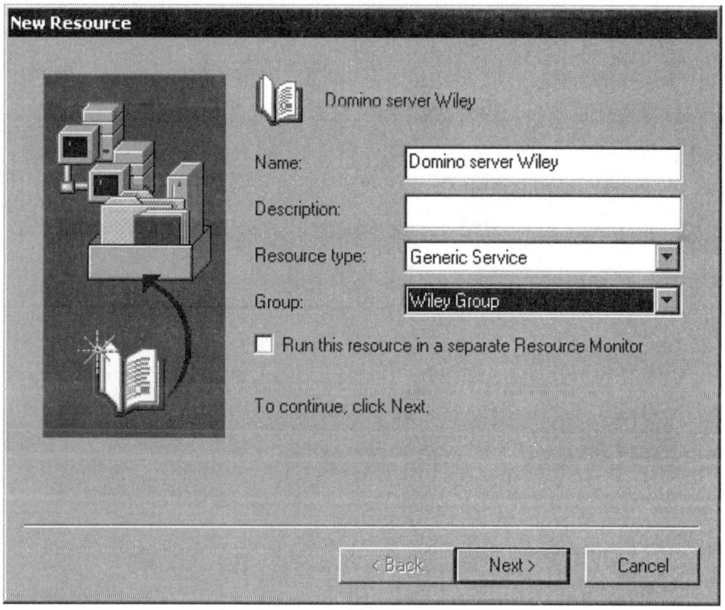

Figure 78. Defining the Domino server resource

3. Set the resource type to be Generic Service from the Resource type drop-down list and select the correct group from the Group drop-down list and click **Next**.
4. The Possible Owners dialog box is displayed. We want both nodes to be able to run Domino, which is the default. Click **Next**.
5. Click **Next** and the Dependencies window will be displayed as shown in Figure 79:

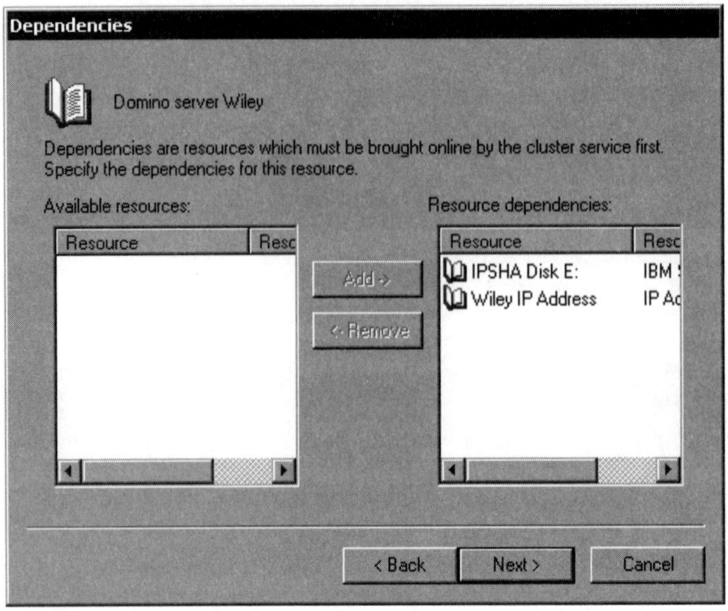

Figure 79. Domino server resource dependencies

6. This dialog box allows you to specify those resources that must be available (that is, active and online) before the Domino server itself can be brought online. Select the physical disk and IP address resources from the Available resources list and add them to the Resource dependencies list. Click **Next** to display the Generic Service Parameters window as in Figure 80:

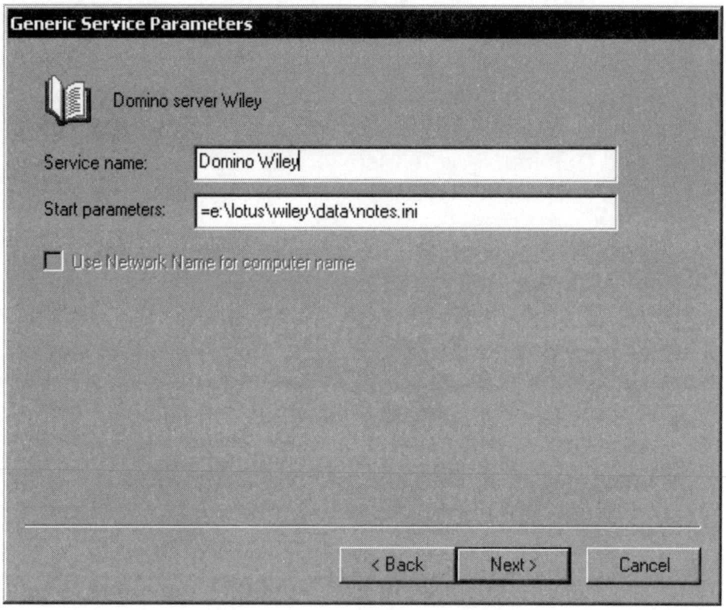

Figure 80. Defining the generic service parameters

Enter the service name for the Domino server. The service name must match the name for the Domino service, which can be found in the Services window, which is opened by clicking **Start -> Settings -> Control Panel -> Administrative Tools -> Services**. The default name for the Domino service is Lotus Domino Server, but it can vary, depending on the way you install Domino. If you look through the list of available services, the one you need will be easy to find. In our case the service is called Domino Wiley.

As we are creating an active-passive configuration, we provide the NOTES.INI file location as the startup parameter.

If you are configuring a Domino server in an active-active Windows 2000 cluster, you would enter the name of the service for the Domino server and leave the Start parameters field empty.

7. Click **Next** to display the Registry Replication settings. We do not need to add registry replications for Domino servers.
8. Click **Finish**.

The steps above are repeated for the second Domino server in an active-active MSCS cluster configuration.

6.4.7 Additional configuration steps for an active-active setup

Some additional steps are required to set up Domino servers in a Windows 2000 cluster with an active-active node configuration. You need to create another resource group that includes the second Domino server service and its own physical disk and IP resources, and each node has to have two partitioned Domino servers installed on it.

> **Partitioned servers**
>
> For active-active configurations, you have to install two Domino servers on each node. To do this you must specify partitioned server installation for both servers by checking **Partitioned Server Installation** in the dialog box following the License Agreement, as shown in Figure 81.
>
> See Appendix A, "Partitioned Domino servers" on page 203 for more information.

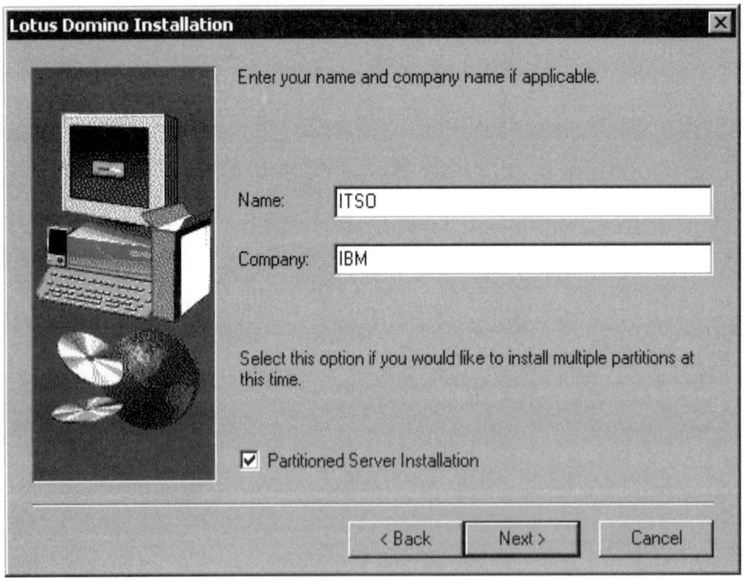

Figure 81. Partitioned server installation

When you install a partitioned Domino server, you select your Domino program and Domino data directories in the same way as for a standard Domino installation. Just as we described in the active-passive configuration, the Domino program directory should be stored on the server's local disk and the Domino data directory should be stored on the common disk subsystem, as shown in Figure 82:

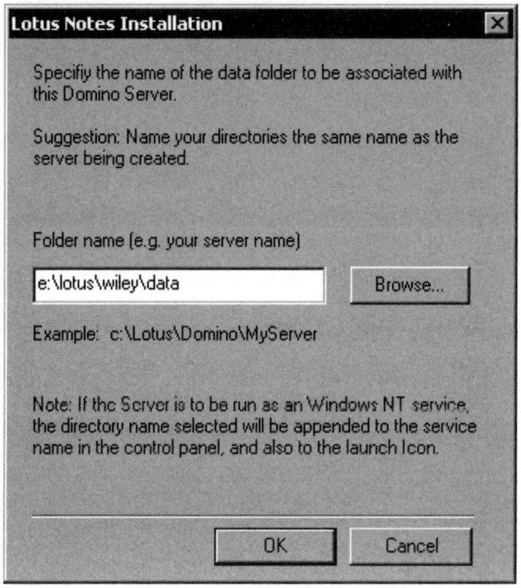

Figure 82. Selecting data directory for partitioned server

Once your first partitioned Domino server installation is complete, you need to follow the configuration steps given in 6.4.4, "Configuration steps for the first node" on page 186, with the exception that you do not have to update the Properties for the Domino server icon. This is because Domino partitioned server installation puts NOTES.INI in the Domino data directory by default and sets the icon's Properties accordingly.

Remember, just as for the active-passive case, you must install the Domino program on the second node using the same data locations as on the first node so that Domino can run on either physical server.

Installing multiple partitions

If you are familiar with partitioned Domino servers, you may know it is also possible to install multiple partitions simultaneously, as discussed in Appendix A, "Partitioned Domino servers" on page 203. We chose to install them separately in our example for the sake of simplicity.

6.4.7.1 Installing the second partitioned Domino server

Once the first partitioned server is installed and can run correctly on either node, you can install the second partitioned server.

1. Move the Domino server resource group to the first node in the Windows 2000 cluster using the Cluster Administration program.
2. Create a new resource group in the Windows 2000 cluster for the second Domino server as described 6.4.2.1, "Creating the resource group" on page 177. The new group name, in our example, is Roadrunner Group.
3. Create a disk resource for the Roadrunner resource group in the same way as described in 6.4.2.2, "Creating the disk resource" on page 178. The new disk resource name in our example is IPSHA Disk F:.
4. Create the IP address in the resource group as described in 6.4.2.3, "Creating the IP address" on page 180. The new IP address resource name is the Roadrunner Domino server IP address.
5. Install the second partitioned Domino server. You can select the same program directory that was used for the first server installation as long as you install the same version of Domino server. Make sure that you locate the data directory on the disk drive in the common subsystem that you configured for the second Domino server. In our example, this is the F: drive.
6. Start the newly installed Domino server and configure the server port in the same way as described earlier for the first server.

   In our example, we defined the IP address for the second Domino server by editing the NOTES.INI file located in the Domino data directory on the shared drive F: to include the following entry:

   ```
   TCPIP_TCPIPAddress=0,9.24.104.5,0
   ```
7. Restart the Domino server and verify the port configuration.
8. Move the resource group for the second Domino server to the second node in the Windows 2000 cluster.
9. Repeat the installation of the second Lotus Domino partitioned server on the second node using the same directories as described in step 5.

6.4.8 Failover and failback in MSCS

Earlier in this chapter we described how the Domino cluster resource is configured as a Generic Service. MSCS supports a range of different types of resource including, as we have already seen, IP addresses and physical disks. For any cluster resource, the MSCS Administrator can set a number of parameters that define the resource behavior if and when it fails. We now examine these parameters.

6.4.8.1 Resource restart settings

Resource restart settings control how a resource's owning node handles failure of the resource. By selecting the Advanced tab of Properties, which can be located by right-clicking the resource, you can examine or modify these settings as shown in Figure 83:

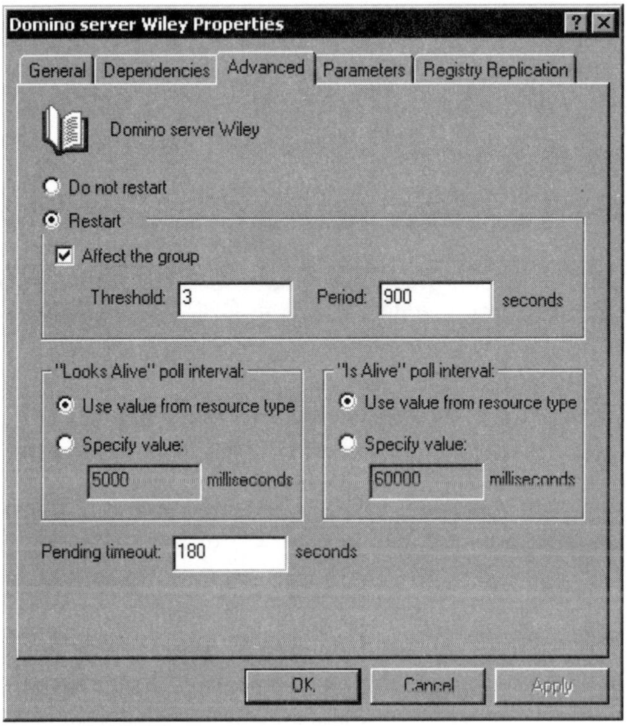

Figure 83. Defining failover properties for a resource

The resource restart settings include:

- Affect the group

  If this check box is selected, failure of this resource will trigger a failover of the owning group. A resource can belong to only one group.

- Threshold

  This is the number of times in the specified period that MSCS will attempt to restart the resource on the same node. If the threshold count is exceeded, the resource will fail, and all other resources in that group fail over to the other node in the cluster.

- Period

  This defines the time in seconds during which the specified number of attempts to restart the resource must occur before the resource is declared to have failed.

- "Looks Alive" and "Is Alive" poll intervals

  These parameters define how often the system should poll the resource to make sure that it is still available and functioning correctly. "Looks alive" uses a simple method that executes quickly but may not detect some failures. The "Is Alive" function is more thorough, and takes more time to execute than "Looks Alive". Under normal circumstances there is no need to change these parameters.

- Pending timeout

  This setting defines how long a resource is allowed to be in a Pending state before it is determined to have failed. Resources assume a Pending state as they make a transition in either direction between being online and offline.

6.4.8.2 Resource group failover settings

The Properties dialog box for a resource group includes two tabs that allow you to control how the group behaves when one of its resources fails. When a resource that has its "Affect the group" check box selected fails, the normal behavior is for the group to fail over to the other node in the cluster. If the nature of the problem, however, is such that the resource fails again on the new node, the cluster will attempt to fail the group back to its original node. This may be desirable, but an unrecoverable error would result in the group flipping from one node to the other continually. The Failover tab (see Figure 84) prevents this from occurring.

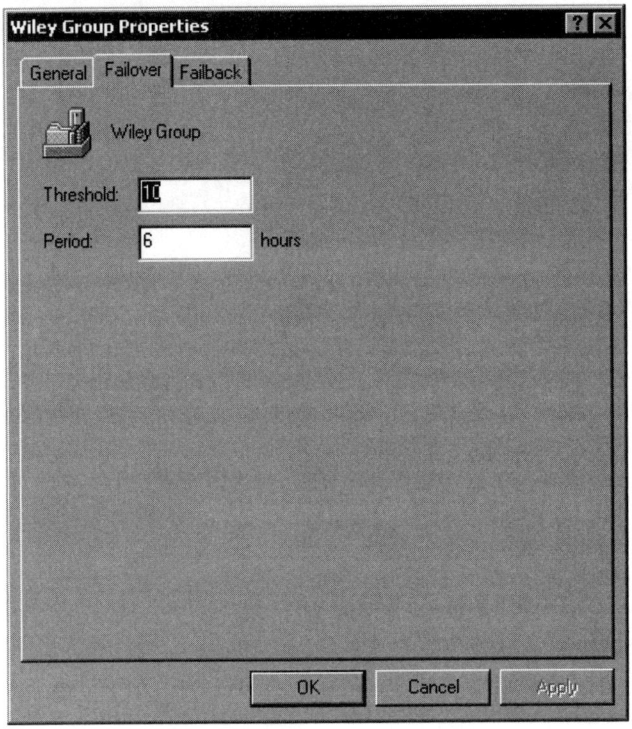

Figure 84. Resource group failover settings

The two parameters shown in Figure 84 let you define the number (Threshold) of failovers that are allowed to occur in a given time (Period), specified in hours. If this number is exceeded, the resource group is deemed to have failed and no further attempts will be made to bring the group online.

6.4.8.3 Resource group failback settings

As we have mentioned previously, MSCS supports the concept of *preferred owners*. When you define a resource group, you can say which node is the preferred host for the virtual server formed by a resource group. (In fact, you can specify multiple preferred nodes, but this is only useful for clusters with more than two nodes.) The preferred owner can also be set or changed by setting a parameter on the General tab in Figure 84.

When a node fails, its groups are transferred to the surviving node. After the problem that caused the failure is resolved, and the failed node is brought back online, those resource groups that have the repaired node defined as their preferred owner are failed back to it. The way that failback operates can be tailored using the Failback tab of the resource group's Properties dialog box as shown in Figure 85:

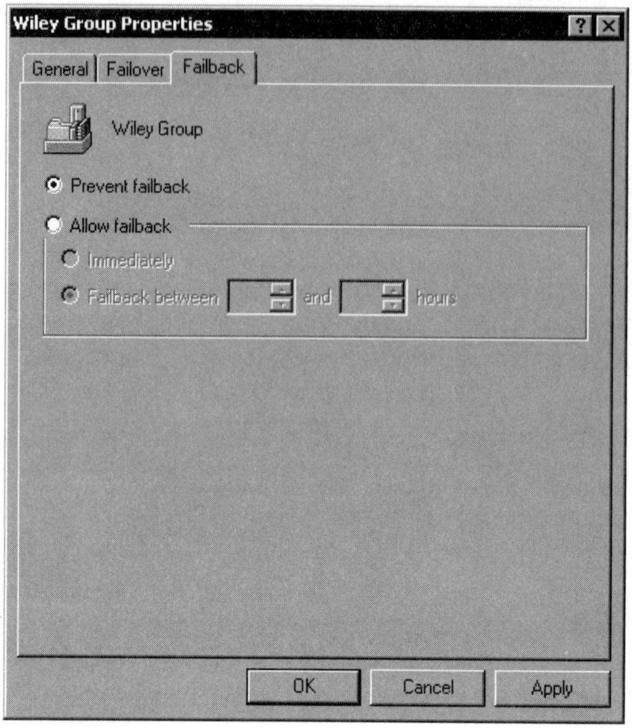

Figure 85. Defining failback settings for resource group

When you create a group, its default failback policy is set to disabled. This means that when a failover occurs, the resources are transferred to the other node and remain there, regardless of whether the preferred node is brought back online again. You can then choose to move the group back to its original owner manually, at a time when it is least disruptive to your users.

By selecting **Allow failback**, you have the option of letting failback occur as soon as possible after the failed server is restored or only allowing the failback to take place during certain hours of the day.

6.5 Combining Domino clusters with MSCS

As we said near the start of this chapter, you can choose to implement MSCS and Domino clusters on the same systems. This solution can be very attractive, for example, if there are several geographical sites in the Notes network, and when high availability is required at each site.

In our next example, there are four Domino servers in the Domino network: Domino servers Mars and Venus at site 1 and Domino servers Jupiter and Pluto at site 2. Both sites have Domino servers installed on Windows 2000 Advanced Servers that have been configured as active-active MSCS clusters.

The servers at site 1 are organized so that, if Domino server Mars fails due to a software or hardware error, Windows 2000 server NodeB takes over that Domino service and runs Mars alongside its "own" Domino server Venus. Domino servers Jupiter and Pluto are organized in a similar way at site 2. This configuration is illustrated in Figure 86:

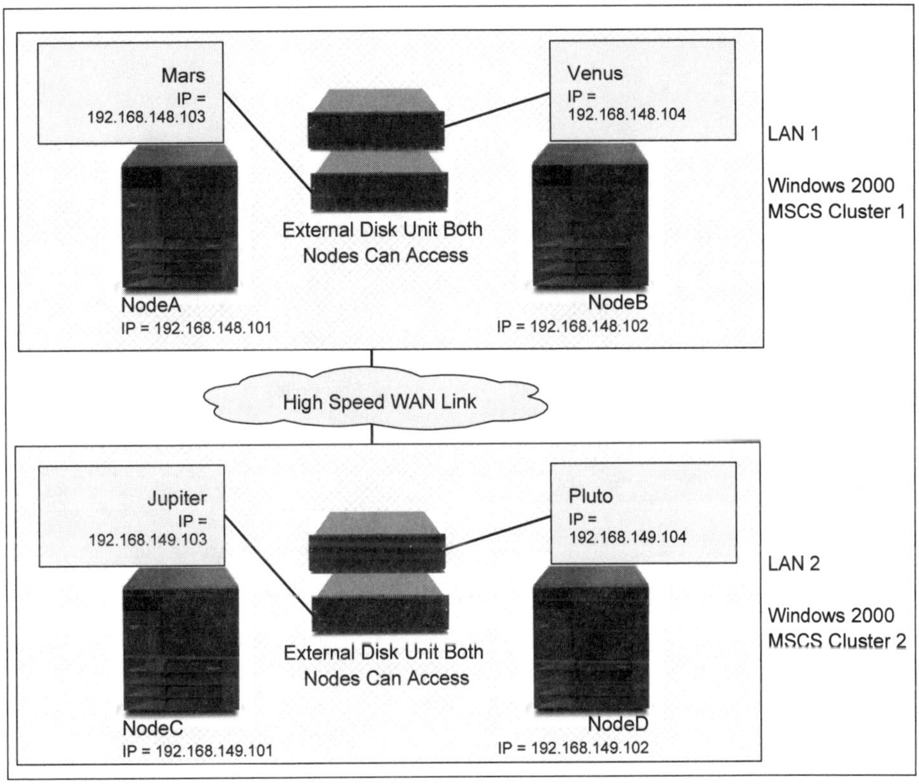

Figure 86. Two MSCS clusters at different sites

This arrangement provides excellent local availability by protecting users against hardware and software errors. Further robustness can be achieved, however, by implementing Domino clustering to ensure system availability even in the case of a total power failure or catastrophic disaster at one of the sites.

In our example, we created two Domino clusters, clustering Mars on site 1 with Jupiter on site 2, and also Venus with Pluto as shown in Figure 87:

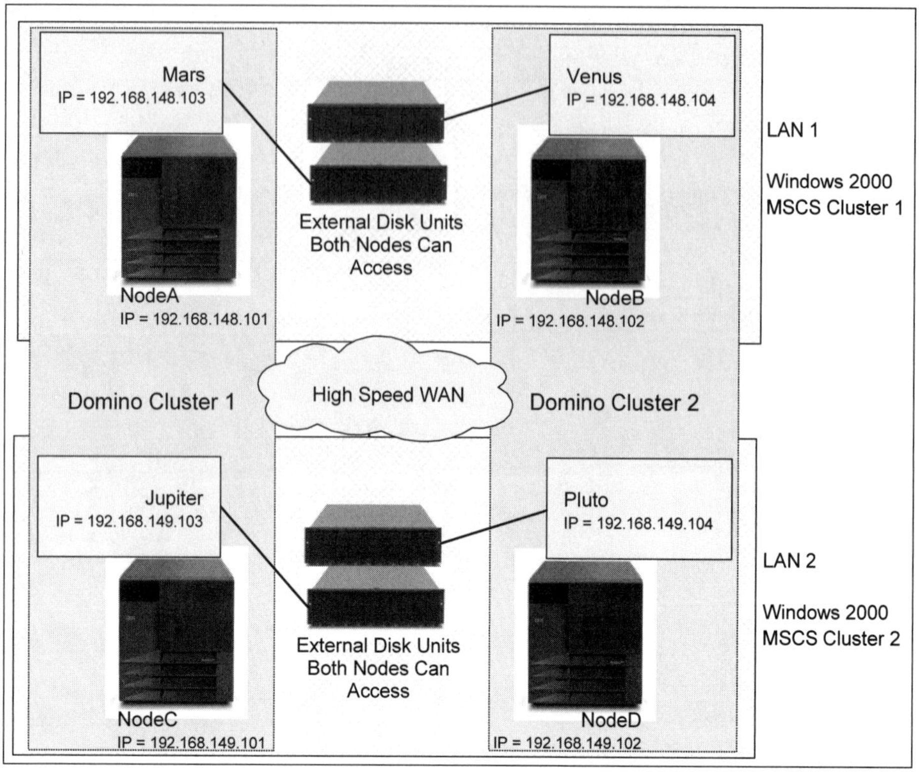

Figure 87. Combining Domino clusters with Windows 2000 clusters

In this setup, there is no cluster replication traffic between the local nodes, and Microsoft Cluster service provides fault tolerance for the servers on one site. Domino cluster replication is used between the geographical sites over a high-speed WAN link. When the servers are configured in this way, even if both servers on site 2 go down, client requests will be forwarded to the replica databases on the servers on site 1 over the high-speed WAN link.

There is one drawback with this configuration. In the unlikely event that you were to suffer both the loss of a site and one of the servers on the other site, the single remaining server has to be able to cope with the load of all four servers. By carefully identifying those resources that are critical and those that can remain unavailable without too much impact on your operations, you can minimize the effect on performance should you be unlucky enough to experience this kind of double failure.

6.6 Summary

Lotus Domino and Microsoft Cluster Services are two different, but complementary, clustering technologies. While Domino clustering is an application level solution, Microsoft Cluster Services works at the operating system level. The implementation and functions provided by the two products are different, and they may be combined to gain an even higher level of availability.

Combining the two products takes more effort to install and set up, in comparison with a simple Domino server installation, but when everything is well planned in advance, the installation is quite straightforward.

Appendix A. Partitioned Domino servers

Domino server partitioning is a feature that allows you to run multiple Domino servers on one physical machine. This is useful in several situations, such as server consolidation, where one large server replaces several smaller systems. Another area where partitioning is particularly useful is in active-active Microsoft Cluster Services configurations, where much improved availability can be achieved, as we have already seen in Chapter 6, "Domino and Windows 2000 clustering" on page 163.

Partitioned servers can share a single network interface card by using TCP/IP port mapping, which allows all partitioned servers on a single machine to use the same IP address for communication. This is achieved by allocating each Domino server its own TCP port. All protocols supported by Lotus Domino can be used with partitioned servers. Protocols other than TCP/IP do not require port mapping.

Windows 2000 allows you to define multiple IP addresses on one physical network adapter card, so you could, instead, dedicate an IP address for each server and avoid the problem of one server being a critical mapper for all the other partitioned servers. You could also install multiple network adapters, assigning each server to a particular adapter, which increases the overall bandwidth to the server. We discuss the advantages of port mapping and unique IP addresses in A.2, "TCP/IP configuration" on page 207.

One benefit of the partitioning feature is to improve the reliability of your applications. By running applications on their own partitioned Domino servers, you offer some protection in the event of a single Domino server or application failure, since an application running in one Domino partition should not be affected if another partition fails.

As we have already mentioned, you can take advantage of partitioned Domino servers for server consolidation. If you have a collection of small Domino servers, you can combine them to run on a single machine. Instead of purchasing, for example, four basic server systems with a standard SCSI disk subsystem, you could invest in a single, more powerful machine that includes a redundant disk subsystem and more memory, and install all four Domino servers on one physical server. The overall hardware expense is likely to be be lower than for the smaller systems. You also have the benefit of reduced administration costs, since there will be only one server to manage.

Domino partitioning is a particularly good option if your Domino servers are in different domains. However, there are also advantages to partitioning when

© Copyright IBM Corp. 1998, 2000

the servers are in the same domain. Even though there is some overhead in managing the additional address books (one per server) in this environment, there are performance advantages to be gained from running several servers rather than combining all servers into one large server on a single box. The distribution of the Domino server tasks, especially on SMP machines, can provide better processing of requests for Domino services, more parallel task execution, smaller mail delivery lists, smaller MAIL.BOX views, and a better distribution of the overhead for processes which must touch every database.

A.1 Installing partitioning

In this section we describe the procedures used to install partitioned Domino servers.

A.1.1 System requirements

Prior to installation, you should decide how many partitioned Domino servers you want to install on your hardware. The number of partitioned servers that you can install depends on the power and capacity of your available hardware.

Lotus recommends that you run partitioned servers on a multi-processor server. It is also recommended that you have at least one, or preferably two, processors for each partitioned Domino server that you plan to run on the system. The basic requirements for running a partitioned Domino server are the same as for a standard Domino server, with some exceptions as noted below. Section 2.3, "Planning cluster hardware" on page 21 provides more detailed information about planning hardware for your specific environment. The following are the additional general requirements provided by Lotus for partitioned servers:

- Add 100 MB of disk space for each additional partitioned server
- Use 128 MB of RAM for each partitioned server
- Configure each partitioned server to use TCP/IP

Additional information for your particular configuration can be obtained from your hardware vendor or at the NotesBench Consortium Web site:

`http://www.notesbench.org`

The NotesBench Consortium is an independent organization dedicated to providing Domino and Notes performance information to customers. Their site contains benchmark reports by various hardware vendors that may be of assistance to you when planning your system. There is also a good server planning tool called Server.Load that you may want to use to plan your hardware. This tool allows you to simulate workloads to obtain server capacity and response time information for your environment. It gives you the ability to evaluate the capacity of your existing servers or to assess planned configurations to determine their requirements for additional CPU and memory. You can download this tool at:

`http://www.lotus.com/itcentral`

A.1.2 Installing the first partitioned server

Installing partitioned servers is similar to installing a single server. Keep in mind that all partitioned servers share the same Domino program directory, but each partition has its own Domino data directory. You can install multiple partitioned servers during a single installation.

You can review basic Domino installation instructions in 4.3.1, "Installing the first Domino server" on page 84. To install multiple partitioned servers, follow these steps:

1. Run the Setup program and follow the directions in each window. Specify that you wish to install partitioned servers by checking **Partitioned Server Installation** in the dialog box following the License Agreement as shown in Figure 88 on page 205. Click **Next**.

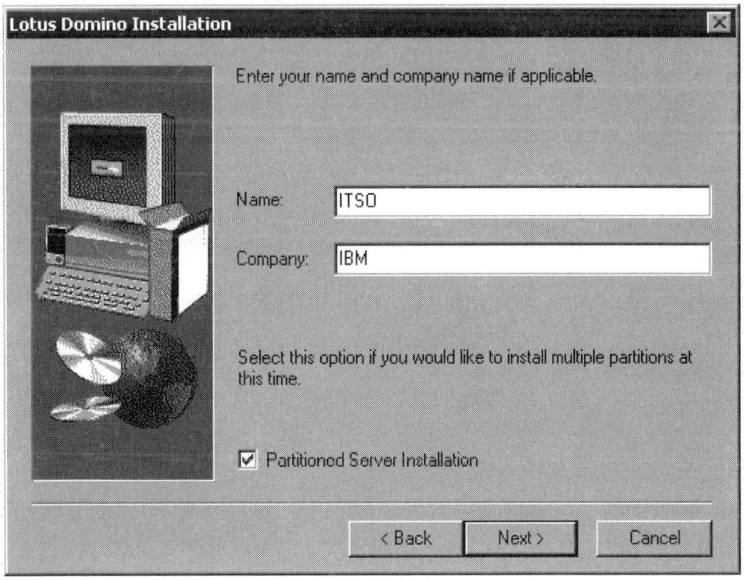

Figure 88. Partitioned server installation

2. Select the location for the Domino program files or accept the default location of C:\Lotus\Domino. All partitioned servers on this system will share the same program files. Click **Next**.
3. Select the type of Domino servers that you wish to install by clicking the appropriate radio button. You have a choice of Domino Application Server, Domino Mail Server, or Domino Enterprise Server.
4. If you wish to run Domino as a Windows service or change the Domino components that will be installed, click **Customize** and check/uncheck the relevant boxes.
5. Click **Next**.
6. Select the locations for the data directories for the individual partitioned servers. In Figure 89 we have selected two locations so that two separate partitioned Domino servers will be installed. Lotus suggests that you choose directory names to match the names of the partitioned servers. Click **Next**.

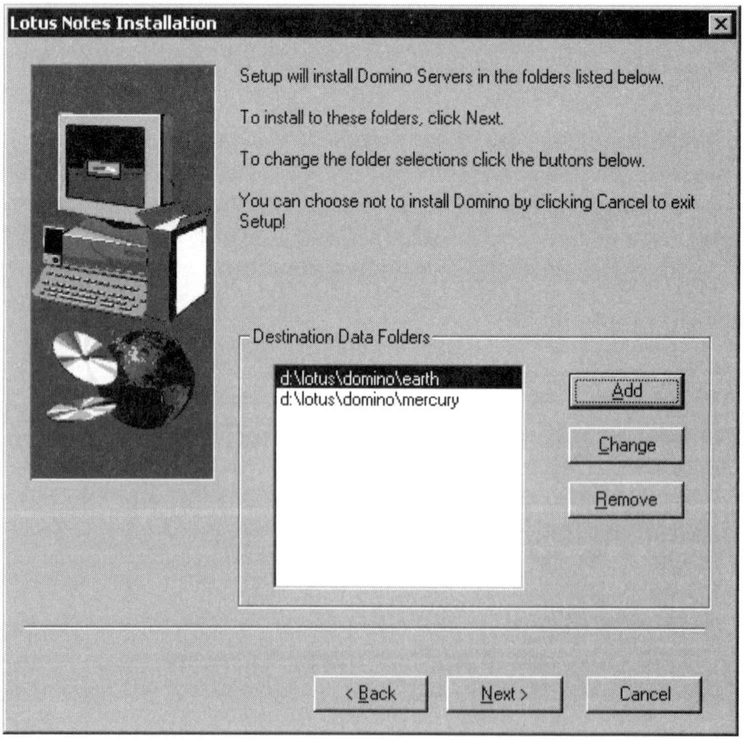

Figure 89. Selecting data directories for partitioned servers

7. Select a Program Folder for the Domino icons and click **Next** to install the software.
8. Click **Finish** to complete the software installation.

Having successfully installed the Domino software, you now need to configure each partitioned server's network settings for TCP/IP. This is covered in the next section. In addition, you need to configure each partitioned server to run the desired services, such as HTTP, IMAP, LDAP, NNTP, or POP3. Detailed instructions can be found in A.3, "Running HTTP and other Internet servers on partitioned servers" on page 210.

A.2 TCP/IP configuration

You can configure the IP settings on your partitioned servers in one of two ways. You can choose to assign a single IP address to the machine and use port mapping, or you can assign separate IP addresses to each partitioned server.

The advantage of using port mapping is that you only need to assign one IP address for the physical server. This is a major advantage if you have only a limited number of IP addresses available. If you want to assign unique IP addresses for each partitioned server, you either have to install multiple network adapters or configure multiple IP addresses for a single network adapter card.

A disadvantage of port mapping is that, if the mapping server is not running, clients cannot establish new connections to other servers running on the same physical machine. This does not affect active connections, which remain open if the port mapping server fails. Port mapping cannot be used if the partitioned servers need to appear in different IP networks; you must assign a unique IP address to each server.

Using multiple network adapters has the benefit of increasing the overall network bandwidth available to the server. Both port mapping and assigning multiple IP addresses to a single adapter can create a bottleneck, depending on the amount of network traffic the server has to handle.

A.2.1 Port mapping

Using port mapping, one IP address is assigned to the physical machine. You nominate one of the partitioned servers as the mapping server and it redirects connection requests to the other partitioned servers as necessary. Port mapping is configured by editing the NOTES.INI file on the server.

Every time a request for a new session on one of the partitioned servers is made, the connection is completed by using the port mapping server, using some system resources and computing time from the mapping server. You may, therefore, want to consider dedicating one partitioned server to handle only port mapping. To do this, remove all other server tasks, such as mail routing and replication, from the server's NOTES.INI file.

Port mapping only works for Notes clients, but you can configure your Domino server to use specific ports for communication when it receives requests for IMAP, LDAP, NNTP, and POP3 services. You can do this by assigning specific port numbers in the Server document in the Domino Directory. Keep in mind that you must make the port number available to clients when they attempt to establish a connection with the server. For example, if you were to assign port number 8080 to the Domino Web server (HTTP) for acme.com, the Web client would use the URL `http://acme.com:8080` to connect to that server.

The port mapping server listens to the standard Notes TCP port, 1352, and redirects the requests to the requested server, which is listening to a non-standard Notes TCP port address. You can select port addresses for the additional servers freely as long as no other application is using that port on the server. The SERVICES file in directory `\winnt\system32\drivers\etc` contains the registered port numbers, which should be avoided. Lotus recommends that you use port numbers 13520 to 13524 for the additional partitioned servers.

To enable port mapping, add these lines to the NOTES.INI file for the port mapping server. Include one line for the port mapping server and one line for each of the additional partitioned servers on the machine. For the port mapping server, enter:

```
TCPIP_TCPIPAddress=0,IPAddress:1352
```

where `TCPIP` is the port name (assigned in the `Port` entry of NOTES.INI), and `IPAddress` is the single IP address assigned to the physical server.

For each additional partitioned server, enter:

```
TCPIP_PortMapping00=CN=Server2/O=Org2,IPAddress:13520
TCPIP_PortMapping01=CN=Server3/O=Org3,IPAddress:13521
TCPIP_PortMapping02=CN=Server4/O=Org4,IPAddress:13522
TCPIP_PortMapping03=CN=Server5/O=Org5,IPAddress:13523
TCPIP_PortMapping04=CN=Server6/O=Org6,IPAddress:13524
```

where `TCPIP` is the port name (assigned in the `Port` entry of NOTES.INI), and `IPAddress` is the same IP address used previously. If you have to change the default port name or configure multiple TCP/IP ports, remember to change the values correspondingly.

The number at the end of each port mapping line defines the port number assigned to a specific partitioned server. For example, Server2/Org2 is assigned port 13520, and Server3/Org3 is assigned 13521.

The variables `TCPIP_PortMappingOn` must be assigned in ascending order, beginning with 00, and ending with the maximum number of 04. If there is a break in the sequence the subsequent entries will be ignored. By implication, a maximum of six partitioned servers can be supported by port mapping.

You now have to add a TCP/IP `port` entry to all of the other partitioned servers' NOTES.INI files. The format for the line is as follows:

```
TCPIP_TCPIPAddress=0,IPAddress:Port
```

where `TCPIP` is the port name, `IPAddress` is the IP address assigned for the Windows 2000 machine and Port is the port number the partitioned server listens on.

To complete the setup:

- In the Net Address field in the Server document for each partitioned server, enter the fully qualified domain name or the common server name for the partitioned server.
- Create a separate entry in DNS, WINS or the local hosts file for each partitioned server name.
- If you want to configure the partitioned servers to use HTTP, POP3, LDAP, IMAP, or NNTP services, assign each protocol a separate port number in the appropriate section on the Server document.

A.2.2 Unique IP addresses (non-port mapping)

Domino partitioned servers can also be assigned unique TCP/IP addresses. The advantage in assigning a unique IP address for each partitioned server is that the servers can be in either the same or different IP networks. If you are using port mapping then the servers are, by definition, using the same IP address and so belong to the same IP network.

To assign an IP address for a server, add the following setting into the server's NOTES.INI file:

```
TCPIP_TCPIPAddress=0,IPAddress:Port
```

where `TCPIP` is the port name used for the client connections (assigned in the `Port` entry of NOTES.INI) and `IPAddress` is the IP address assigned to the network interface the Domino server is using. The last parameter, `Port`, should be set to zero or the default Domino port, 1352. If the port is set to something other than 1352 or zero, clients will not be able to open connections to the server unless they are individually configured to use the correct port number.

Configuration is the same whether you have multiple IP addresses assigned to a single network adapter or the system has multiple adapters, each with its own address.

A.3 Running HTTP and other Internet servers on partitioned servers

When running Internet servers such as HTTP, POP3 and IMAP on partitioned servers, you need to perform some additional configuration steps if you intend to run these services on more than one partitioned server.

A.3.1 Configuration with unique IP addresses

If you are using a unique IP address for each server, you need to bind the host name with the HTTP server. Otherwise, all the HTTP servers would try to use the same host name and a conflict would occur. To make this binding, edit the Server document and enter the host name or IP address of the server in the Host name(s): field on the Internet Protocols-HTTP tab. Then select **Enabled** in the Bind to host name: field.

To configure other Internet services when using unique IP addresses, you need to edit the NOTES.INI file for each partitioned server. The following table defines the service name and the corresponding line to be added in the server's NOTES.INI file:

Table 12. Binding host names to services

Service	**NOTES.INI entry**
POP3 server	`POP3Address=hostname`
IMAP server	`IMAPAddress=hostname`
NNTP server	`NNTPAddress=hostname`
LDAP server	`LDAPAddress=hostname`

where `hostname` is the IP address or the fully qualified domain name of the server.

A.3.2 Configuration with port mapping

To assign unique port numbers to different Internet services such as HTTP, IMAP, LDAP, NNTP, and POP3, you need to define the port numbers in the respective Server document. Assign the port numbers in the "TCP/IP port number" field on the appropriate sections found by selecting the **Ports -> Internet Ports** tabs of the Server document.

Keep in mind that when you change the port number for a server, the same port number needs to be defined for the clients when opening connections. For example, if the assigned port number is 8080 for HTTP server acme.com, the client would open the connection by using the following URL:

```
http://acme.com:8080/
```

This applies to other servers as well. For example, if you are running POP3 server on more than one partitioned server, each POP3 server must be listening on a TCP port of its own and the clients must explicitly connect to that port.

A.4 Hints and tips for partitioning

The following section includes some hints and tips for Domino partitioned server installation and maintenance.

A.4.1 Installing partitioned servers as Windows 2000 services

Unlike earlier versions of Domino, which only installed a single Domino service, Lotus Domino R5 installs a service for each partitioned server. This means that all partitioned servers on a single system can be started without intervention. Achieving this used to require manual configuration and editing of the Windows Registry.

A.4.2 Server not responding

There are several problems that could cause the error message, `Server not responding`.

1. If the destination server is sharing a network interface card with a port mapper server, first check that the port mapper server (the listener) is running. You cannot establish a new connection to a server sharing the port mapper's network interface card (IP address), unless the port mapper is able to redirect the traffic to the port your destination server is listening on.

2. In the port mapper server's NOTES.INI file, there are entries that reference the other partitioned servers on that machine. If the lines containing the port mapping information are not working, you will get the error message `Server not responding` or `Server's name changed`. If the port numbers are incorrect, edit the port mapper's NOTES.INI file and make sure that the port mappers are listed in numerical order, as in the following example:

   ```
   TCPIP_PortMapping00=
   TCPIP_PortMapping01=
   TCPIP_PortMapping02=
   TCPIP_PortMapping03=
   ```

   After modifying the port mapper's NOTES.INI, you must shut down and restart the server for the changes to take effect.

3. Check the port mapper's NOTES.INI file. Make sure that the port number appended to the destination server's IP address matches the port number in the NOTES.INI of the destination server. Also, verify that the server name and organization are entered correctly in the port mapper's NOTES.INI. If changes to the NOTES.INI are required, you must shut down and restart the server whose NOTES.INI file you changed. The following lines show the typical NOTES.INI settings:

   In the port mapper's NOTES.INI (line that assigns the destination server's IP address and port number):

   ```
   TCPIP_PortMapping00=CN=Server1/O=Org1,130.103.40.26:13520
   ```

   In the destination server's NOTES.INI:

   ```
   TCPIP_TCPIPAddress=0,130.103.40.26:13520
   ```

A.5 Managing partitioned servers

This section highlights some useful tips that specifically relate to partitioned servers.

A.5.1 NOTES.INI settings for partitioned servers

If you have significant concurrent usage on your partitioned server and you are running into performance problems, use the `Server_Max_Concurrent_Trans` setting in the NOTES.INI file to limit the number of concurrently scheduled transactions for each server. Studies show that the optimal number of concurrent transactions when using Windows NT is 20. So, for example, if you have two partitioned servers on the system, set each partitioned server's `Server_Max_Concurrent_Trans` value to 10. Equivalent data for Windows 2000 is not yet available, so we suggest using the Windows NT figure as a starting point.

Limiting the number of concurrently scheduled transactions optimizes system resource utilization among the servers, thereby significantly improving performance of all the partitioned servers on the system.

To set the value, edit each server's NOTES.INI file to add the following entry:

```
Server_Max_Concurrent_Trans=<setting>
```

To limit the number of active users on a partitioned server, use the `Server_MaxUsers` setting in NOTES.INI. If this limit is reached, service is denied to any additional users of that partition.

To set the value, edit each server's NOTES.INI file to include this entry:

```
Server_MaxUsers=<setting>
```

We recommend that you also include the entry:

```
KillProcess=1
```

in each partitioned server's NOTES.INI to enable the shutdown procedure that cleans up a partitioned server's processes if it suffers an unplanned shutdown. This will allow one partitioned server to crash and be re-loaded without having to shut down the entire machine to restart the server.

In Release 5.04, support was added for a new NOTES.INI setting that allows administrators to limit the amount of physical memory allocated to each partition on the server. For example, to limit a specific partitioned server to use up to 65% of memory, add the following entry to its NOTES.INI file:

```
PercentAvailSysResources=65
```

Assuming there were two partitions on this particular system, the other server's NOTES.INI should contain this entry:

```
PercentAvailSysResources=35
```

The range for the variable is auto limited between 2 to 100. If this parameter is used then `NSF_Buffer_Pool_Size` should not be used unless advised by Lotus Support.

A.5.2 Monitoring partitioned servers

Monitoring a partitioned server is no different from monitoring a single Domino server. Partitioned servers include the same set of tools as a single Domino server.

What is important to remember is that a particular Domino partitioned server may be taking advantage of system resources and denying the resources to another partitioned server on the same system. For example, the indexer on one partitioned server may be taking a large percentage of the CPU cycles, resulting in another partitioned server providing a slower than usual response time to its users.

It is important to look at system resources along with Domino statistics to determine which partitioned server is using the system resources. Using the Windows 2000 Performance tool is an excellent way to monitor usage of operating system resources alongside Domino server statistics. When monitoring partitioned servers, you should monitor all of the partitioned servers on a single system as a group, to ensure that one server's effect on another's performance is taken into consideration.

A.5.3 Analyzing and optimizing

You use the same set of tools to analyze Domino partitioned servers that you would use to analyze the activities of a single Domino server.

Partitioned servers are monitored differently from single Domino servers. Keep in mind that the partitioned servers are sharing the resources of the same physical machine, so bad server performance on one partitioned server could be the result of a task on another partitioned server.

When analyzing server performance you should look past individual server statistics. Instead, look at system resources as a whole and then compare the statistics for each individual server. If you find that one server is using significant system resources, you may want to consider removing that partitioned server from the machine.

A.6 Partitioning within clustering

We have already seen, in 6.3.2, "Active-active configuration" on page 172, how partitioning can be effectively used in conjunction with Microsoft Cluster Services. Domino clusters can also be introduced into the partitioned server environment. Domino clustering of servers provides for increased server availability and scalability, and, when combined with the cost-effective server administration and hardware consolidation provided by partitioning servers, it provides another option for an efficient Domino server environment.

Note that although you could theoretically create a cluster of partitioned servers on a single machine, we do not recommend this, nor is it supported. Doing so would, anyway, defeat the purpose of clustering, as a failure of the physical system would cause the loss of all cluster members.

Instead, if you have a machine with partitioned servers, and server availability is a high priority, consider clustering all or some of the partitioned servers on another machine running partitioned servers.

For example, suppose you have a machine, Machine1, that has four partitioned servers, ServerA, ServerB, ServerC and ServerD. It is determined that the data on one or some of these servers is important and they are therefore introduced into a clustered Domino environment to increase the availability of these important databases.

Add a new machine, Machine2, with four partitioned servers, ServerW, ServerX, ServerY and ServerZ and build clusters as follows:

- Cluster ServerA on Machine1 with ServerW on Machine2
- Cluster ServerB on Machine1 with ServerX on Machine2
- Cluster ServerC on Machine1 with ServerY on Machine2
- Cluster ServerD on Machine1 with ServerZ on Machine2

You should make sure that both servers in a single cluster are not the port mappers for their respective sibling partitions. Instead, assign the port mappers to different clusters. Otherwise, for example, if ServerA and ServerW are both port-mapping servers that belong to the same cluster and an application that is running within this cluster is causing server problems, you have the potential of making all eight servers unavailable.

Another possibility is to cluster only a subset of the partitioned servers:

- Cluster ServerA on Machine1 with ServerW on Machine2
- Cluster ServerB on Machine1 with ServerX on Machine2
- Do not cluster ServerC or ServerD

For the clustered servers, you may want to consider having the users primarily access ServerW and ServerX because they are a group of two partitioned servers and ServerA and ServerB are in a group of four partitioned servers. This is assuming ServerW and ServerX make better use of resources because they belong to a partition of two servers.

To force users to use ServerW and ServerX, put ServerA and ServerB in the Busy state and this will make users fail over to ServerW and ServerX. If ServerW or ServerX experience problems, the users will fail over to ServerA and ServerB. Remember, if the only available server is a Busy server, the user will be allowed access.

Appendix B. Tuning Domino clusters

You can determine how your cluster is performing by viewing cluster statistics, and adjusting your cluster settings for optimal performance. You can also view transaction logging statistics and Internet Cluster Manager statistics to further optimize your cluster's performance. In this appendix you will find information to help you fine-tune your cluster.

B.1 Cluster statistics

There are different types of statistics parameters related to clustering. These include NOTES.INI variables, fields in the server document, and Administration Process tasks. All of the statistics parameters on your server can be viewed by typing the following command at the server console:

```
show statistic
```

or its short form:

```
sh stat
```

You can do this from the remote console in the Domino Administrator client. Use the live console mode, as shown in Figure 90 on page 218, to see the statistics parameters immediately.

© Copyright IBM Corp. 1998, 2000

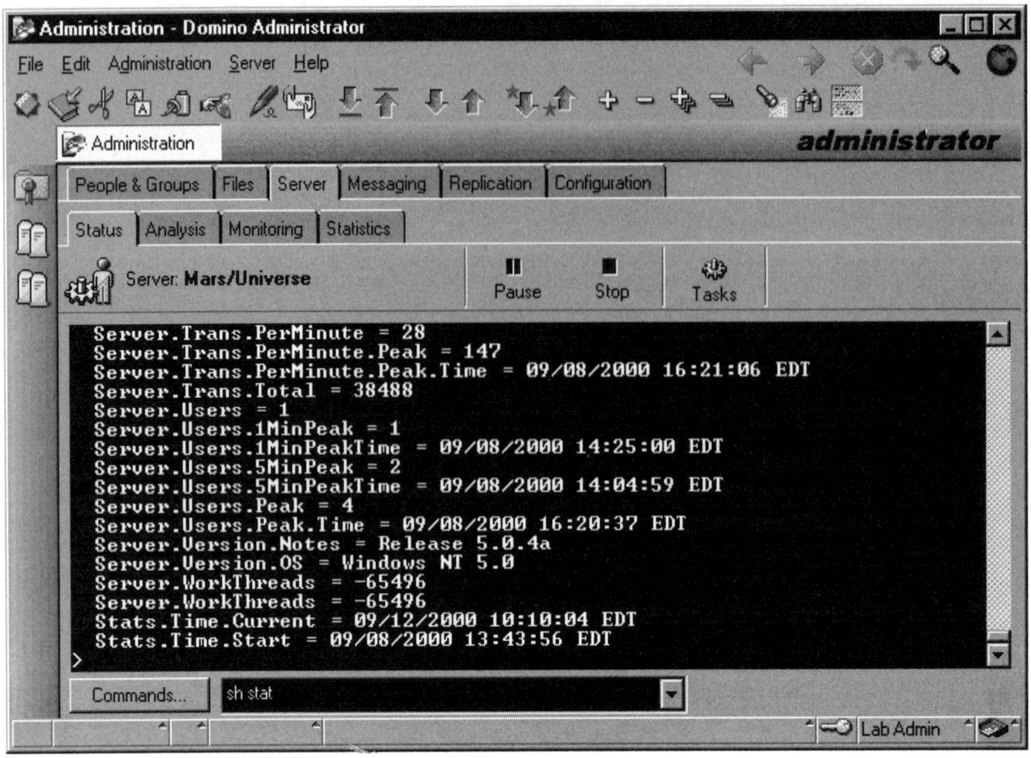

Figure 90. Show statistic command

You can also type this command at the server console and then view the results in the Notes log database (LOG.NSF). The `show statistic` command returns a large amount of information, so you may want to view the log entry for this command to perform a more detailed analysis of the results.

Some of these settings are recorded on a hourly basis in the Statistics Reports database (STATREP.NSF). Cluster-related statistics can be viewed in the Statistics Reports - Clusters view.

You can also view all statistics for your servers, including cluster-related statistics, in the Domino Administrator client. To view the statistics, select the **Server -> Statistics** tabs in the Administrator client, as shown in Figure 91:

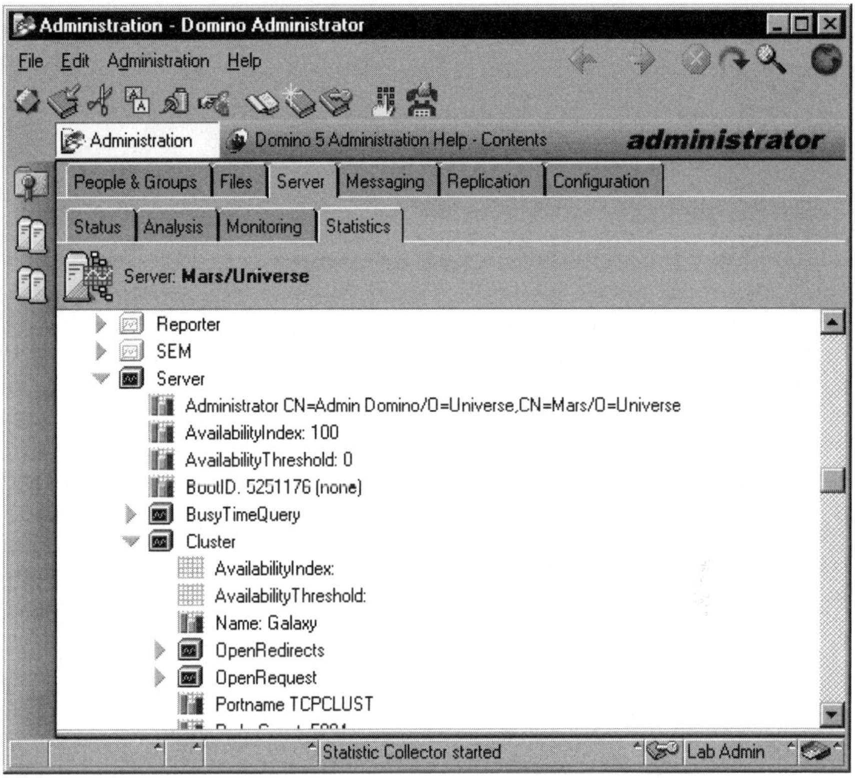

Figure 91. Server -> Statistics tabs in the Domino Administrator client

This windows allows you to view various server statistics quickly and easily. Since all server statistics are displayed in this section, the Statistics tab is a good tool to use when you need to gather a variety of information about your server's performance quickly.

B.2 Statistics variables descriptions

There are different types of cluster statistics parameters. Server.Cluster and Replica.Cluster statistics relate to Domino clustering. Statistics beginning with ICM relate to the Internet Cluster Manager. There are many other parameters available. For details, review the Domino Administrator help database, shipped with the product. In this section we list some of the most useful, along with their descriptions.

- Server.AvailabilityIndex

  Shows the current percentage or index of a server's availability. The value may range from 0-100, inclusive, where zero (0) indicates the server has virtually no available resources, and 100 indicates that the server is essentially idle. This statistic was called Server.Cluster.AvailabilityIndex in Release 4.

- Server.AvailabilityThreshold

  Shows the current setting of a server's availability threshold. The value is compared against the value of the Server.AvailabilityIndex. If the availability index drops below the threshold, the server enters the Busy state. This statistic was called Server.Cluster.AvailabilityThreshold in Release 4.

- Server.Cluster.Member.<ServerName>.Index

  There is one instance of this parameter for each server in the cluster. It shows the availability index between 0 and 100 if the server is in the Available state, or the cluster state of each cluster member.

- Server.Cluster.Name

  Shows the name of the cluster in which this server is participating, if any.

- Server.Cluster.OpenRedirects.FailoverByPath.Successful

  Shows the number of times that this server was able to redirect a client to another cluster member after the client was unable to open a database by path name on a cluster member.

- Server.Cluster.OpenRedirects.FailoverByPath.Unsuccessful

  Shows the number of times that this server was not able to redirect a client to another cluster member after the client was unable to open a database by path name on a cluster member.

  This is an important statistic to monitor when determining if replica copies of databases should be added to other cluster members.

- Server.Cluster.OpenRedirects.Failover.Successful

  Shows the number of times that this server was able to redirect a client to another cluster member after the client was unable to open a database by replica ID on a cluster member.

- Server.Cluster.OpenRedirects.Failover.Unsuccessful

  Shows the number of times that this server was unable to redirect a client to another cluster member after the client was unable to open a database by replica ID on this cluster member.

This is an important statistic to monitor when determining if replica copies of databases should be added to other cluster members.

- Server.Cluster.OpenRedirects.LoadBalanceByPath.Successful

  Shows the number of times that this server was able to redirect a client to another cluster member after the client attempted to open a database by path name on this cluster member while it was in the Busy state.

- Server.Cluster.OpenRedirects.LoadBalanceByPath.Unsuccessful

  Shows the number of times that this server was unable to redirect a client to another cluster member after the client attempted to open a database by path name on this cluster member while it was in the Busy state.

  This is an important statistic to monitor when determining if replica copies of databases should be added to other cluster members or when adjusting the server availability index.

- Server.Cluster.OpenRedirects.LoadBalance.Successful

  Shows the number of times that this server was able to redirect a client to another cluster member after the client attempted to open a database by replica ID on this cluster member while it was in the Busy state.

- Server.Cluster.OpenRedirects.LoadBalance.Unsuccessful

  Shows the number of times that this server was unable to redirect a client to another cluster member after the client attempted to open a database by replica ID on this cluster member while it was in the Busy state.

  When this occurs, this cluster member will open the database even though it is in the Busy state.

  This is an important statistic to monitor when determining if replica copies of databases should be added to other cluster members or when adjusting the server availability index.

- Server.Cluster.OpenRequest.ClusterBusy

  Shows the number of times that a client attempted to open a database on this cluster member when it was in the Busy state, as well as every other available member of the cluster.

  This is an important statistic to monitor when determining if servers should be added to your cluster or when adjusting the server availability index.

- Server.Cluster.OpenRequest.DatabaseOutOfService

  Shows the number of times that a client attempted to open a database that has been marked as out of service on this cluster member.

This is a useful statistic to monitor when determining if users are attempting to access a database that is marked out of service.

- Server.Cluster.OpenRequest.LoadBalanced

  Shows the number of times a client attempted to open a database on this cluster member when it was in the Busy state.

  This is a useful statistic to monitor when determining if your server is utilizing the cluster functionality.

- Server.Cluster.PortName

  Shows the name of the default port being used for intra-cluster network traffic. An asterisk (*) indicates that there is no default port and that any available and active port could be used for intra-cluster traffic.

- Server.Cluster.ProbeCount

  Shows the number of times that this cluster member has completed a probe request of one of the cluster members.

- Server.Cluster.ProbeError

  Shows the number of times that this cluster member has received an error when probing another cluster member.

- Server.Cluster.ProbeTimeout(mins)

  Shows the interval at which the intra-cluster probe or cluster member heartbeat occurs.

  By default the interval is one minute (60 seconds), but this is tunable by setting the `Server_Cluster_Probe_Timeout` parameter in NOTES.INI.

- Server.OpenRequest.MaxUsers

  Shows the number of times that a client has attempted to open a database on this server when the server was at its MaxUsers limit.

  This is a useful statistic to monitor when determining the number of workload requests to your server.

- Server.OpenRequest.PreV4Client

  Shows the number of times that Notes R3 (or earlier) clients attempted to open a database on this server.

- Server.OpenRequest.Restricted

  Shows the number of times that a client has attempted to open a database on this server when the server was in the Restricted state.

  This is a useful statistic to monitor when determining the number of workload requests to your server.

- Server.OpenRequest.V4Client

  Shows the number of times that Notes R4 (or later) clients attempted to open a database on this server.

- Replica.Cluster.Docs.Added

  Shows the number of new documents pushed to other replicas by the Cluster Replicator.

- Replica.Cluster.Docs.Deleted

  Shows the number of document deletions pushed to other replicas by the Cluster Replicator.

- Replica.Cluster.Docs.Updated

  Shows the number of document updates pushed to other replicas by the Cluster Replicator.

- Replica.Cluster.Failed

  Shows the number of failed replications that have occurred since server startup. A failure can occur when the target server is not started, or when there is an error with a specific database such as an access control list preventing access by this server.

  To gather more information on specific failures, the Replication Events log entries recorded by the Cluster Replicator should be examined. See also Replica.Cluster. Retry.Skipped and Replica.Cluster.Retry.Waiting.

- Replica.Cluster.Files.Local

  Shows the number of databases on this server that are being replicated to other servers in the cluster through cluster replication. If this number appears to be lower or higher than expected, examine the Cluster Database Directory (CLDBDIR.NSF) to see which local databases have replicas on other servers in the cluster. Also, remember that cluster replication can be disabled for specific databases in the Cluster Database Directory. This statistic will not count any local database for which cluster replication has been disabled.

- Replica.Cluster.Files.Remote

  Shows the number of replicas on other servers in the cluster that are receiving changes through cluster replication from this server. If this number appears to be lower or higher than expected, examine the Cluster Database Directory (CLDBDIR.NSF) to see which remote databases are replicas of local databases.

- Replica.Cluster.Retry.Skipped

  Shows the number of times the Cluster Replicator had database modifications to replicate, but did not attempt to replicate them because the destination server was known to be unreachable or the database was waiting for another retry attempt. See also Replica.Cluster.Failed and Replica.Cluster.Retry.Waiting.

- Replica.Cluster.Retry.Waiting

  Shows the number of replicas that are waiting for retry attempts at the current time. See also Replica.Cluster.Retry.Skipped and Replica.Cluster.Failed.

- Replica.Cluster.SecondsOnQueue

  Shows the amount of time in seconds that the last database replicated spent on the Cluster Replicator's work queue before being replicated to other servers. This statistic can be an important indicator of the ability of the Cluster Replicator to keep up with modifications being made to local databases. Since the Cluster Replicator checks its work queue every 15 seconds, a value of less than 15 would normally be seen under a light workload. As the number of databases being modified increases, or the time it takes to replicate to remote servers increases, this value may rise as a backlog of work develops. If the value is consistently more than 30 seconds, you may benefit from the addition of another Cluster Replicator task to help reduce the backlog.

- Replica.Cluster.SecondsOnQueue.Avg

  Shows the average amount of time in seconds that modified databases spent on the Cluster Replicator's work queue before being replicated to other servers. See also Replica.Cluster.SecondsOnQueue.

- Replica.Cluster.SecondsOnQueue.Max

  Shows the maximum number of time in seconds that a modified database spent on the Cluster Replicator's work queue before being replicated to other servers. Note that a large value here doesn't necessarily warrant the addition of more Cluster Replicator tasks, since it is a recording of the highest value seen since server startup. This value is not reset when you increase the number of Cluster Replicator tasks, so this statistic may represent a value seen before the addition of Cluster Replicator tasks. See also Replica.Cluster.SecondsOnQueue.

- Replica.Cluster.Servers

  Shows the number of other servers in the cluster that are receiving changes through cluster replication from this server.

This value does not include the local server. If this value is lower or higher than expected, examine the Cluster Database Directory to see which servers contain replicas of local databases.

- Replica.Cluster.SessionBytes.In

  Shows the total number of bytes received while performing cluster replication.

  This is a useful statistic to monitor when determining the network traffic due to cluster replication.

- Replica.Cluster.SessionBytes.Out

  Shows the total number of bytes sent while performing cluster replication.

  This is a useful statistic to monitor when determining the network traffic due to cluster replication.

- Replica.Cluster.Successful

  Shows the number of successful cluster replications that have occurred since server startup.

- Replica.Cluster.WorkQueueDepth

  Shows the current number of modified databases that the Cluster Replicator needs to replicate to the other servers in the cluster. If this number is consistently greater than zero, additional Cluster Replicator task instances may help to bring the number down by increasing replication throughput. See also Replica.Cluster.SecondsOnQueue.

  This is an important statistic to monitor when determining if additional CLREPL tasks should be added to your server.

- Replica.Cluster.WorkQueueDepth.Avg

  Shows the average work queue depth since the server has started. See also Replica.Cluster.WorkQueueDepth.

- Replica.Cluster.WorkQueueDepth.Max

  Shows the highest work queue depth since the server has started. See also Replica.Cluster.WorkQueueDepth.

- ICM.AvailabilityIndex

  Shows the current measure or index of a server's availability. Zero (0) indicates no available resources. 100 indicates that the server is essentially idle.

- ICM.Command.Total

  Indicates the number of URL commands that the ICM has received.

- ICM.Command.Unknown

  Shows the number of URL commands that the ICM did not recognize.

- ICM.Receive.Error

  Shows the number of times that the ICM could not process a client request because of a communication problem between the client and the ICM.

- ICM.Command.Redirects.Successful

  Indicates the number of times the ICM successfully redirected a client URL request to a cluster member.

- ICM.Command.Redirects.Unsuccessful

  Shows the number of times that the ICM could not redirect a client URL request to a cluster member.

- ICM.Command.Redirects.ClusterBusy

  Indicates the number of times that the ICM received a client request when all servers in the cluster were in the Busy state.

- ICM.Requests.Per1Hour.Total

  Shows the number of HTTP requests that the ICM received in the past hour.

- ICM.Requests.Per1Minute.Total

  Shows the number of HTTP requests that the ICM received in the past minute.

- ICM.Requests.Per5Minutes.Total

  Shows the number of HTTP requests that the ICM received in the past five minutes.

B.3 Adjusting settings on clustered servers

There are several settings that you can adjust on your servers to improve cluster performance. You should view the statistics for your cluster prior to changing any settings, and adjust the settings accordingly. You should also monitor other server statistics that are not related to clustering. Periodically reviewing and adjusting your servers will ensure that you provide the highest level of availability and the best server performance for your users. Keep in mind that if your original server configuration was not sized correctly, you may need to make adjustments to your hardware to notice any appreciable improvement in performance.

The two NOTES.INI variables that help to make cluster failover run smoothly are Server_Availability_Threshold and Server_TransInfo_Normalize. These parameters help the Domino server anticipate the point at which it should start denying new user connections, prior to its reaching the maximum level of connections. This ensures that currently connected users get good response times, and new connections, once redirected to a less busy server in the cluster, will also have good response times.

The Server_Availability_Threshold parameter is directly related to the server statistic Server.AvailabilityIndex. When this statistic reaches the threshold set in the Server_Availability_Threshold parameter, new connection requests are rejected. Setting this threshold high (between 95 and 97) may help ensure smooth failover.

To further tune your cluster failover, the Server_Transinfo_Normalize parameter should be set. This parameter helps create more consistent response times and will ensure that failover processing will only occur when it is actually necessary. You can tune this variable to suit your clustered environment.

Since it is difficult to predict database growth rates, user count increases, and other configuration changes that often occur in the real world, checking your cluster's statistics and adjusting the parameters accordingly is the best way to maintain consistent high availability and good server performance.

Appendix C. NOTES.INI variables

This appendix lists the NOTES.INI parameters related to clustering and partitioning settings. Many of these settings can be configured using the Domino Administrator graphical user interface. Those that cannot, can be modified in the NOTES.INI Settings tab of the Configuration document in the Domino Directory.

C.1 NOTES.INI entries relevant to Domino clusters

- `Log_Replication`

  Controls the logging level of cluster replication and standard Notes replication events. Values of 0 through 4 result in increasingly more information being logged.

  0: Do not log replication events
  1: Log that a database is replicating
  2: Log summary information about each database
  3: Log information about each replicated document (both design and data documents)
  4: Log information about each replicated field

  There is no default value.

- `Log_Sessions`

  Specifies whether individual sessions are recorded in the log file and displayed on the console:

  0: Do not log individual sessions
  1: Log individual sessions

  There is no default value.

- `MailClusterFailover`

  This setting was introduced in Domino R4 and it is still necessary to set it on all Domino R4 mail servers in your domain. When set to 1, it enables Mail Router to fail over and delivers mail to the replica copy of the mail file while the home mail server is unavailable.

  In Domino R5, cluster failover is enabled for the last hop by default. If you want to disable it or enable it for all transfers in domain, you should modify the Configuration document in the Domino Directory **Router/SMTP -> Advanced -> Controls -> Additional Controls** section.

© Copyright IBM Corp. 1998, 2000

- `RTR_Logging`

  Monitors activity of the Cluster Replicator when set to 1.

- `Server_Cluster_Default_Port`

  Specifies the port used for intra-cluster network traffic. This variable is used to set the port for cluster replication.

- `Server_Cluster_Probe_Port`

  Specifies the port used for probing server members in the cluster.

- `Server_Cluster_On`

  Controls whether the Cluster Manager is enabled (1) or disabled (0) on a server in a cluster. This variable is updated during cluster addition or cluster deletion. This variable should not be modified manually; it is the AdminP process that modifies it when you move a server in or out of a cluster, since it changes the Cluster Name field in the Server document in a Domino Directory.

- `Server_MaxUsers`

  Restricts the number of active users accessing a server to the specified number of users. If set to 0, the number of users is unlimited.

  Use the `Server_MaxUsers` setting to specify the maximum number of user sessions allowed on a server. When the server reaches this limit, the server goes into a MaxUsers state. The Cluster Manager then attempts to redirect new user requests to other servers in the cluster.

  To see how often requests are being redirected, check the log file for failover events. If redirection of the user request is unsuccessful, the user receives a message, and is not allowed access to the server.

  You can use the `Server_MaxUsers` setting for any Domino server. This setting is not restricted to cluster members.

- `Server_Availability_Threshold`

  Helps you balance the workload across the cluster servers. This variable is set by the Domino administrator. If the `Server_Availability_Index` is less than the `Server_Availability_Threshold` the server will enter the Busy state.

  The `Server_Availability_Threshold` setting lets you specify the maximum availability level beyond which the server attempts to redirect new user requests to other servers in the cluster, and works in the following way. A server's availability index is recalculated each minute and compared against the threshold value set. If the index falls below the server threshold, the server becomes Busy. The Cluster Manager redirects access requests from a Busy server to other servers in the cluster. If the attempt to redirect is unsuccessful, the user receives access to the Busy server.

A `Server_Availability_Threshold` value of zero (0) indicates a fully available state and workload balancing is disabled. A `Server_Availability_Threshold` value of 100 indicates the server is Busy, since the availability index can never be greater than 100.

The server's availability index is derived from the ratio between the current response time and the response time in optimum conditions (with no Domino transactions). Response times taken into account are server-based and do not include any consideration for network time. The Cluster Manager process on each server monitors the average response time of a set of server operations over approximately the last 75 seconds.

- `Server_MaxSessions`

  Specifies the maximum number of sessions that can run concurrently on the server. You can use the `Server_Maxsessions` setting for any Domino server, but it is particularly useful for workload balancing.

- `Server_Restricted`

  Restricts access to the server when set to 1 or 2. If set to 0, the server is unrestricted. If set to 1 or 2, the server enters the restricted state. If set to 1, once the server is rebooted this variable is set to 0; if set to 2 the server will stay restricted until this variable is manually modified.

  The `Server_Restricted` setting enables a server to deny new open database requests. Users with active connections to databases retain their connections. The Cluster Manager attempts to redirect new requests to other servers in the cluster. When an attempt to redirect is unsuccessful, the user receives a message and is not allowed access to the server. For each redirection attempt, Domino generates a failover event in the log file.

  You can use the `Server_Restricted` setting for any Domino server. This setting is not restricted to clusters.

- `ServerTasks`

  Contains the list of server add-in tasks to run at server startup. For a clustered server, it should contain one instance of CLDBDIR and one or more instances of CLREPL. These tasks are added or removed during cluster addition or cluster deletion. If you start a task manually (for example an additional Cluster Replicator) and decide you wish to run it permanently, be sure to update the ServerTasks setting in NOTES.INI. If edited manually, make sure all CLREPL tasks are listed after the CLDBDIR task as the Cluster Replicator relies on information provided by the Cluster Directory Manager.

- `Server_TransInfo_Max`

  Controls the number of update intervals that are factored into the load balance computation. The default value is 5.

- `Server_TransInfo_Normalize`

  Domino server uses this setting when calculating the server availability index to “normalize” the response times observed at the server. It divides the observed response times by this value. This setting was undocumented prior to Domino R4.6.

  For the availability index calculation to work properly, the normalize value should be approximately equal to 100 times the average Domino transaction time in milliseconds. The default value is 3000, corresponding to an average response time of 30 ms per transaction. This default value was appropriate for “the average system” when clustering was first shipped several years ago, but it is too large for the current generation of servers. You should use a lower normalize value with today’s faster servers.

- `Server_TransInfo_Update_Interval`

  Controls how frequently (in seconds) the load balance data is recomputed. The default value is 15.

- `<TCPIP Port Name>_TCPIPAddress=0,a.b.c.d:1352`

  The IP address a.b.c.d must be the same that is set in the server’s Server document in the Domino Directory, found by clicking the **Ports -> Notes Network Ports** tabs for the specified port name.

  Our recommendation is to install and configure two network adapters in each Domino server in a cluster. Then you can dedicate one of them for client-to-server traffic and the other for intra-cluster traffic.

- `<TCPIP Port Name>_PortMappingNN=CN=servername /O=organization, IPAddress:TCP/IP portnumber`

  This parameter is used only for partitioned servers using TCP/IP port mapping. It specifies the TCP/IP port number of each partitioned server sharing the IP address of the port mapper server. This entry is valid only in the NOTES.INI file of the port mapper server. Currently supported values for NN are 00 to 04. Numbers must be assigned in ascending order, because an invalid break in the number sequence causes subsequent entries in the NOTES.INI file to be ignored. TCPIP is the name of the TCP port. For example:

```
TCPIP_PortMapping00=CN=Sun/O=Universe,192.168.148.101:13520
TCPIP_PortMapping01=CN=Mars/O=Universe,192.168.148.101:13521
TCPIP_PortMapping02=CN=Venus/O=Universe,192.168.148.101:13522
```

The last number in this setting is the port number assigned to each partitioned server. This number must be an available number, as specified in Assigned Numbers RFC 1340.

Appendix D. Special notices

This publication is intended to help Domino implementors and administrators to design, plan, install and manage clusters of Domino servers running on Windows 2000 and Linux. The information in this publication is not intended as the specification of any programming interfaces that are provided by Lotus Domino Server, Microsoft Windows 2000, or Linux.

References in this publication to IBM products, programs or services do not imply that IBM intends to make these available in all countries in which IBM operates. Any reference to an IBM product, program, or service is not intended to state or imply that only IBM's product, program, or service may be used. Any functionally equivalent program that does not infringe any of IBM's intellectual property rights may be used instead of the IBM product, program or service.

Information in this book was developed in conjunction with use of the equipment specified, and is limited in application to those specific hardware and software products and levels.

IBM may have patents or pending patent applications covering subject matter in this document. The furnishing of this document does not give you any license to these patents. You can send license inquiries, in writing, to the IBM Director of Licensing, IBM Corporation, North Castle Drive, Armonk, NY 10504-1785.

Licensees of this program who wish to have information about it for the purpose of enabling: (i) the exchange of information between independently created programs and other programs (including this one) and (ii) the mutual use of the information which has been exchanged, should contact IBM Corporation, Dept. 600A, Mail Drop 1329, Somers, NY 10589 USA.

Such information may be available, subject to appropriate terms and conditions, including in some cases, payment of a fee.

The information contained in this document has not been submitted to any formal IBM test and is distributed AS IS. The use of this information or the implementation of any of these techniques is a customer responsibility and depends on the customer's ability to evaluate and integrate them into the customer's operational environment. While each item may have been reviewed by IBM for accuracy in a specific situation, there is no guarantee that the same or similar results will be obtained elsewhere. Customers attempting to adapt these techniques to their own environments do so at their own risk.

© Copyright IBM Corp. 1998, 2000

Any pointers in this publication to external Web sites are provided for convenience only and do not in any manner serve as an endorsement of these Web sites.

The following terms are trademarks of the International Business Machines Corporation in the United States and/or other countries:

AIX	S/390
AS/400	ServeRAID
DB2	ServerProven
e (logo)® @	SP
IBM ®	System/390
Netfinity	TechConnect
Netfinity Manager	WorkPad
OS/2	Lotus
OS/390	cc:Mail
Redbooks	Lotus Notes
Redbooks Logo	Domino
RS/6000	Notes

The following terms are trademarks of other companies:

Tivoli, Manage. Anything. Anywhere.,The Power To Manage., Anything. Anywhere.,TME, NetView, Cross-Site, Tivoli Ready, Tivoli Certified, Planet Tivoli, and Tivoli Enterprise are trademarks or registered trademarks of Tivoli Systems Inc., an IBM company, in the United States, other countries, or both. In Denmark, Tivoli is a trademark licensed from Kjøbenhavns Sommer - Tivoli A/S.

C-bus is a trademark of Corollary, Inc. in the United States and/or other countries.

Java and all Java-based trademarks and logos are trademarks or registered trademarks of Sun Microsystems, Inc. in the United States and/or other countries.

Microsoft, Windows, Windows NT, and the Windows logo are trademarks of Microsoft Corporation in the United States and/or other countries.

PC Direct is a trademark of Ziff Communications Company in the United States and/or other countries and is used by IBM Corporation under license.

ActionMedia, LANDesk, MMX, Pentium and ProShare are trademarks of Intel Corporation in the United States and/or other countries.

UNIX is a registered trademark in the United States and other countries licensed exclusively through The Open Group.

SET, SET Secure Electronic Transaction, and the SET Logo are trademarks owned by SET Secure Electronic Transaction LLC.

Other company, product, and service names may be trademarks or service marks of others.

Appendix E. Related publications

The publications listed in this section are considered particularly suitable for a more detailed discussion of the topics covered in this redbook.

E.1 IBM Redbooks

For information on ordering these publications see "How to get IBM Redbooks" on page 241.

- *Netfinity Server Disk Subsystems*, SG24-2098
- *Tuning Netfinity Servers for Performance*, SG24-5287 (PDF file only. Hard copy available as ISBN 0-13-040612-0)
- *Netfinity and Domino R5.0 Integration Guide*, SG24-5313
- *Lotus Domino R5 for Linux on IBM Netfinity Servers,* SG24-5968
- *IBM @server xSeries Clustering Planning Guide*, SG24-5845
- *Red Hat Linux and Netfinity Server Integration Guide,* SG24-5853
- *Netfinity and Caldera OpenLinux Integration Guide*, SG24-5861
- *Netfinity and TurboLinux Integration Guide*, SG24-5862
- *Netfinity and SuSE Linux Integration Guide*, SG24-5863

E.2 IBM Redbooks collections

Redbooks are also available on the following CD-ROMs. Click the CD-ROMs button at ibm.com/redbooks for information about all the CD-ROMs offered, updates and formats.

CD-ROM Title	Collection Kit Number
IBM System/390 Redbooks Collection	SK2T-2177
IBM Networking Redbooks Collection	SK2T-6022
IBM Transaction Processing and Data Management Redbooks Collection	SK2T-8038
IBM Lotus Redbooks Collection	SK2T-8039
Tivoli Redbooks Collection	SK2T-8044
IBM AS/400 Redbooks Collection	SK2T-2849
IBM Netfinity Hardware and Software Redbooks Collection	SK2T-8046
IBM RS/6000 Redbooks Collection	SK2T-8043
IBM Application Development Redbooks Collection	SK2T-8037
IBM Enterprise Storage and Systems Management Solutions	SK3T-3694

© Copyright IBM Corp. 1998, 2000

E.3 Referenced Web sites

These Web sites are also relevant as further information sources:

- `http://www.support.lotus.com` Lotus support
- `http://www.lotus.com/itcentral` Load.Planner tool
- `http://www.microsoft.com` Microsoft
- `http://www.microsoft.com/hcl` Microsoft hardware compatibility list
- `http://www.microsoft.com/technet/win2000/clustep.asp` Microsoft clustering information
- `http://www.microsoft.com/technet/win2000/win2ksrv/technote/clustsrv.asp` Microsoft clustering information
- `http://www.notesbench.org` NotesBench Consortium
- `http://www.notes.net` Domino technical information
- `http://www.pc.ibm.com/us/eserver/xseries/index.html` IBM xSeries and Netfinity servers
- `http://www.pc.ibm.com/ww/eserver/xseries/clustering/index.html` IBM clustering information
- `http://www.pc.ibm.com/us/compat/nos/ms.shtml` IBM ServerProven compatibility list

How to get IBM Redbooks

This section explains how both customers and IBM employees can find out about IBM Redbooks, redpieces, and CD-ROMs. A form for ordering books and CD-ROMs by fax or e-mail is also provided.

- **Redbooks Web Site ibm.com/redbooks**

  Search for, view, download, or order hardcopy/CD-ROM Redbooks from the Redbooks Web site. Also read redpieces and download additional materials (code samples or diskette/CD-ROM images) from this Redbooks site.

  Redpieces are Redbooks in progress; not all Redbooks become redpieces and sometimes just a few chapters will be published this way. The intent is to get the information out much quicker than the formal publishing process allows.

- **E-mail Orders**

  Send orders by e-mail including information from the IBM Redbooks fax order form to:

	e-mail address
In United States or Canada	pubscan@us.ibm.com
Outside North America	Contact information is in the "How to Order" section at this site: http://www.elink.ibmlink.ibm.com/pbl/pbl

- **Telephone Orders**

United States (toll free)	1-800-879-2755
Canada (toll free)	1-800-IBM-4YOU
Outside North America	Country coordinator phone number is in the "How to Order" section at this site: http://www.elink.ibmlink.ibm.com/pbl/pbl

- **Fax Orders**

United States (toll free)	1-800-445-9269
Canada	1-403-267-4455
Outside North America	Fax phone number is in the "How to Order" section at this site: http://www.elink.ibmlink.ibm.com/pbl/pbl

This information was current at the time of publication, but is continually subject to change. The latest information may be found at the Redbooks Web site.

IBM Intranet for Employees

IBM employees may register for information on workshops, residencies, and Redbooks by accessing the IBM Intranet Web site at http://w3.itso.ibm.com/ and clicking the ITSO Mailing List button. Look in the Materials repository for workshops, presentations, papers, and Web pages developed and written by the ITSO technical professionals; click the Additional Materials button. Employees may access MyNews at http://w3.ibm.com/ for redbook, residency, and workshop announcements.

© Copyright IBM Corp. 1998, 2000

IBM Redbooks fax order form

Please send me the following:

Title	Order Number	Quantity

First name　　Last name

Company

Address

City　　Postal code　　Country

Telephone number　　Telefax number　　VAT number

☐ Invoice to customer number ______________________

☐ Credit card number ______________________

Credit card expiration date　　Card issued to　　Signature

We accept American Express, Diners, Eurocard, Master Card, and Visa. Payment by credit card not available in all countries. Signature mandatory for credit card payment.

Abbreviations and acronyms

ACL	access control list
AIX	advanced interactive executive
API	application programming interface
ASM	Advanced Systems Management
ATM	asynchronous transfer mode
BIOS	basic input/output system
CD-ROM	compact disk read-only memory
CPU	central processing unit
DNS	Domain Name System
ECC	error checking and correcting
EST	Eastern Standard Time
FDDI	fiber distributed data interface
GB	gigabytes
GMT	Greenwich Mean Time
HACMP	High Availability Cluster Multiprocessing
HTML	hypertext markup language
HTTP	Hypertext Transfer Protocol
HTTPS	secure form of HTTP
I/O	input/output
IBM	International Business Machines Corporation
ICM	Internet Cluster Manager
IDE	integrated drive electronics
IIS	Microsoft's Internet Information Server
IMAP	Internet Message Access Protocol
IP	Internet Protocol
IPX	Internetwork Packet eXchange
IT	information technology
ITSO	International Technical Support Organization
KB	kilobytes
LAN	local area network
LDAP	Lightweight Directory Access Protocol
MB	megabytes
MSCS	Microsoft Cluster Services
MTA	mail transfer agent
NIC	network interface card
NNTP	Network News Transfer Protocol
ODS	on disk structure
OLE	Object Linking and Embedding
OS	operating system
OU	organizational unit
PABX	private automatic branch exchange
PCI	peripheral component interconnect
PDA	personal digital assistant
PFA	predictive failure analysis
RAID	redundant array of independent disks
RAM	random access memory
RFC	Request for Comments
ROM	read only memory
RPC	Remote Procedure Call
SCOS	Single Copy Object Store
SCSI	small computer system interface
SMP	symmetric multiprocessing
SMTP	Simple Mail Transfer Protocol
SPX	Sequenced Packet eXchange

© Copyright IBM Corp. 1998, 2000

SQL	structured query language
SSL	Secure Sockets Layer
TCP/IP	Transmission Control Protocol/Internet Protocol
UDP	User Datagram Protocol
UPS	uninterruptible power supply
WAN	wide area network
WINS	Windows Internet name service

Index

Numerics

A

B

C

© Copyright IBM Corp. 1998, 2000

D

M

N

O

P

Q

R

T

U

V

IBM Redbooks review

Your feedback is valued by the Redbook authors. In particular we are interested in situations where a Redbook "made the difference" in a task or problem you encountered. Using one of the following methods, **please review the Redbook, addressing value, subject matter, structure, depth and quality as appropriate.**

- Use the online **Contact us** review redbook form found at **ibm.com**/redbooks
- Fax this form to: USA International Access Code + 1 845 432 8264
- Send your comments in an Internet note to redbook@us.ibm.com

Document Number **Redbook Title**	SG24-5141-01 Lotus Domino R5 Clustering
Review	
What other subjects would you like to see IBM Redbooks address?	
Please rate your overall satisfaction:	O Very Good O Good O Average O Poor
Please identify yourself as belonging to one of the following groups:	O Customer O Business Partner O Solution Developer O IBM, Lotus or Tivoli Employee O None of the above
Your email address: The data you provide here may be used to provide you with information from IBM or our business partners about our products, services or activities.	O Please do not use the information collected here for future marketing or promotional contacts or other communications beyond the scope of this transaction.
Questions about IBM's privacy policy?	The following link explains how we protect your personal information. **ibm.com**/privacy/yourprivacy/

© Copyright IBM Corp. 1998, 2000

InformIT™

Solutions from experts you know and trust.

Articles | Free Library | eBooks | Expert Q & A | Training | Career Center | Downloads | MyInformIT

Login | Register | About InformIT

Topics

Operating Systems
Web Development
Programming
Networking
Certification
and more...

www.informit.com

- Free, in-depth articles and supplements
- Master the skills you need, when you need them
- Choose from industry leading books, ebooks, and training products
- Get answers when you need them - from live experts or InformIT's comprehensive library
- Achieve industry certification and advance your career

Expert Access

Free Content

Visit InformIT™ today and get great content from PH PTR

Prentice Hall and InformIT are trademarks of Pearson plc /
Copyright © 2000 Pearson

Prentice Hall: Professional Technical Reference

Back Forward Reload Home Search Guide Images Print Security Stop

PH PTR

http://www.phptr.com/

PRENTICE HALL

Professional Technical Reference

Tomorrow's Solutions for Today's Professionals.

www.phptr.com

Keep Up-to-Date with

PH PTR Online!

We strive to stay on the cutting edge of what's happening in professional computer science and engineering. Here's a bit of what you'll find when you stop by **www.phptr.com**:

- **Special interest areas** offering our latest books, book series, software, features of the month, related links and other useful information to help you get the job done.

- **Deals, deals, deals!** Come to our promotions section for the latest bargains offered to you exclusively from our retailers.

- **Need to find a bookstore?** Chances are, there's a bookseller near you that carries a broad selection of PTR titles. Locate a Magnet bookstore near you at www.phptr.com.

- **What's new at PH PTR?** We don't just publish books for the professional community, we're a part of it. Check out our convention schedule, join an author chat, get the latest reviews and press releases on topics of interest to you.

- **Subscribe today! Join PH PTR's monthly email newsletter!**

  Want to be kept up-to-date on your area of interest? Choose a targeted category on our website, and we'll keep you informed of the latest PH PTR products, author events, reviews and conferences in your interest area.

Visit our mailroom to subscribe today! **http://www.phptr.com/mail_lists**